STEM IN EARLY CHILDHOOD EDUCATION

Bringing together a diverse cohort of experts, *STEM in Early Childhood Education* explores the ways STEM can be integrated into early childhood curricula, highlighting recent research and innovations in the field, and implications for both practice and policy.

Based on the argument that high-quality STEM education needs to start early, this book emphasizes that early childhood education must include science, technology, engineering, and mathematics in developmentally appropriate ways based on the latest research and theories. Experienced chapter authors address the theoretical underpinnings of teaching STEM in the early years, while contextualizing these ideas for the real world using illustrative examples from the classroom. This cutting-edge collection also looks beyond the classroom to how STEM learning can be facilitated in museums, nature-based learning outdoors, and after-school programs.

STEM in Early Childhood Education is an excellent resource for aspiring and veteran educators alike, exploring the latest research, providing inspiration, and advancing best practices for teaching STEM in the early years.

Lynn E. Cohen is Professor at Long Island University, USA.

Sandra Waite-Stupiansky is Professor Emerita at Edinboro University of Pennsylvania, USA.

STEM IN EARLY CHILDHOOD EDUCATION

How Science, Technology, Engineering, and Mathematics Strengthen Learning

Edited by Lynn E. Cohen and Sandra Waite-Stupiansky

Routledge
Taylor & Francis Group

NEW YORK AND LONDON

First published 2020
by Routledge
52 Vanderbilt Avenue, New York, NY 10017

and by Routledge
2 Park Square, Milton Park, Abingdon, Oxon OX14 4RN

Routledge is an imprint of the Taylor & Francis Group, an informa business

© 2020 Taylor & Francis

The right of Lynn E. Cohen and Sandra Waite-Stupiansky to be identified as the authors of the editorial material, and of the authors for their individual chapters, has been asserted in accordance with sections 77 and 78 of the Copyright, Designs and Patents Act 1988.

Library of Congress Cataloging-in-Publication Data
A catalog record for this title has been requested

ISBN: 978-1-138-31983-7 (hbk)
ISBN: 978-1-138-31984-4 (pbk)
ISBN: 978-0-429-45375-5 (ebk)

Typeset in Bembo
by Taylor & Francis Books

To our parents, our first and most important STEM teachers:

Leroy and Lorraine Schieferstein – Lynn
Mary and Paul Waite – Sandra

CONTENTS

FIGURES

TABLES

ACKNOWLEDGMENTS

The editors would like to thank all the contributors to this book.

Lynn and Sandi would like to thank John-Paul McCaffrey, Director of Information Technology, and Andrew Rogers, Instructional Technologist, at Long Island University/Post for their technical support with this book.

FOREWORD

Chip Donohue

A Perfect Storm: Science, Technology, Engineering, and Mathematics in the Early Years

At the time I didn't realize it, but 2016 was the beginning of a professional whirl-wind around STEM for young children—a perfect storm of activities, events, research findings and reports that would help establish principles and guidelines and translate research into classroom practices for the "S," "T," "E," and "M" of STEM teaching and learning. The "grown-ups" in this STEM perfect storm included researchers, policy makers, funders, developers, teacher educators, early childhood practitioners, staff from children's libraries, museums and other informal learning environments, parents, and all other adults involved in the parenting process for young children growing and learning in the digital age.

Early STEM-focused convenings like the 2016 *Fostering STEM Trajectories: Bridging ECE Research, Practice, & Policy*, co-hosted by the Joan Ganz Cooney Center and New America and funded by the National Science Foundation, and the *Early STEM Learning Symposium* organized by the White House in partnership with the US Departments of Education and Health and Human Services, brought together thought leaders in the STEM disciplines to articulate a vision and goals to realize the promise of early STEM. Now, in 2019, this book brings together 15 of today's thought leaders to continue that dialogue and advance our understanding of how early STEM experiences enhance learning for young children—in the classroom and beyond.

These events were catalysts for a series of influential reports that were published in 2016–2018.

Shelley Pasnik and Naomi Hupert from Education Development Center (EDC), published *Early STEM Learning and the Roles of Technologies* in mid-2016.

The FrameWorks Institute developed and shared a suite of resources about STEM Learning and early STEM during 2017. The Early Childhood STEM Working Group released *Early STEM Matters. Providing High-Quality STEM Experiences for All Young Learners* as 2017 began. I was honored to be a member of the Working Group and to have the opportunity to learn with and from early science visionary Karen Worth, who has contributed a chapter on Science Learning in Early Learning Environments to this book and references the Early STEM Matters report.

Also, in early 2017, the Joan Ganz Cooney Center published *STEM Starts Early: Grounding Science, Technology, Engineering, and Math Education in Early Childhood,* written by Elizabeth McClure, Lisa Guernsey, Doug Clements, Susan Nall Bales, Jennifer Nichols, Nat Kendall-Taylor, and Michael Levine. In Chapter 4, you'll hear from Doug Clements, who is co-author with Julie Sarama, of Mathematics in Early Learning Environments.

In 2018, the Center for Childhood Creativity at the Bay Area Discovery Museum added an important piece of the puzzle with their review of the literature and evidence-based practices, *The Roots of STEM Success: Changing Early Learning Experiences to Build Lifelong Thinking Skills.* The same year, EDC and SRI Education released, *What Parents Talk About When They Talk About Learning: A National Survey About Young Children and Science,* providing fascinating insights into how parents feel about and think about science and their role in supporting STEM learning for their children.

Each of these reports provides a perspective on the four STEM disciplines, describes both domain specific knowledge and the integration of STEM content areas, and reviews the research about young children and STEM learning (Donohue, 2017). Taken together these events and reports created a perfect storm that provided me with the provocations and nudges to develop a deeper understanding of the "T" in STEM in my work at the Technology in Early Childhood Center at Erikson Institute in Chicago and the Fred Rogers Center for Early Learning and Children's Media at Saint Vincent College in Latrobe, Pennsylvania. And yes, it was a thrill to be invited to the Obama White House.

Are you ready to step into STEM?

Before you turn the page and start reading Chapter 1, let me offer four provocations to set the stage as you explore why early STEM matters and STEM starts early. These provocations, and a gentle nudge or two, will point you toward the key concepts and big ideas you are about to discover in every chapter of this book.

Provocation 1–21st century skills are any/every century skills

Lists of 21st century skills tend to include skills and dispositions like the following:

- Communication;
- Collaboration;

- Critical thinking;
- Problem solving;
- Creativity;
- Curiosity;
- Adaptability;
- Self-awareness;
- Grit and resilience;
- Persistence; and
- Playing well with others.

Helping young children gain the dispositions and skills on this list is nothing new for early childhood educators and has long been part of fostering a love of learning and developing lifelong learning skills in young children. Perhaps what makes them 21st century dispositions and skills is that we have new tools and technologies, new understandings, new methods, and new frameworks to support child development and early learning in this digital age.

Healthy child development and high-quality early STEM learning requires parents and educators to play an active role as STEM learning companions and mentors. The children will not get there on their own. Children are...

> inherently curious and equipped with basic capacities and dispositions to make sense of the world around them...These natural abilities are necessary to develop understandings of STEM disciplines, but they are not sufficient. Children may be curious to explore and eager to affect the world around them, but without support, their curiosity does not persist or motivate sustained investigation.
>
> *Early Childhood STEM Working Group (2017, p. 13)*

The grown-ups in young children's lives play an essential role in introducing early STEM learning by helping children develop their natural curiosity about the world around them and their capacity to learn on their own in the 21st century or in any and every century.

Provocation 2—The goal of early STEM is not to prepare young children for STEM careers in the future

Early STEM experiences should not be designed to prepare a 4-year-old for a future STEM career, and early coding, computational thinking, and robotics experiences for 5-year-olds need to be about what the child is learning today through authentic and engaging learning experiences, not about turning out future programmers. Do not worry, children will be future-ready when the time comes, but for today, let us focus on early STEM experiences like those described by the contributing authors in this book that emphasize...

- Being curious and gaining a sense of wonder about the world.
- Asking questions—Why? What? How? When?
- Figuring out how things work.
- Using tools for inquiry and discovery.
- Imagining and pretending.
- Playing and practicing.
- Making and tinkering.
- Observing and noticing.
- Exploring, experimenting, testing, debugging, and trying again.
- Using open-ended materials and manipulatives.
- Using digital tools for communication, documentation, and collaboration.

Teach for today and tomorrow will take care of itself is a lesson I learned when I visited the schools of Reggio Emilia. Great todays = future-ready children. Let a 4-year-old be 4, not a child on the way to being 5. The thought leaders in this book offer many examples of early STEM experiences for right now.

Provocation 3—It takes an ecosystem to support early STEM learning in your community

When I think about early STEM, I get excited about inviting and engaging new partners and exploring collaborative opportunities for developing an expanded eco-system that increases access to quality STEM learning at home, in school, and in the community. My list of essential partners includes parents, caregivers, family members, and other grown-ups at home and in neighborhoods; early childhood educators in formal settings and home-based programs; informal educators in libraries, museums, zoos and nature centers and out-of-school time programs, pediatricians and pediatric health professionals; teacher educators; researchers; funders and policy makers; public broadcasters; and, children's media developers (Donohue, 2017).

Who is already on your list? Who are your early STEM partners today? Whom do you need to recruit and add? Read on and I guarantee the authors of each chapter will help expand your list and your notion of who needs to be an early STEM partner in your community.

Provocation 4—Put both the "t" and the "T" in STEM

The Early STEM Matters report defines technology broadly to mean "anything human-made that is used to solve a problem or fulfill a desire. Technology can be an object, a system, or a process that results in the modification of the natural world to meet human needs and wants" (Early Childhood STEM Working Group, 2017, p. 8).

Unlike other STEM disciplines, technology is not a content area to be studied by young children but rather an important tool that can support learning in

STEM and across the curriculum. This perspective suggests that the "T" in STEM should be considered differently from Science, Engineering, and Math (Early Childhood STEM Working Group, 2017).

In the early childhood years, technology is a powerful tool for learning, exploration, discovery, communicating, telling a story, documenting, sharing, saving, revisiting, and reflecting. In the earliest years, technology tools for STEM learning at home and in early childhood settings should emphasize communication, relationships and joint engagement—interactive tools that invite interactions with others.

In my "T" in STEM work at the TEC Center, I have described a simple framework that uses a lower case "t" and an upper case "T" to describe a developmental progression through the early childhood years from 3–5.

- **t = learn *how to use* technology**—*Children gain basic tech handling skills, beginning experiences with technology selection and us, and technology experiences are playful and social.*

- **t = learn *with* technology**—*Children use tech as tools for learning across the STEM disciplines all day long, throughout the environment and across the curriculum.*

- **T = learn *about* technology**—*Children are makers and media creators not just consumers, and coding, computational thinking, and tangible technology are introduced.*

My four provocations are meant to whet your appetite for what is to come. There are more provocations to discover in the pages that follow and much to learn from this remarkable and inspiring collection of thought leaders. This book is a call to action for everyone interested in early STEM teaching and learning. And it offers a gentle nudge to educators and the grown-ups in the lives of young children to embrace the STEM disciplines and create your own perfect storm.

You play an essential role in introducing early STEM learning. When you model curiosity and imagination and demonstrate your disposition and skills for inquiry, information gathering, solution seeking, learning from mistakes, risk taking, and collaborating, children will catch your enthusiasm. But when in doubt, just let the real early STEM experts show you the way.

References

Center for Childhood Creativity at the Bay Area Discovery Museum (2018). *The Roots of STEM Success: Changing Early Learning Experiences to Build Lifelong Thinking Skills*. San Francisco, CA: Center for Childhood Creativity. https://centerforchildhoodcreativity. org/roots-stem-success/

Donohue, C. (2017). Putting the "T" in STEM for the youngest learners: How caregivers can support parents in the digital age. *Zero to Three Journal*, 37(5), 45–52. https://eric.ed.gov/?id=EJ1143056

Early Childhood STEM Working Group. (2017). *Early STEM Matters: Providing High-quality STEM Experiences for all Young Learners*. Chicago, IL: University of Chicago Center for Elementary Mathematics and Science Education. http://ecstem.uchicago.edu

FrameWorks Institute. (2017). *STEM Learning*. https://www.frameworksinstitute.org/stem-learning.html#early

McClure, E. R., Guernsey, L., Clements, D. H., Bales, S. N., Nichols, J., Kendall-Taylor, N., & Levine, M. H. (2017). *STEM Starts Early: Grounding Science, Technology, Engineering, and Math Education in Early Childhood*. http://joanganzcooneycenter.org/publication/stem-starts-early/

Pasnik, S., & Hupert, N. (2016). *Early STEM Learning and the Roles of Technologies*. Waltham, MA: Education Development Center, Inc. http://ltd.edc.org/early-STEM-tech-white-paper

Silander, M., Grindal, T., Hupert, N., Garcia, E., Anderson, K., Vahey, P., & Pasnik, S. (2018). *What Parents Talk About When They Talk About Learning: A National Survey About Young Children and Science*. New York, NY, & Menlo Park, CA: Education Development Center, Inc., & SRI International. https://www.edc.org/sites/default/files/uploads/EDC_SRI_What_Parents_Talk_About.pdf

PREFACE

The idea for this book began around ten years ago. The co-editors, who are both teacher educators with decades of kindergarten teaching experience between them, lamented that there were plenty of resources on the hows of teaching STEM to young children, but very few authoritative sources on the theoretical underpinnings for the approaches that practitioners were urged to try, in other words, the whys of teaching STEM. Many sources for curriculum theories for STEM instruction of older students were available, but not so for teachers of very young children. To fulfill the dream of offering a source that was approachable, founded on accepted theories of how children learn, and based on up-to-date research, we approached experts who had a proven track record and the respect of the education field. We asked each of them to write a succinct chapter that addresses what we know about the best practices for STEM in early childhood settings. To our delight and amazement, they all agreed. So what you find in the pages that follow are the fruits of their extensive years of labor.

One of our first challenges was to decide if we wanted the focus to be on STEM in its purest sense of science, technology, engineering, and mathematics, or the various spin-offs which include the arts, social studies, language arts, and so on. Early on we decided to keep the focus on the four disciplines at the core of STEM, with acknowledgment that learning does not occur in a vacuum, and children learn best in an interdisciplinary, integrated curriculum. Yet, we wanted to put the focus on the four roots of STEM in its original form.

The book is divided into three parts. Part I delves into the definitions and theoretical underpinnings of each of the four STEM disciplines by authors whose voices have garnered respect within and outside education circles for decades. The authors of the first four chapters set the foundation for the rest of the book by defining the parameters and definitions of science, technology, engineering, and mathematics (in that order), connecting theories to practice, grounding the theories on current research, and introducing some of the policy implications for current and future practices.

In Chapter 1, Karen Worth, whose work in science for young children is well-known to early childhood educators, introduces the readers to the science of learning science on the part of young children. Her use of vignettes illustrates what science education, based on best practices, looks and sounds like in real classrooms. Chapter 2's author, Lynn Hartle, examines technology using the bioecological concepts of process, person, context, and time, giving fresh insights into how technology impacts the teaching and learning systems for today's children. Demetra Evangelou and Aikaterini Bagiati, in Chapter 3, show how engineering, specifically early engineering, is a fundamental approach to learning and development expressed each time a child alters the environment to solve a problem. The authors of Chapter 4, Douglas Clements and Julie Sarama, focus on mathematics, arguing that children follow learning trajectories as they master abstract concepts under the guidance of informed teachers.

Part II addresses the processes of STEM and higher order thinking. Questions relating to thinking and STEM are woven throughout this section, including the following: How do we assess children's computational thinking? How do we teach invention and design to young minds? And, what does tinkering and making, which is hitting the US by storm, have to do with STEM? The three chapters in this section take the ideas from Section I and put them into a context of thinking and doing STEM in the real world. In Chapter 5, Emily Relkin and Marina Bers argue that computational thinking (CT) can be assessed using KIBO robotics, in playful programming activities to measure young children's skills and abilities. Engineering design is addressed by Pamela Lottero-Perdue in Chapter 6, as she answers the question of teaching inventive modes of thinking by scaffolding design challenges as she illustrates with vignettes of four skillful teachers. Chapter 7, the last chapter of this section, Olga Jarrett, with Aliya Jafri, take the readers into the world of tinkering and making with their personal stories of how they came to use both these processes as a means for social equality and justice in their own lives and the lives of their students.

Part III takes readers outside the classroom and illustrates how learning STEM occurs in the wider world. All of the authors of the chapters in this section have experience working with children in settings not typically thought of as formal schooling as they put forth convincing arguments that these settings are powerful contexts for teaching and learning STEM. The authors of the three chapters in this section are creative and innovative entrepreneurs who have developed materials and settings for children to learn STEM outside of school hours and outside school walls. Children's museums provide such a setting, as argued by Gina Svarovsky in Chapter 8, as she demonstrates how they have become visible, accessible settings for families to explore STEM together. Janet Emmons and Lynn Cohen introduce readers to Blockspot® in Chapter 9, an innovative model which uses unit blocks in creative, educational, and fun ways to challenge children to use STEM. The model they use can be a prototype for other entrepreneurs who want to make STEM accessible in public spaces. Finally, STEM goes outdoors in Chapter 10 with Monica Wiedel-Lubinski, where readers will learn how nature is a powerful teacher with skilled adults guiding the process.

The voices in this book combine to provide a new tool for addressing the whys—and wheres—for teaching and learning STEM in the early years, which we think is a perfect complement to the many sources on the market that already address the hows.

Lynn E. Cohen and Sandra Waite-Stupiansky, Co-Editors

PART I

STEM in Early Childhood Environments

1

SCIENCE IN EARLY LEARNING ENVIRONMENTS

Karen Worth

This book is about science, technology, engineering, and mathematics (STEM). While it is useful to separate these domains for examination, young children do not learn about their world in narrowly defined subject matter domains nor are these domains entirely separate. In quality learning environments, the STEM domains overlap in multiple ways. Figure 1.1 suggests the nature of this overlap and the need to integrate the STEM areas, but it also acknowledges the need, at times, to focus on each separately to highlight domain specific skills and concepts.

This chapter will focus on the S of STEM. It will examine some of the research and theoretical foundations, some of the implications for learning settings for young children, and some of the attendant policy issues.

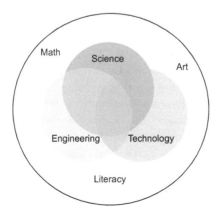

FIGURE 1.1 The Integration of STEM

The Concern

In a world filled with the products of scientific inquiry, scientific literacy has become a necessity for everyone. Everyone needs to use scientific information to make choices that arise every day. Everyone needs to be able to engage intelligently in public discourse and debate about important issues that involve science and technology. And everyone deserves to share in the excitement and personal fulfillment that can come from understanding and learning about the natural world (National Research Council, 1996).

In recent years, there has been an increase in concern over the quality of science education and a great deal of rhetoric about the need to improve science teaching and learning in pre-college education. However, it is important to acknowledge that this concern is not new. The early 60s saw the development of innovative elementary and secondary science curricula. In 1989, the American Association for the Advancement of Science (AAAS) began its Project 2061 and published *Science for All Americans* (Rutherford & Ahlgren, 1989). In 1996, the National Science Education Standards (National Research Council, 1986) and the Benchmarks for Science Literacy (AAAS, 1993) were published.

Even improved science education for early childhood has been more than a recent subject of concern. Over the past 20 years there has been a growing acknowledgment and understanding that STEM education should begin in these early years. Many reports and publications support and illuminate the reasons, including a *Dialogue on Early Childhood Science, Mathematics, and Technology Education* (AAAS, 1999), *Eager to Learn* (National Research Council, 2001), and *STEM in Early Education and Development Conference (SEED): Collected Papers*, (University of Illinois, 2010). In 2014, the National Science Teachers Association (NSTA) published a *Early Childhood Science Education: A Position Statement of the National Science Teachers Association* (NSTA, 2014) that was endorsed by the National Association for the Education of Young Children (NAEYC). Recently two new reports were issued: *Early STEM Matters Providing High-Quality STEM Experiences for All Young Learners* (Early Childhood STEM Working Group, 2017) and *STEM Starts Early: Grounding Science, Technology, Engineering, and Math Education in Early Childhood* (McClure et al., 2017).

These documents support the belief that science education in early childhood is critical both for later science learning as well as for the development of basic cognitive skills and attitudes towards learning. These reports also present a relatively uniform understanding of the need for a child-centered, play-based, and inquiry-based approach. However, significant change in the role of science in the early childhood years is still a distant goal. The amount and quality of science taught in the younger grades as well as in childcare settings is still low. In the early grades, even the use of materials may be limited. In many settings, the new knowledge about children's cognitive potential is not being used to broaden and deepen the science curriculum to include more in-depth and challenging experiences. Science activities often are vehicles for the development of literacy and mathematics skills as an increasing concern about reading has reinforced the almost singular focus on learning basic skills of literacy, numeracy, and socialization. This focus on the "basics" is also bringing to the early childhood setting increased pressure for accountability, leaving little room for children's rich play and exploration of the world around them. The rhetoric and the publicity around STEM are strong, but a real public understanding of its importance, what to do about it, and how to implement change is far less so.

What We Know

Research on science learning in K-12 has a long history, but what we know about very young children's science learning is limited as most of the research focuses on the later elementary years and beyond. Even within the years considered early childhood—ages 3 through 8 or PreK through third grade—much of the research is focused on grades 1–3. A recent publication, *Research in Early Childhood Science Education* (Trundle & Sackes, 2015) is one of the latest additions to surveys of existing research. The authors have covered a great deal but virtually all bemoan the lack of research and the virtual absence of longitudinal efforts. This may be due in part to a lack of a priority on early childhood in research funding, but it is also important to acknowledge the difficulty of research into science knowledge and understanding with the very young where language, both oral and written, may not reveal children's skills, reasoning, and understanding. Therefore, much of what we know about the learning and teaching of science in early childhood is based on reasonable assumptions from developmental research, philosophical commitments, the observations and experiences of educators of young children, and the existing research into the later elementary years. There are several of those assumptions about young children's learning that emerge from this foundation that are key to our understanding of how children learn science and, as we will see, map onto the nature of science and science inquiry, underscoring the importance of science as a major focus of the early years.

Curiosity

A baby throws her plate on the ground over and over. Four- and five-year-olds bombard us with questions: Why is the sky blue? Why does the worm wriggle like that? Where do babies come from? What happens if I jump off this rock? They make rock or shell collections, and make mixtures of sand and dirt and water to build structures. They catch and release insects and worms over and over. Six- and seven-year-olds play with flashlights and mirrors wondering about the moving light beams or identify places to find critters in the neighborhood. These kinds of actions make visible a drive to know the world. Fundamental to the thinking about science learning has been the research on very young children and the nature of this curiosity. Based on their research with infants, Gopnik, Meltzoff, and Kuhl (1999) conclude that from birth there is an innate drive to make sense of and understand the world. Babies and young children are curious because they need to reduce uncertainty and make the world a predictable place. A plate always crashes to the ground when let go. A child can jump from a small rock and not get hurt, but a big one is dangerous. A worm will quickly go underground if let go. Gopnick et al. (1999) argue that young children are driven to understand and take satisfaction in understanding. More recently, Jirout and Klahr (2012) are providing interesting support for this idea. Gopnick et al. (1999) go on to compare the drive of the scientist and that of the very young child. By titling their book, *The Scientist in the Crib* (and using the phrase "children are natural scientists"), they are making the case that science, in its aims and processes, resembles what young children do naturally. This idea of the relationship between young children's drive to understand and the nature of science is reflected in the statement in *Eager to Learn* (National Research Council, 2001) that science is a privileged domain in the younger years, as is language and mathematical thinking.

> Because these [mathematics and science] are "privileged domains," that is, domains in which children have a natural proclivity to learn, experiment, and explore, they allow for nurturing and extending the boundaries of the learning in which children are already actively engaged.
>
> *(pp. 8–9)*

This relationship between children's curiosity and play and science is delight-fully expressed by the neuro-scientist, Beau Lotto (Lotto, 2017). He describes science as a way of being that is based on five principles: 1) uncertainty, 2) openness to possibility, 3) cooperation, 4) intrinsic motivation (i.e., it is its own reward), and 5) intentional action. He then writes,

> Remarkably, principles one through 4 are defined by one word: play. By "play" I don't so much mean a literal activity as an attitude. It is about embodying playful qualities in how one approaches a problem or situation or conflict.... What do you get if you add intention to play? Science.
>
> *(Lotto, 2017, pp. 272, 274)*

Early Reasoning Abilities and Theories

Young children are not just curious questioners, they are active doers and thin-kers. Motivated by the need to know, they work to make sense of the world. In doing so they engage in many of what we now call practices of science inquiry. These capabilities have been seriously underappreciated (Akman, 2015). As stated in *Taking Science to School* (National Research Council, 2007) "… research shows that children's thinking is surprisingly sophisticated …. Children can use a wide range of reasoning processes that form the underpinnings of scientific thinking, even though their experience is variable and they have much more to learn" (pp. 2–3). Even very young children, who may naturally ask questions and explore, also create theories and build skills in many of the science practices if supported in learning environments that spark wonder and curiosity and build on their interests and experiences.

In addition to our general domain knowledge of development, science specific research provides insight into some of what children know and the theories they have formed, although these tend to be from children at the upper age levels of early childhood. Examples include the belief that clouds are solids (Sackes, 2015), that matter is solid and inanimate (Hadzigeorgiou, 2015), and that trees are not plants (Akerson, Weikand, & Fouad, 2015). Early ideas such as these demonstrate that children construct reasoned theories about how the world works. While these naïve ideas tend to be perception bound and vary depending on an individual child's experiences, they show the power of their reasoning and their attempts to connect what they know and to build a theory that reduces uncertainty and seems to make sense.

The Importance of Adults and Peers

Science is a collaborative endeavor. While exploration of the natural world is driven by an innate need to know and satisfaction in knowing, and while children engage in their play in some aspects of science inquiry and its practices, this work is encouraged, guided, and deepened by adults who model, mentor, challenge, guide, and provide stimulating environments and carefully designed experiences with the natural world. Developing understanding, whether by scientists or young children, comes not only through direct experiences but also through children's relationships with others, peers and adults, as they cooperate and collaborate, share their thinking, listen to and debate the ideas of others.

THE DEVELOPMENTALLY APPROPRIATE CLASSROOM

The scene is in a PreK classroom of 20 children a teacher and an aide. Much would be familiar to those who have been in such classrooms. There are areas set up around the room: a corner with books and soft cushions, a block area, a meeting area, a table and an easel for art work near the sink, a sand table with very wet sand, two round tables for different kinds of activities, shelves with a variety of materials, and colorfully decorated walls. A closer look suggests this is not quite so familiar. The book area has a preponderance of books on topics such as buildings, animal structures, and homes. The block area is enlarged, the usual props such as human figures, animals, and vehicles are on the sidelines. And on the walls is a mirror, images of structures, and photographs of children's structures with brief captions. On two of the tables there are different kinds of small blocks including colored cubes, mini-unit blocks, and straws and connectors. A third table has only Kapla blocks. The art area has clay, and cardboard boxes, and other 3-D materials. There are partially completed creations on a nearby shelf. Through the windows can be seen in the play yard some large block structures as well as a "lean-to" made of sticks and burlap. At the meeting area, three questions are pinned to a chart: How can we make things stand up? What do we think makes things fall? What materials work best for each structure? There are children in each area building, talking, and, in some cases, sitting with clipboards and paper drawing images of their work. As the children work, the adults engage with them, observing, listening, guiding, modeling, challenging with new materials and carefully considered comments and questions, and documenting the work. Group meetings take place several times a week, to talk about the big questions and share structures and new ideas.

> The teacher is engaged with the children in a study that may last for weeks on the science of materials and structures. She has created a stimulating environment with a variety of carefully chosen materials that allow the children to create their own pathways, challenges, and explorations as they broaden their experiences with the phenomena, extend their ideas, and engage in science practices. Language, mathematics, and engineering are rich partners.

This brief PreK classroom description is in sharp contrast to a more traditional setting where individual areas may have little relationship to one another, and literacy and early numeracy are central. Science is confined to a science table and weekly activities with limited engagement in science inquiry and its practices.

The next vignette is from a second-grade classroom in a formal setting where there is a standards-based district curriculum to guide teachers but one that allows for flexibility to support children's and teachers' interests.

> In a second-grade classroom, children are beginning a unit on earth materials. The questions that guide their work over 6–8 weeks are as follows: "What is soil?" and "Where does soil come from?" In the first 8-week segment, they are looking at the role of living things in creating the organic component of soil (Brookline Public Schools, 2018). In the classroom, there is a bin with a large rotting log that is kept moist. A book for observations hangs nearby. On a shelf in another area are vials filled with soil with labels indicating where they came from. Some are part of an investigation into the components of the soil with a focus on the amount of humus. In a corner is a booklet entitled *Observations*

from the Wormery where children enter interesting comments. Books on soil abound both in the library corner and near the on-going activities. A box holds the children's science notebooks that are used on a regular basis for documenting investigations, collecting data, reflecting, and drawing conclusions. Several charts suggest the nature of the science talks that occur regularly and the progression of children's thinking about the questions that guide the unit.

> The guiding questions of the unit speak to the larger concepts the children are working with. However, there are many pathways that depend on the children's interests. While outside looking at soil in the school yard, some children become fascinated with the pill bugs that "appeared." Others talk excitedly about the little piles of "sawdust" they see forming under the decaying log. Still others are only interested in the worms. The teacher is supporting these varied interests, encouraging children to observe closely, document their work, and report to the class as she skillfully guides them to make connections to the conceptual focus of the unit.

This description contrasts with what is happening in many classrooms where science is limited to once- or twice-a-week sessions of directed experimentation, text-based instruction, or even non-existent. The final vignette describes an example of the science that can emerge from a typical informal out-of-school setting.

> In a small playground, two young children are playing on the slide. One comes shooting down; the other comes more slowly. They do this again and again, changing speeds in a variety of ways. After a few times, the adult muses out loud, "I wonder how you make yourself go slowly or fast." Some discussion ensues. "I wonder if you can stop in the middle?" As the children seem to tire, she asks, "What else do you think we could slide down the slide?" As the children find pebbles and twigs and handfuls of sand, the adult asks, "Do you think it's going to roll?"
>
> This brief snapshot suggests the potential of the small events of children's daily lives if caregivers understand and support their children's curiosity about their world around them.

Good science learning and teaching can only take place in the context of the total classroom environment. It does not exist on its own. Therefore, to look at the implications of what we know for teaching science, the first step is to underline the importance of some general criteria for learning environments for young children. These are described in the position statement of NAEYC's *Position Statement: Developmentally Appropriate Practice in Early Childhood Program Serving Children from Birth* and in more detail in the book by the same name, edited by Copple and Bredekamp (2009). These documents provide a framework for best practice.

> Developmentally appropriate practice requires both meeting children where they are—which means that teachers must get to know them well—and enabling them to reach goals that are both challenging and achievable. All teaching practices should be appropriate to children's age and developmental status, attuned to them as unique individuals, and responsive to the social and cultural contexts in which they live. Developmentally appropriate practice does not mean making things easier for children. Rather, it means ensuring that goals and experiences are suited to their learning. (NAEYC, 2009, p. xii)

It is in such a caring classroom community with its child-centered, playful, family-oriented, and culturally inclusive culture, and teaching that enhances children's development and learning that inquiry science teaching can take place

Another way of thinking about appropriate classrooms for young children is to look at some of the characteristics of such classrooms related to the children, the curriculum, and the culture or environment as described in Table 1.1.

The classroom environment includes the physical environment as well. The work of the educators in Reggio Emilia, Italy, provide an important reminder. The learning spaces in Reggio reflect the idea of the environment as a third teacher able to influence the teaching and learning (Edwards, Gandini, & Forman, 2012; Wurm, 2005). In an earlier article, Gandini (1993) writes,

TABLE 1.1 Characteristics Related to Children, the Curriculum, and Classroom Environment.

The Children	<ul><li>play, wonder, and are curious</li><li>engage in intellectually challenging activity</li><li>collaborate with others</li><li>communicate with others in multiple ways</li><li>take risks and overcome problems</li><li>have confidence and take leadership in their own learning</li><li>feel appreciated for their individual and cultural differences</li></ul>
The Curriculum	<ul><li>is relevant to the interests, questions and wonderings of children</li><li>is individual and child-centered, meeting children where they are</li><li>builds and applies skills in cognitive, physical, emotional, and social domains</li></ul>
The Culture	<ul><li>has time and space for children to engage, struggle and succeed</li><li>is responsive to diverse social, cultural, and individual experiences</li><li>values families and their role in the education of their child</li></ul>

The layout of physical space in the school encourages encounters, communication, and relationships. The arrangement of structures, objects, and
activities encourages choices, problem solving, and discoveries in the process
of learning. In preparing the space teachers offer the possibility for children
to be with the teachers and many of the other children, or with just a few, or
even alone. (p. 6)

In learning environments based on these ideas, inquiry-based science can thrive,
and, in many instances, be the core of children's work. In the sections that follow
are descriptions of key elements of science teaching and learning.

Elements of Science Teaching and Learning

Given what we know about development and developmentally appropriate
practice, what we know from the research and experience, as well as what we
understand to be the nature of science—the way scientists go about their
work—there is a reasonably broad consensus on the nature of experiences that
provide opportunities for children to develop understanding of science concepts
and the nature of science, as well as develop their abilities to engage in the
practices of science inquiry. Areas of importance to consider in planning and
designing learning environments and guiding student learning are highlighted
and hinted at in the vignettes. These are discussed broadly to apply to children
4-years to 8-years of age and child care settings as well as formal schooling. A
more detailed piece would need to consider the differences within this developmental range in terms of skills and experiences, as well as the implications of
the formal school context with its curriculum and assessments and its focus on
literacy and mathematics.

Science Inquiry and Its Practices

Many of us have grown up with the understanding that there is a science
method: a fixed sequence of steps that describes how scientists do their work.
The publication, *A Framework for K-12 Science Education* (National Research
Council, 2011), as well as the *Next Generation Science Standards* (NGSS, 2013), has
moved the dial by describing what scientists do, not as the application of a
method, but rather as a set of practices that are used by scientists in many ways
depending on the focus of their work. Table 1.2 is a list of those practices with
elaboration for the early childhood years. Although presented here as a list, the
practices are not intended to be "practiced" individually, learned as a set of skills,
or used always in sequence. Rather they are embedded in the work and play of
children as they investigate interesting phenomena and questions over time.

As is clear from Table 1.2, this understanding of science inquiry goes beyond
asking questions and doing experiments. It also includes making meaning, making

TABLE 1.2 Ways Young Children Demonstrate Next Generation Science Standards

Next generation science standards practices	Ways in which young children might demonstrate these practices
Ask questions	• displaying curiosity • observing and asking questions about observable phenomena (objects, materials, organisms or events)
Plan and carry out investigations	• drawing on prior knowledge and experience to predict what might happen and to inform investigations • planning and implementing investigations using simple equipment • using their senses and simple tools to observe, gather, and record data using words, drawings, photographs, charts, and graphs
Make meaning from experience and data	• describing in many ways what happened during an investigation; comparing, sorting, classifying, and ordering • talking and thinking about (reflecting on) what happened during an investigation and why what happened might have happened
Use mathematics and computational thinking	• counting and measuring using non-standard and standard units and learning to use standard units when appropriate to support science understanding • using mathematical language to describe attributes such as position (*next to*), motion (*backwards*), speed (*fast*), shape (*circle*), size (*tall*)
Construct explanations/theories	• looking for and describing patterns and relationships • constructing theories/explanations based in experience about what might be going on • using evidence to support a theory
Develop and use models	• using representations, and simple models to help develop explanations of their experiences
Engage in discussion/ argument from evidence	• engaging in discussion before, during and after investigations • sharing ideas and listening to new perspectives • supporting thinking with evidence • using evidence, representations, and simple models to communicate with others
Obtain, evaluate, and talk about information	• documenting experiences and thinking to communicate with others • using basic science terms and vocabulary • using first-hand interactions with objects and organisms, media, and books to gather information

models, constructing explanations and engaging in argumentation (National Research Council, 2011). It makes clear that literacy and mathematics are key to these practices and highlights the thinking, reasoning, and communication that are essential to science practice and science learning. All are naturally integrated in science inquiry. If we compare this with the table of characteristics of appropriate classrooms, it is clear that there is substantial overlap. This suggests that engaging in the practices of science inquiry not only supports science learning but also provides children with opportunities for developing language and mathematics skills, social skills, and key thinking and learning skills (Greenfield, 2018).

The Inquiry Learning Cycle

The so-called scientific method has been discredited. In its place, a simple learning cycle (see Figure 1.2) can be used to describe and guide classroom-based science inquiry experiences.

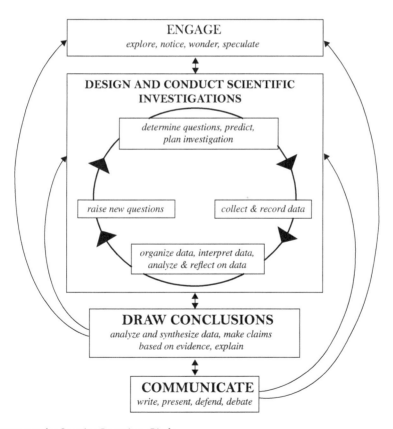

FIGURE 1.2 An Inquiry Learning Circle

Arguably, similar to how scientists conduct their work, the cycle begins with an extended period of engagement where children explore the selected phenomenon and materials, experiencing what they are and can do, wondering about them, raising questions, and sharing ideas. This allows children with a range of backgrounds and interests to engage with the phenomena, structured largely by the materials themselves, as well as their interactions with peers, and observations and informal comments from adults. During this stage, they begin to make connections to their daily experiences, wonder about the phenomena, and identify questions and interests. In the vignette on structures, the children had explored the various structures' materials before focusing in on their specific questions as well as the over-arching questions. The cycle continues with a more guided stage as questions are identified that might be further investigated. While some children may move naturally into this stage, most benefit from guidance by an adult using the conceptual focus of the content (see below) as a guide. Some of the questions may be the children's questions, others may be introduced by the teacher, but their purpose is to begin the process of more focused and deeper inquiry involving prediction, planning next steps, collecting and recording data, and reflecting on their work. As children's experiences mount up the adult role becomes one of listening and observing, questioning, adding resources, and challenging the children to look for patterns and relationships. Given enough experience, the children move to a third stage where they work with their peers, guided by an adult, to discuss, debate, and make sense of their work, leading some of the time to new ideas and conclusions and at other times to more questions. Finally, they may share their ideas, communicating them in a variety of ways. This structure is not rigid, nor is it linear—thus the many arrows. It is used here to suggest to adults working with children a scaffold for inquiry-based science teaching and learning (Worth & Grollman, 2003).

The Content

Practices are not learned in a vacuum. Young children need to engage in science inquiry in the context of interesting and basic science concepts. State and national standards are an attempt to define what content is important to know. On the national level, the Next Generation Science Standards K-12 (NGSS, 2013) define important concepts and, with grade-by-grade standards, articulate a progression of deepening learning from K–12. Locally, many states have begun to include PreK standards in science. Some are articulated from PreK to 12th grade, including those in Massachusetts (Massachusetts Department of Elementary and Secondary Education, 2016) and Pennsylvania (Pennsylvania Department of Education and Department of Human Services, 2016). Standards identify important concepts, but more specific content, the actual topics and phenomena children engage with, must also meet the following criteria (Worth & Grollman, 2003):

a   They are interesting and engaging
b   They are drawn from and emerge from children's experience
c   They can be explored directly
d   They are open to deep exploration over time
e   They are developmentally appropriate

In the PreK vignette, the over-arching concepts involved are properties of materials and forces. Given the children's interest in building things, the topic—the phenomena they are investigating—is how structures stand up. In the second-grade vignette, the concepts explored are the nature and properties of earth materials with the topic being the different soils in the school yard and the role of the living things in that soil. Standards provide guidelines for what is to be taught and criteria such as those listed in the guide topic selection but the individual needs and interests of children are still important drivers for the specific investigations. Their interests and questions—within the broad conceptual context—are key. While the overall concept of the nature of soil underlies the children's work in the example above, should the study of some of the local critters become a passion of some or all, a teacher might take advantage of this interest and include in the goals a study of the life cycle or animal habitats. Beneath these choices is a careful and shifting balance among concept goals, practice goals, children's interests, and their developmental levels.

Investigations over Time

Doing science takes time. The Inquiry Learning Cycle discussed on pages 13-14 has several stages and multiple iterations. Constructing understanding may mean weeks of focus on one or two concepts using a range of materials and events as in the vignettes. Too often science is taught once or twice a week at the end of the day, if there is time, or not at all. What we understand about young children's learning and the nature of inquiry teaching and learning, suggests strongly that science must be a basic subject permeating the days and weeks. Children need time to play, try out ideas, try them in different contexts, reflect on what they are observing, and come to new conclusions.

Science across the Domains

We often hear that mathematics is the language of science and science investigations certainly offer many opportunities for children to use mathematical skills. There are opportunities to count, to balance, to explore two- and three-dimensional shapes, and even think about scale. What we hear less often is that language is the language of science. Children's talk is as critical to the development of ideas as the direct experiences. It encourages movement from phenomenon-based reasoning to relation-based reasoning as ideas must be voiced and shared with others. Confusion about the ideas of others requires explication and detail. Differences in ideas need discussion and debate. Even PreK children can engage in "science talks" in small groups and sometimes as a class providing opportunities for children to listen to the ideas of their peers, defend their own ideas, ask more refined or focused questions, develop deeper conceptual understanding, and become more aware of the collaborative nature of science.

Documentation and representation go together with children's talk. Collecting and recording data and documenting investigations and ideas are critical to science and serve to both support children's participation in discussions and their own reflections. It is part of the nature of science and even PreK children can keep their own or a class science notebook with drawings and words "just as scientists do" (Worth, Winokur, Crissman, & Heller-Winokur, 2009). Books and other media provide access to images, information, and models of language structures.

Integration goes beyond the STEM disciplines and literacy. Creative teachers will see in a structured unit opportunities for a social studies study of buildings and homes, and in a soil study there are many implications for studies of the environment. The acronym STEAM in current use suggests the role of art in science documentation as well as the role of the science of materials and color in art.

The Role of the Teacher

A well-designed environment with appropriately selected content provides the context for children's learning. In such an environment, children's natural curiosity and motivation to understand leads to playful engagement but for deeper and more challenging inquiry, informed and educated adult guidance is essential. The teacher's role is critical to children's science learning, and it is a complex one that is informed by knowledge of children, of teaching and learning, and of pedagogical science knowledge.

Understand and Focus on the Content

Children's scientific inquiry is guided by the teacher's explicit understanding of the important underlying science concepts of the focus chosen. For example, the children's work with structures described in the vignette is indeed about buildings, but it is also about concepts related to forces, balance, and properties of materials. While explicit teaching of the concepts is not appropriate, the structure of the experiences and the teacher's facilitation is guided by an understanding of the concepts and how children learn them. Children's work may take them in many directions. They may build a structure to house a dinosaur or a temporary home for a snail. The challenge for the teacher is to join in and incorporate those ideas into interactions around the concept. A teacher might ask, "How can you make it really strong? Do you think it is big enough for the dinosaur? How might you make a roof? What will the snail need?" Questions, comments, and probes such as these draw the children's attention to the guiding concepts and the children's interests and questions draw the teacher into theirs. In the study of soil in a second-grade classroom, the children were interested in lots of things, in particular the animals themselves. While supporting these interests, the teacher also must skillfully guide them to notice how the behavior of the animals plays a role in soil formation. This kind of teacher guidance and facilitation encourages children to notice and reflect on key aspects of the phenomenon they are exploring.

Model Inquiry and Science Practices

Modeling may be a very new role for many teachers whose science background is limited and who have themselves never had the opportunity to engage in science inquiry. Yet modeling of the practices from curiosity to risk taking, to learning from mistakes, to open discussion, to seeking information provides children with examples and images of what the practices look like and sound like.

Identify Appropriate Expectations

There is some research on progressions of children's use of practices and their understanding of science concepts especially in the later years of early childhood (Harlan & Qualter, 2014). However, much still falls on teachers to observe and listen to assess what and how children are thinking, where their interests and questions lie, and to determine appropriate challenges to guide their interactions.

Encourage/Facilitate Discussion

Under emphasized, especially at the very young levels, science talks (large or small group) are key for student reflection and theory building (Worth & Grollman, 2003). Skills in guiding these conversations are complex drawing on teachers' knowledge of children, observations of their work, and an understanding of the science conceptual goals. It also requires a reorientation of the role of the teacher in discussion from a more traditional teacher–child interaction to one that fosters authentic dialogue among children.

Integrate Documentation and Representation

Science requires that experiences be documented. Teachers need to encourage and support children's documentation of their work using a wide range of media from writing and drawing, to photography and video, to dance and music. In addition, teacher documentation plays a key role in guiding children's reflections and assessing their understanding, requiring new skills in both observation and the use of a range of media (Worth et al., 2009; Wurm, 2005).

This brief description of the role of the teacher makes clear that high-quality science teaching demands a great deal from teachers in addition to the knowledge and skill that is required to create the basic culture of the classroom. Yet many teachers are uncomfortable with science, have little science background, and lack confidence in their abilities to teach science to children. Many of the following policy recommendations concern this reality and the need to rethink the preparation and on-going support for teachers of young children.

Implications for Policy

The reality that science education for early childhood has been a concern for at least two decades, that there is consensus on what it should look like, and that changes have been slow, suggests that increasing children's experiences with quality science programs requires actions at the policy level. These actions are not mysterious. The difficulty in implementing them is as much about will, economics, and politics as it is about crafting implementation strategies. Two recent reports have focused specifically on policy issues that need to be addressed if STEM education in early childhood is to change (Early STEM Working Group, 2017; McClure et al., 2017). Each lists a set of recommendations. While these recommendations vary slightly in how they are presented and the particular emphasis, there is enormous overlap. Below is a list that draws heavily from these reports. Readers are encouraged to read the full reports.

- Improve pre-service and in-service STEM-related professional development and training for early childhood teachers.
- Improve institutional supports and make high-quality early STEM resources and implementation guidance available to practitioners.
- Professionalize the role and pay of teachers of PreK.
- Build a sustainable and aligned system of high-quality early learning from birth through age 8 and ensure that early learning and development standards explicitly address the STEM disciplines and align with K-12 standards.
- Develop and support a research agenda that informs developmental trajectories, effective resources, and best practices in early childhood STEM education. Support researcher–practitioner partnerships in which practitioners are involved as on-going partners as early as the research design stage, play an essential role in supporting the iterative process of education reform.
- Establish initiatives, resources, and supports that promote parents' and families' involvement and engagement in their young children's STEM education.
- Raise the profile of early childhood STEM education using insights from communications science to build public will for and understanding of early STEM learning.
- Support and expand the out-of-school web of STEM learning "charging stations" available to children.

Closure

For many years, early childhood education has focused on children's social, emotional, and physical development as well as basic skills in language and mathematics. Yet the exploration of the natural world is the stuff of childhood. Science, when viewed as a process of constructing theories and new understandings, is a natural focus in early childhood programs. The growing understanding and recognition of the power of children's early thinking and learning and their potential to learn, and their drive to make sense of the natural world, argues strongly for early childhood settings that provide rich and challenging environments for science learning. Guided by skillful teachers, children's inquiry into appropriate natural phenomena is not only the place to build foundational experiences in science learning and appreciation for the natural world, it also is fertile ground in which children can develop their approaches to learning, practice many basic skills of literacy and mathematics, and learn to collaborate with others (Worth, 2010).

References

Akerson, V., Weikand, I., & Fouad, K. (2015). Children's ideas about life science concepts. In K. Trundle & M. Sackes (Eds.) *Research in early childhood science education.* (pp. 99–123). Dordrecht, Netherlands: Springer Netherlands.

Akman, O. (2015). Role of play in teaching science in the early years. In K. Trundle, & M. Sackes (Eds.). *Research in early childhood science education.* (pp. 237–259). Dordrecht, Netherlands: Springer Netherlands.

American Association for the Advancement of Science (AAAS): Project 2061. (1993). *Benchmarks for science.* Washington, DC: American Association for the Advancement of Science.

American Association for the Advancement of Science. (1999). *Dialogue on early childhood science, mathematics, and technology education.* Washington, DC: American Association for the Advancement of Science.

Brookline Public Schools. *K-8 learning expectations.* Retrieved from https://www.brookline.k12.ma.us//site/Default.aspx?PageID=1792

Copple, C., & Bredekamp, S. (Eds.) (2008). *Developmentally appropriate practice in early childhood programs serving children from birth through age 8.* Washington, DC: National Association for the Education of Young Children.

Early Childhood STEM Working Group. (2017). *Early STEM matters providing high-quality STEM experiences for all young learners: A policy report.* Retrieved from http://ecstem.uchicago.edu

Edwards, C., Gandini, L., & Forman, G. (Eds.) (2012). *The hundred languages of children: The Reggio Emilia experience in transformation.* Santa Barbara, CA: Praeger.

Gandini, L. (1993). Fundamentals of the Reggio Emilia approach to early childhood education. *Young Children, 49*(1), 4–8.

Gopnik, A., Meltzoff, A. N., & Kuhl, P. K. (1999). *The scientist in the crib: Minds, brains, and how children learn.* New York: Harper Collins.

Greenfield, D. (2018). Approaches to learning and science education in Head Start: Examining bidirectionality. *Early Childhood Research Quarterly, 44*(3), 34–42. doi:10.1016/j.ecresq

Hadzigeorgiou, Y. (2015). Young children's ideas about physical science concepts. In K. Trundle, & M. Sackes (Eds.) *Research in early childhood science education.* (pp. 37–97). Dordrecht, Netherlands: Springer Netherlands.

Harlen, W., & Qualter, A. (2014). *The teaching of science in primary schools.* New York, NY: Routledge.

Jirout, J., & Klahr, D. (2012). Children's scientific curiosity: In search of an operational definition of an elusive concept. *Developmental Review, 32,* 125–160. doi:10.1016/j.dr.2012.04.002

Lotto, B. (2017). *Deviate: The science of seeing differently.* New York, NY: Hachette Books.

Massachusetts Department of Elementary and Secondary Education. (2016). *Massachusetts science and technology/engineering curriculum framework 2016.* Retrieved from http://www.doe.mass.edu/frameworks

McClure, E., Guernsey, L., Clements, D., Bales, S., Nichols, J., Kendall-Taylor, N., & Levine, M. (2017). *STEM starts early: Grounding science, technology, engineering, and math education in early childhood.* New York, NY: The Joan Ganz Cooney Center at Sesame Workshop.

National Association for the Education of Young Children (NAYC). (2009). Position statement: Developmentally appropriate practice in early childhood programs serving children from birth through age 8. Retrieved from https://www.naeyc.org/resources/topics/dap/position-statement

National Research Council. (1996). *The national science education standards.* Washington, DC: National Academies Press.

National Research Council. (2007). *Taking science to school: Learning and teaching science in grades K–8.* Washington, DC: National Academies Press.

National Research Council. (2001). *Eager to learn: Educating our preschoolers.* Washington, DC: National Academies Press.

National Research Council. (2007). *Ready, set, science.* Washington, DC: National Academy Press.

National Research Council. (2011). *A framework for K-12 science education: Practices, crosscutting concepts, and core ideas.* Washington, DC: The National Academies Press.

National Science Teachers Association (NSTA). (2014). *Early childhood science education: A position statement of the National Science Teachers Association* and endorsed by the National Association for the Education of Young Children. Washington, DC: National Science Teachers Association.

NGSS Lead States. (2013). *The Next Generation Science Standards: For States, By States.* Washington, DC: The National Academies Press. doi:10.17226/18290

Pennsylvania Department of Education and Department of Human Services: Office of Child Development and Early Learning. (2016). *2014/2016 Pennsylvania learning standards for early childhood.* Retrieved from http://www.pdesas.org/Page/Viewer/ViewPage/11

Rutherford, J., & Ahlgren, H. (1989). *Science for all Americans.* Washington, DC: Oxford University Press.

Sackes, M. (2015). Young children's ideas about earth and space science concepts. In K. Trundle, & M. Sackes. (Eds.) *Research in early childhood science education.* (pp. 35–65). Dordrecht, Netherlands: Springer Netherlands.

Trundle, K., & Sackes, M. (Eds.). (2015). *Research in early childhood science education.* Dordrecht, Netherlands: Springer Netherlands.

University of Illinois. (2010). STEM in Early Education and Development Conference: Collected Papers. *Early Childhood Research and Practice, Beyond this Issue, 12*(2).

Worth, K. (2010). Science in early childhood classrooms: Content and process. *Early Childhood Research & Practice, Beyond This Issue. Collected Papers from the STEM in Early Education and Development Conference, 12*(2).

Worth, K., & Grollman, S. (2003). *Worms, shadows, and whirlpools: Science in the early childhood classroom.* Portsmouth, NH: Heinemann.

Worth, K., Winokur, J., Crissman, S., & Heller-Winokur, M. (2009). *The essentials of science and literacy: A guide for teachers.* Portsmouth, NH: Heinemann.

Wurm, J. (2005). *Working in the Reggio way: Beginner's guide for American teachers.* St. Paul, MN: Redleaf Press.

2

TECHNOLOGY AND YOUNG CHILDREN

Processes, Context, Research, and Practice

Lynn C. Hartle

Most children growing up after the rapid expansion of digital technologies and the internet in the 1990s cannot imagine a world without technology. They live in a world where a few clicks on a computer, tablet, or mobile phone bring up a wealth of information from the internet, connects us face to face for a video chat, or even turn off our lights at home. Humans throughout history have involved technologies—objects, systems, or processes to modify the natural world to meet human needs and wants. Rapidly emerging and advancing technologies in science, engineering, and mathematics fields will impact the future life, work, health, and education of young children in ways society has yet to imagine (Early Childhood STEM Working Group, 2017).

Experts in business (Cearley, Burke, Searle, & Walker, 2017) predict technology trends in business and commercial applications, some of which are moving faster than PreK–12 education (Kinshuk Huang, Sampson, & Chen, 2013; Lim, Zhao, Tondeur, Chai, & Tsai, 2013). As an expert on emerging technologies, Chris Dede (2011, 2017), Harvard University Professor in Learning Technologies, Technology, Innovation, and Education Programs, suggests that preparation at all levels of education should not focus on knowledge and skills for jobs of today. Schools need to prepare students with thinking and collaboration skills needed for careers yet to be developed and will change as technologies change.

Two of the current trends in technology application include Artificial Intelligences (AI) and the Internet of Things (IoT). AI that learn from patterns of data are already making the way into the mainstream, such as facial recognition security for mobile phones and fluid language translations. Self-driving cars are the next AI devices that today's young children will own during their lifetimes. Intelligent Apps, the human interface to AI, provide targeted feedback to users, for example in game-based learning, learning a second language, or monitoring home or school energy uses. Immersive experiences, such as augmented reality (AR), virtual reality (VR), and mixed reality experiences, are readily available as virtual labs and virtual and interactive museum tours and field trips, as well as simulations that can be used for teacher training. Finally, Wearable Technology is still relatively new, but catching on, such as smart watches and exercise monitors, wearable and touch devices that can conduct a medical grade EKG and send the results to a phone app, VR headsets, and a second iteration of Google glasses.

While technology uses are pervasive in ever-changing digital contemporary society, young children's involvement in appropriate interactive media and selected types of technologies requires intentional guidance to optimize cognitive, social, emotional, physical, and linguistic learning and development. Challenges exist (Voogt, Erstad, Dede, & Mishra, 2013), but research studies report the benefits of carefully selected developmentally appropriate and interactive technology tools and materials to enhance children's learning and development as effectively as playing and working with non-technology materials (Hartle & Berson, 2012; Simon & Nemeth, 2012).

While science, engineering, and math are content areas or subjects, non-digital technologies (e.g., pencils, blocks), digital technologies, and interactive media are actually not a subject, but are important tools, processes, or systems. Technologies can support learning in other content areas (e.g., literacy) and usually involve problem solving resulting in modifications of the natural world to solve the problem to meet human needs or desires (Early Childhood STEM Working Group, 2017). Mitchell Resnick (2006, 2017), head of the Life Long Kindergarten group of engineers at the Massachusetts Institute of Technology, suggests that computers and their uses should be considered more like paint brushes to create, imagine, and play, than like TVs for passive viewing. Additionally, not all technologies require sitting in front of a computer screen; some technologies engage robotics and mechanized gears. Marina Bers (2018), one of Resnick's former students, focuses on the development of technology-rich experiences for children that are modeled like digital coding and computational thinking "playgrounds." Her team has developed technology toys with which children can do what they naturally do—move, explore, invent, collaborate with peers and adults, and even resolve conflicts. Older technologies, such as tape recorders, light tables, DVD players, and overhead projectors, can also still be valuable resources; but interactive media that utilize tablets, interactive whiteboards (IWBs), mobile phones, digital cameras, digital microscopes, and computers are quickly finding their way into schools and homes.

The following sections couch the expanding world of the young child through a bioecological perspective, a practical framework for contextualization of developmentally appropriate technology interactions. Support for this perspective is research on the impact of children's engagement with digital technologies. While limited, research is central to the development of approaches to guide appropriate interactive technology experiences and related adult guidance to support science, math, and engineering for young children in formal and informal settings.

Conceptual Framework

A bioecological perspective (Rosa & Tudge, 2013; Tudge, Merçon-Vargas, Liang,& Payir, 2017) provides a practical framework for contextualization of developmentally appropriate technology use (McClure et al., 2017; Rosen & Jaruszewicz, 2009; Wang, Berson, Jaruszewicz, Hartle, & Rosen, 2010). This model affords an evolving system for studying human development over time and extends Bronfenbrenner's original model (1979). The model supports the study of the many new changes as technologies impact the world of young children as they move through school and into a world of work in ways society can only begin to predict. Children, families, schools, and communities need a better understanding of how the multiple realities of digital representation can be one of many strategies to enhance children's experiences now and in the future.

Process-Person-Context-Time (PPCT) Model

This bioecological perspective emphasizes understanding children's development and the child's reciprocal interactions with people, objects, and symbols in a variety of social contexts as well as the interrelation among the various settings or spheres in which the child functions. The PPCT Model expands on the influences on children's development (Rosa & Tudge, 2013; Tudge et al., 2017). Children's affordances, access to Information and Communication Technologies (ICT), as well as family beliefs about technology uses, impact how technologies are used to enhance development. The concept of "exposure," the extent of the contact of engagement (frequency, duration, interruption, timing, and intensity) and proximal processes are key to understanding developmental changes in learning (Bronfenbrenner & Morris, 2006). The child's experiences with ICT, if repeated and personally relevant, will enhance success with those technologies (time and process). Each child's unique personal characteristics, skills, cognition, and limitations due to any special needs play a part in both how the child progresses, what the child learns, and how the child uses technology (person). How children utilize and how often children utilize technologies throughout their life spans, as well as the timing of the cultural climate in history, shape agency in each child's own learning and development (Rosa & Tudge, 2013).

Proximal Processes

Human development over a lifetime involves engagement in progressively more complex reciprocal interactions with persons, objects, and symbols in their immediate environment. When these interactions are sustained or repeated over extended periods-of-time, children gain competence. Bronfenbrenner and Morris (2006) coined these enduring forms of interaction *proximal processes*; these processes are so important to this model and theory that Bronfenbrenner considered proximal processes the *engines of development*.

These proximal processes, enduring everyday activities and interactions with people and materials (of recent including new ICT) that change rapidly, are continually influenced by the person (the child, teachers, family), the context, and time to vary in form, power, and direction to then influence each child's development (Tudge et al., 2017). There is still controversy about whether (a) young children should use digital technologies at all; (b) how much technology is enough; and (c) what might be the right technologies for young children. The rapid growth of technology into every segment of society suggests that a central part of children's future lives and work will rely on knowledge and skills in ICT. Learning and development will depend on children developing through relevant, repeated and appropriate proximal processes.

A study by the RAND Corporation (Daugherty, Dossani, Johnson, & Oguz, 2014) takes the perspective that early childhood education can play a central role in bridging the digital divide between low- and high-income families. They discuss the need for children to have early access and develop a trajectory of skills (through repeated substantive exposure and adult guidance) that they will use in future careers and lives. Those who use technology in the workplace earn 14–27% more than those who do not; and the findings are clear that children, especially those from families with low incomes who participate in early childhood education, achieve better life and career skills. The Early Childhood STEM Working Group (2017) takes the stand that the proximal processes in early childhood education and family life should include foundational technology literacy skills.

Person Characteristics

Children are naturally curious and want to learn; while physical interactions with people and objects are central to young children's development (NAEYC, 2009), the technologies that are all around them are enticing. The child (person) should be at the center of all learning decisions. Three types of developmentally instigative characteristics of the developing person include *demand, resource*, and *force*. Demand characteristics or personal stimulus are those first impressions of initial visual characteristics, such as color, shape, or blinking lights as well as initial impressions or comparisons to what the child knows, such as "Is this toy fun?" or "Is this teacher friendly?" Resource characteristics are developed from previous experiences, such as learning to read and knowing ways to play, so these impact children's comfort level as well as ability to try new technology materials and experiences. Force characteristics have to do with children's developed belief systems, temperament, motivation, and persistence, and impact children's ability to stay on task or finish an activity (Tudge et al., 2017).

Understanding and developing those characteristics is not only important to the child, but also to those who interact with the child. Teachers' or parents' demand characteristics impact the children if they limit or expand their children's technology experiences depending on, for example the gender of a child or if the child seems shy. Resource characteristics of teachers or parents with limited experiences with technologies may not be able to or willing to support children's uses with technologies; while adults with more experiences may expand experiences for children. Belief systems, force characteristics of parents and teachers, have the potential to afford them the motivation and persistence (or not) to work with children who are not as easy to teach as other children (Tudge et al., 2017).

Contexts

Bioecological theory (Tudge et al., 2017) connects the child's personal characteristics with spheres of influence and contexts to provide a lens to explore how current and emerging digital technologies and experiences through the internet stretch the boundaries of these spheres to provide new contexts in which children interact and learn (Wang et al., 2010). The **Microsystem** context consists of the spheres of influence of home, school, place of worship, community settings and people with whom the child interacts. The **Mesosystem** is not really its own sphere but includes relations between microsystems that directly affect the child. The **Exosystem** includes linkages that indirectly affect the child, such as societal structures, standards/regulations, research, and institutions (Rosa & Tudge, 2013). Finally, the **Macrosystem** is of the highest order.

> The macrosystem consists of the overarching pattern of micro-, meso-, and exosystems characteristic of a given culture, subculture, or other broader social context, with particular reference to the developmentally-investigative belief systems, resources, hazards, life styles, opportunity structures, life course options, and patterns of social exchange that are embedded in each of these systems. The macrosystem may be thought of a societal blueprint for a particular culture, subculture, or other broader social context. (Bronfenbrenner, 1989, p. 228)

Young children in the 21st century continue to have strong and frequent connections to their immediate **Microsystem** spheres of home, school, and community activities, but these spheres are "stretched" through children's growing involvement with the ever-expanding digital worlds of TV, internet videos, online games, and virtual chats with friends and family. In their chapter "Young Children's Technology Experiences in Multiple Contexts: Bronfenbrenner's Ecological Theory Reconsidered," Wang et al. (2010) describe the world of a young child in contemporary society who seamlessly shifts connections from her immediate world of home, family, and school to other worlds through the use of the internet. Modern computer interfaces allow for more distanced interactions with relative ease and with a few clicks, children can interact virtually with other friends to play video games, complete online homework, and communicate with distant friends and family. Relationships with adults and peers in real-life contexts continue to be an integral part of children's immediate world as children can and do move fluidly between virtual and real worlds to bring other internet users into their immediate worlds; a paradox of immediate vs virtual that can raise concerns.

Family life is changing as more technologies make their way into daily life. These new digital spheres of technologies were not available when many of the parents of today were growing up, so they lack experiences or knowledge on how or when to balance virtual world and real-world experiences to best enhance children's development. Over half of families in a survey by the Joan Ganz Cooney Center (Rideout, 2014) reported that parents want more guidance on selection and uses of quality educational media to support learning. Some parents feel that uses of "devices" at home takes away too much time from other activities, such as playing, gardening, and cooking together. For those families who are using the internet at home, 77% of the parents reported that they helped their children use digital technology, and 53% said their children helped them.

Yet, for some families, their sphere of influence and choices of how to guide their children is limited, and they need to rely on community assets in their microsystems. Families with lower incomes do not have access to these technologies or to high-speed internet: 33% do not have access to high-speed internet at home for children to do homework and cannot afford experiences with technologies at museums or science centers (Guernsey & Levine, 2017). Parents earning less than $50,000 per year report that libraries are a great resource for the internet, quiet study spaces, interactive learning, and e-books. When children are not home and are in the library, they could still benefit from "media mentors," but according to the Association for Library Service to Children, only 22% of libraries offer device mentoring and only 2% of those offer services for emerging bilingual children (Campbell, Haines, Koester, & Stoltz, 2015). Young children from low-income families may only interact with technologies briefly while in libraries and during their school day.

Young children engage in academic learning in school and informal learning experiences in libraries, museums, cultural events, and other extracurricular activities. Besides the systematic view of children's development in multiple contexts, bioecological theory also emphasizes the importance of investigating the **Mesosystem**—interrelations among the various contexts, formal and informal, and how these are interconnected, dynamic, and fluid (Tudge et al., 2017). Teachers, schools, libraries, and community organizations have an important role to select activities based on the age, interests, cultural, and abilities of each child. Technology play should not replace other real-world activities crucial for young children's development, such as block play, social interactions, story reading, outdoor play, drawing, painting, singing, and more (Hartle, 2015).

Conflicting views, activities, and practices involving technology in different contexts can lead to adverse consequences. For example, if teachers limit use of technology to drill and practice activities with fill-in-the-blank electronic worksheets or restrict technology to an extra activity once the "real" work is completed, children may not value technology for learning. They may view technology experiences at home and other informal settings as distinct from school experiences. At home, if children engage in excessive use of video games and television, this reinforces a dichotomy of technology: boring learning at school vs. exciting gaming at home. Negative technology experiences can evoke negative connotations and detract from potential, rich opportunities to promote transformative learning and knowledge building (Wang et al., 2010).

The report *STEM Starts Early* by the Joan Ganz Cooney Center at Sesame Street Workshop points out how children's learning is supported and enriched when their formal school learning is connected to informal experiences (McClure et al., 2017). They suggest that formal and informal learning spaces can create a web of "charging stations" where children can power up to extend their STEM learning and hence STEM fluency. Environments that are well coordinated between home, school, and the community in terms of practices, activities, and systems of learning tend to enhance children's development. An example of a coordinated practice could include a visit to a museum followed by a school's use of inquiry-based technology experiences with take home activities. Children explore the museum, bring additional questions back to the classroom, and investigate the answers on the internet later at home with their parents. The report for the Cooney Center by Shapiro (2018), *Digital Play for Global Citizens*, takes it a step further by providing fun and meaningful activities that teachers can do in school and then extend with families at home to help "… children learn about, understand and engage with our increasingly interconnected world" (p. 4) so children can become "macro-minded" global citizens.

Technology can be a valuable bridge between the microsystems of home and school. A study by the RAND Corporation (Daugherty, Dossani, Johnson, & Wright, 2014) found that if teachers carefully choose and use technologies that families have and use (e.g., text, email, websites), communication between home and school improves, as does school-based parental involvement. Children may not recall what they did at school when they get home. Having children's work posted on a system like *Seesaw* that parents can access from an application on their phones, provides a conduit for home school connections.

The **Exosystem** includes societal structures that indirectly affect the child. McClure and colleagues (2017) reviewed educational policies, one of the social structures that impacts student learning in STEM. They found that inconsistencies with policy expectations and instruments as well as lack of continuity of instruction across grade levels impact how well children are developing STEM skills. Policies that promote seamless pathways of the infrastructure (standards, curricula, assessment, and professional development) from PreK–third grade are needed. Similar professional learning is needed for PreK teachers as well as K–third grade teachers because shared goals and instructional strategies lead to increased student performance. Teachers need to implement concepts with technologies by building from lower to higher skills in a learning trajectory (Sarama & Clements, 2013). Following national standards, such as those from the International Society for Technology in Education (ISTE, 2016), provides a sequential road map for learning based on research-based principles and practices.

Another indirect influence is the limited funding for comprehensive research-practice partnerships on the impacts of technology uses with young children. In a comprehensive analysis of grants funded, McClure and colleagues (2017) found that some federal monies support math and science concept development for young children, but modest research dollars were used or available for studying technology uses with young children (see also Paciga & Donohue, 2017). Without adequate dollars for research, teachers and families have limited knowledge on best practices for engaging children in types, amount of time, or appropriate technologies that afford children the skills they need for the 21st century.

In the Joan Ganz Cooney Center report *How to Bring Early Learning and Family Engagement into the Digital Age*, Guernsey and Levine (2017) recommend a comprehensive plan to strengthen and bridge the societal structures impacting children's STEM development. This comprehensive plan includes four interlocking and progressive action steps to help communities prioritize and advance the agenda for families, communities, and schools. They include the following:

1. Take stock of family engagement offerings currently in place, online connectivity, and keep an eye on equity and diversity.
2. Develop professional learning programs that build corps of media mentors (see also Donohue, 2017).
3. Invest in physical infrastructure that promotes internet connectivity for homes, schools, and community centers and foster meaningful participation across these systems.
4. Insure success, create a continuous cycle of improvement using research and evaluation to continue to improve the systems.

Children are indirectly impacted by research, national organizations, and public policy, but these are dynamic as new technologies and beliefs about new technologies change with increased availability in daily life, work, and school. The overarching **Macrosystem** of family norms, cultural norms, patterns of beliefs, values are passed on from one generation to the next, but throughout the course of history are also evolving into new societal structures. The Frameworks Institute interviewed experts, researchers, and members of the American public (i.e., laypersons, families) about STEM learning environments. They analyzed and compared public understandings with those of experts to identify gaps, similarities, and differences to provide a starting place on how to connect children's STEM learning environments effectively with the goal to improve learning. In their report, *Crossing the Boundaries: Mapping the Gaps between Expert and Public Understandings of Bridging STEM Learning Environments*, Levay, Volmert, and Kendall-

Taylor (2018) found two sets of common assumptions and understandings or "cultural models" that shaped how respondents thought about the role of technology in children's learning.

"Technology as Artificial Distraction," was the metaphor for those who fit the dominant cultural model regarding technology uses. The dominant culture viewed technology as something that is not real, not authentic learning and can isolate children and even distract or impede them from real learning. The less dominant way of thinking about technology, the "Engaging Technology" model, considers ways open-ended, interactive gaming computer programs, robotics, virtual graphics, or internet searches can facilitate learning by increasing children's interest and engagement with content. An example of how technology can and should be responsive to children's input and how engagement is fundamental to effective learning is *Minecraft*, where players move virtual blocks to create and learn how to survive in those worlds they create.

As cultures evolve, values shift to make way for the continuing impact and influences of technology in the child's near and virtual spheres of influence. Communicators (teachers, parents, media, organizations, schools) need to know how to reframe the research on best practices with technologies to enhance children's learning in school, home, community, and now virtual worlds, on the internet.

Time

More than once thought, young children are capable of engaging in all STEM practices, and, in fact, opportunities for learning and developing STEM habits may be missed if schools and homes wait until later years (McClure et al., 2017). We are now living in a "connected" world so children should be prepared in connected ways to value global citizenship (Shapiro, 2018). Implications of technology uses over time are illustrated by a survey of more than 10,000 North American families on the uses of technologies as children matured. Samuel (2015) found that parents could be grouped into three groups based on their responses.

One-third of the responders (almost half of the parents of teens) were termed "enablers." They allowed their children to use their phones and computers as much as they wanted, allowing their children to set the family's tech agenda. Another third, on the opposite end of the spectrum (including half of the parents of preschoolers), were called the "limiters," and said they heeded warnings about the impact of technology to reduce children's attention spans and interpersonal skills, so they limited technologies at every opportunity. While another third, the "digital mentors," actively guided their children on internet uses (half of the digital mentors do so at least once per week), and they connected with their children through technology such as playing video games with them. The extent of the contact of engagement and context of exposure, frequency, duration, interruption, timing, and intensity (Bronfenbrenner & Evans, 2000) by the "media mentors" proved most successful for preparing their children for appropriate uses of technology. The children of the "digital mentors" were less likely to engage as teenagers in problematic behaviors such as posting rude comments to students or watching pornography. Children of "limiters," without training and guidance, were less likely to have the skills needed to engage with media in productive ways as teens. Digital "mentors" over digital "limiters" used an approach to digital parenting that could sustain a family long term and prepare their children for the world where technologies are prevalent.

Research: Navigating Spheres of Influence and Informing Intentional Technology Decisions

While children are drawn to new virtual worlds and technologies, questions arise about whether or not those who influence children's worlds (e.g., families and teachers) have equal access to these technology tools and if they have the knowledge, skills, and experiences to use data driven decisions as they guide and implement technologies with young children. In a meta-analysis of 595 pieces of literature on young children and technology published from 2012–2017, Pagica and Donohue (2017) found that there is growing interest in this topic, but that the research is limited. Much of the research they did find focused on access to and frequency of uses of technologies. Many studies do not contain live observations of children using the technology and provide few details about the social and emotional contexts in which children are using technologies.

A 2017 survey of families, *Common Sense Census: Media Use by Kids Zero to Eight*, reported findings compared to their 2011 and 2013 surveys designed to illuminate the uses of the ever-changing digital technologies (Common Sense Media, 2017). Television watching still outnumbers the minutes on any other device at 58 minutes per day, but almost 98% of children 0–8 years live in a home with a mobile device (95% have smartphones; 78% have a tablet). Since 2011, the time young children spend on mobile devices tripled to 48 minutes per day. A growing trend by 2017 in homes with young children is that 11% have VR headsets, 10% have smart toys, and 9% report having a voice activated virtual assistant device. However, print is still valued; young children still preferred printed over digital materials (just 3 minutes per day on electronic devices and 26 minutes on printed books).

The 2017 survey also found that challenges remain. Even though the digital divide has narrowed between lower vs. higher income households (74% of lower income households, up from 42% in 2011, have digital devices). Also, contrary to recommendations by American Academy of Pediatrics Council on Communications and Media (2016), 49% of parents report their young children watch television or play videos in the hour before bedtime; and 42% report the TV is always or almost always on, even though negative effects have been found in terms of quality sleep and distractions from concentration, impacting school engagement. Fortunately, 67% of families whose children use screen media reported that it helps their children, and they reported wanting to know more about appropriate uses of technology. Since their children have technologies at home and in school, this adds to the number of hours and uses of digital media. Research indicates, though, that this varies by what media schools have, teacher attitudes about media uses, and how much professional development teachers have.

In their study, Callaghan and Reich (2018) found that while half of all application software (apps) on the market is for preschool children, their analysis of the apps' features revealed that few of the apps provided scaffolded feedback. Other features were also found lacking, including (1) Simplicity and Clarity of Goals (learning goals and features of enjoyment, types of prompts, modeling goals, in-play guidance), (2) Feedback and Rewards (consistency of guidance, quality of feedback, reward systems), (3) Structure of Challenge (leveling, scaffolded challenge), and (4) Mobile App-Based Interactions (touchscreen interactions, mobile-device capabilities). One app that does meet these qualities and has research-based child outcomes is from the Bedtime Math Foundation; it extends family bedtime routines with fun, learning activities. One study found that first graders who used this app at least once per week were three months ahead of their peers on the *Woodcock-Johnson-III Tests of Achievement* (Berkowitz et al., 2015).

The type of device children use matters as well. Roskos, Burstein, Shang, and Gray (2014) studied the differences between children's engagement behaviors (looking, touching, moving, gesturing) while using an iPod, an iPad, and desktop touchscreen computer. Relevant to the importance of young children's engagement through touch, researchers found the iPod more than the desktop touchscreen computer led to more tapping, swiping, dragging, and pulling. The iPod also stimulated more moving, gesturing, and looking behaviors. Considering the research on the value of multi-modality to motivate and increase the relevance of the visual effects, these findings further support the value of looking through a bioecological lens to understand the connections between child behaviors, adult mentoring, and affordance of materials.

Simon, Nameth, and McManis (2013) conducted research on the availability of technologies (N=485; 369 teachers and 116 administrators). Findings indicated that 95% of the early childhood classrooms had desktop or laptop computers available for the children; 44% were using IWBs; 37% were using tablet computers, but fewer were using smartpens, ebook readers, or iPod Touch (19%), smartphones (16%), or multi-touch tables or surfaces (6%). Seventy-five percent of teachers used technology because the children enjoy it. Of those, 67% used technology to extend concepts and skills, and 67% used technology indirectly to support the introduction of concepts and skills, as well as for children to learn how to use the technology itself. Teachers were using technologies in more large-group, teacher-directed ways; for example, about 60% of the teachers said they use the classroom computer (63%) or tablet (58%) less than 30 minutes per day, but 67% of teachers reported using IWBs for more than 30 minutes per day (Simon et al., 2013).

Wartella, Blackwell, Lauricella, and Robb (2013) reported a collaborative research study with the Center on Media and Human Development at Northwestern University, The Fred Rogers Center, and NAEYC. They found that while early childhood teachers increased in levels of confidence with using technologies, 92% had access to digital cameras, but only 61% used them once a week. Of the 84% with computers, only 45% used them once per week. Reasons for limited uses included the need for necessary technical assistance to implement the technology and the need for necessary professional development.

Teachers in both studies reported that they needed professional development to support young children's learning. This is consistent with a national trend that educational technology training has declined over time and lags behind the amount of technologies available to teachers. The number of laptops, tablets, netbooks, and Chromebooks shipped annually to US K-12 schools grew by 363% (more than 14 million devices shipped in 2015, compared to just over 3 million devices in 2010). Although schools have more technological resources, the percentage of fourth graders with math teachers who had received training on integrating technology into instruction ranged from 59% for the highest-poverty schools to 69% for the lowest-poverty schools. While trends in education technology require more creative and critical thinking skills, students report using computers most often for rote learning (Davis, 2017; Education Week Research Center, 2017).

Implications for Appropriate and Intentional Early Childhood Practices

Young children (birth to age 8) are ready and eager to engage in STEM experiences (McClure et al., 2017). Since the early 1990s, the National Association for the Education of Young Children has been involved in researching and understanding best practices with ICT as these almost burst into learning environments. Their first position paper, *Technology and Young Children—Ages 3 through 8* (NAEYC, 1996), led the way to guiding what was then known about how young should utilize technologies. Over the next 20 years, the types, quality, and quantity of technologies changed and continue to change all aspects of society. Additional research led to the updated position statement by National Association for the Education of Young Children and the Fred Rogers Center for Early Learning and Children's Media at Saint Vincent College (FRC) *Technology and Interactive Media as Tools in Early Childhood Programs Serving Children from Birth to Age Eight* (2012).

While science, math, and engineering STEM subjects have been accepted into early childhood classrooms, the education community is divided about how the rapidly changing world of technology should be integrated into early education. There are also concerns that "screen time" may replace the important developmentally appropriate activities such as pretend play, outdoor play, storytelling, and hands-on arts and building experiences (American Academy of Pediatrics

Council on Communications and Media, 2016; Levin, 2013). While there exists some conflicting evidence on the value of technology for young children, Wainwright and Linebarger (2006) found no evidence of harm to children. Rather they suggest that the educational content and children's use of technology support the use of selected digital media and interactive technologies. Developmentally appropriate practices must guide decisions about what, how, when, and where technology is integrated (NAEYC, 2009).

From 2012 to 2018, other major position papers from government, medicine, media, higher education, and research leaders in the field of early childhood education and educational technology brought to the public research on appropriate uses of technologies with young children and translated research into practices of how adults should guide children's engagement (See Table 2.1).

TABLE 2.1 Position Papers: Technology and Children

- Levay, K., Volmert, A. and Kendall-Taylor, N. (April, 2018). *Crossing the boundaries: Mapping the gaps between expert and public understandings of bridging STEM learning environments.* http://www.frameworksinstitute. org/stem-learning.html
- Levine, M. H. (April, 2018). "What does the research say about tech and kids' learning?" Part 1 & 2. New York: NY: The Joan Ganz Cooney Center at Sesame Street Workshop. http://joanganzcooneycenter.org/blog/
- Shapiro, J. (March 2, 2018). *Digital play for global citizens. New York: The Joan Ganz Cooney Center at Sesame Workshop.* http://joanganzcooney center.org/publication/digital-play-for-global-citizens/
- Early Childhood STEM Working Group (January, 2017). *Early STEM matters: Providing high-quality STEM experiences for all young learners.* Chicago, IL: author. Retrieved at http://ecstem.uchicago.edu
- Common Sense Media. (2017). *Common sense census: Media use by kids zero to eight.* San Francisco, CA: Author. https://www.commonsensem edia.org/research
- Paciga, K. A. and Donohue, C. (2017). *Technology and interactive media for young children: A whole child approach connecting the vision of Fred Rogers with research and practice.* Latrobe, PA: Fred Rogers Center for Early Learning and Children's Media at Saint Vincent College. http://www.fre drogerscenter.org/frctecreport
- U.S. Department of Education, Office of Educational Technology. (October, 2016). *Early learning and educational technology policy brief.* Washington, DC: Author. https://tech.ed.gov/files/2016/10/Early-Lea rning-Tech-Policy-Brief.pdf
- American Academy of Pediatrics Council on Communications and Media. (2016). Media and young minds. *Pediatrics, 138* (5). http://pediatrics. aappublications.org/content/138/5/e20162591.full

- Epstein, A. S. (February 3, 2015). Using technology appropriately in the preschool classroom. *Exchange Focus*.https://www.childcareexchange.com/using-technology-appropriately-in-the-preschool-classroom/
- Daugherty, L., Dossani, R., Johnson, E. E., and Oguz, M. (2014). Using early childhood education to bridge the digital divide. Santa Monica, CA: RAND Corporation, PE-119-PNC. https://www.rand.org/pubs/perspectives/PE119.html
- Lerner, C., and Barr, R. (2014). Screen sense, setting the record straight: Research-based guidelines for screen use for children under 3 years old. https://www.zerotothree.org/resources/series/screen-sense

While each report included unique and directed messages, there was consensus about key issues (Donohue & Schomburg, 2017). All position statements agree that technology, when used properly, can be a tool for learning, but strongly endorse always putting the child first, with caring relationships taking precedence over technologies. Another hallmark of any technologically connected classroom is that carefully selected materials should promote collaborative rather than isolated uses that promote children's critical thinking, collaboration, creativity, and communication that children will need to be successful in the 21st-century workforce (Zimmerman, 2018).

Technology, if used appropriately, is one of the many literacies (broader than reading and writing) children can use to understand, explore, and document their learning. Multi-literacy examples include researching a question or topic, reviewing the merit of the content found at selected internet sites, taking and using digital photographs to capture understanding, and using a story creation app to document what children learn. These digital literacies stretch the analog world to other dimensions of visual, signs, symbols to deeper aesthetic understandings (Hartle & Jaruszewicz, 2009).

Technologies should be selected carefully based on how each enriches learning and enriches other early childhood hands-on activities, rather than by marketing claims. Experiences with technology should be interactive, engaging, culturally sensitive, and developmentally appropriate. As with any learning tool, Hirsh-Pasek, Zosh, Golinkoff, Gray, Robb, and Kaufman (2015) illustrate experience should be in the context of scaffolded exploration. Technologies and apps should initiate the four learning science pillars: active involvement, engagement with the materials, meaningful personally relevant experiences, and social interaction with peers and adults. Beyond those affordances, compared with traditional play materials, ICT materials may provide more than physical objects can, such as viewing a 3-D object on the computer from multiple angles. Computer-generated images can also be revisited multiple times to enhance reflection and new ideas (Sarama & Clements, 2013).

Teaching trends supported by the ISTE are making their way into PreK–third grade classrooms to support children's seamless uses of both high tech and lower technologies in all subjects (Randles, 2018). The ISTE standards for students is a framework to guide students to become empowered learners, digital citizens, knowledge constructors, innovative designers, computational thinkers, creative communicators, and global collaborators (ISTE, 2016). These standards shift the agenda away from warning students about the risks of computers to empowering them to leverage digital media for creation, social justice, and equity. The Brookings Institute supports these skills for a changing world (Care, Kim, Anderson, & Gustafsson-Wright, 2017). Freeman, Adams Becker, Cummins, Davis, and Hall Giesinger's (2017) research found that two of the trends that are accelerating K-12 education technology adoption in the next two years are "coding as literacy" and the rise of Science, Technology, Engineering, (with and through the) Arts, Math (STEAM) learning.

Marina Bers, co-founder of KinderLab Robotics, studies the design and implementation of innovative learning technologies to promote young children's positive development through coding. Bers' coding systems support STEAM learning. Through a lengthy research and development process, Bers and her team created KIBO, a block-based coding language. Children use the platform by sequencing and snapping together the coded physical 3-D command blocks to control their robots' movements, sounds, and lights. They can work alone or work with others to decorate their robots, create paper costumes for their robots, and engage their robots to tell stories. The blocks are color and gender neutral to support all children of all backgrounds and genders to engage in STEAM (Bers, 2018). Bers (2012) teaches children coding so they develop fluency in a new set of tools for self-expression and development of cognitive skills as they solve a problem (e.g., teach the robot new commands) through sequencing the KIBO blocks. When children solve a problem through coding, they are using an engineering design process: identify a problem, imagine and plan, build and test, then share the new creation. KIBO is an effective programming tool because the coding blocks are 3-D, concrete, tangible blocks that children can manipulate, the way young children naturally play to learn. Once children are comfortable with the processes of coding through concrete block programming, children can begin using Scratch Jr., another coding language Bers and colleagues created. Using a Scratch Jr. program on a tablet or computer, children snap together digital (rather than 3-D) coding blocks to make characters move, jump, and sing to tell stories. Children can add their own voice and photos to plan, develop, edit, and create stories, games, or movies.

Children live in a digital world and can engage in developmentally appropriate uses such as KIBO and Scratch Jr. to develop critical and creative thinking and tools they will need for the future. Since the research shows that limiting or considering technology as artificial and distinct from real does not support better uses as teenagers (Levay, Volmert, & Kendall-Taylor, 2018; Samuel, 2015), why not prepare young children with the media literacy skills and digital citizenship to make good decisions about technology uses? Faith Rogow (2012) in her book, *The Case for Digital Media Literacy in Early Childhood Education*, reminds teachers and families that learning to use technologies, like learning to use any other tool, is not culturally neutral—demand, resource, and force personal characteristics interact with the overarching macrosystem of culture, impact decisions about selecting or using technologies. Adults need to be willing to address and reduce biases and stereotypes that could limit children's chances of success. While society should be concerned that all children, regardless of income, have access to technologies and guidance to use devices productively. Media literacy also includes developing the habits of inquiry and skills of expression to question media influences and choices, while respecting family, school, and community cultures. Rogow (2015) has developed a set of six developmentally appropriate and achievable outcomes to guide teachers and parents to lay the foundation for young children's media literacy:

1. Routinely ask relevant questions about ideas and information and use at least two different strategies for finding credible answers.
2. Exhibit the habit of linking answers to specific evidence.
3. Demonstrate knowledge that media are made by people who make choices about what to include and what to leave out (i.e., that all media messages are "constructed").
4. Choose appropriate pictures to accompany a story or report they have created and provide a basic explanation for their choice.
5. Create and share original stories and reports using images, sounds, and words.
6. Identify media technologies as tools that people use for learning, communication, and persuasion, and that (with permission) they can use, too. (p. 94)

Since technologies are changing rapidly and the schools must keep pace, ongoing teacher professional learning is also needed to enhance the school's sphere of influence. National reports such as those by NAEYC and the Fred Rogers Center (2012), Institute of Medicine (IOM) and the National Research Council (NRC) (2015), U.S. Department of Education, Office of Educational Technology (2016), the Joan Ganz Cooney Center at Sesame Workshop, (McClure et al., 2017), and the Early Childhood STEM Working Group (2017), recommend early childhood teacher training programs make needed changes to include additional content and experience-based STEM pedagogy to guide children for 21st-century careers and life. Professional learning (rather than "development") that is intensive, sustained over time, seamlessly incorporated into professional life, and includes reflective practice are key elements to teachers' success in implementing any new tool, but especially technologies, if teachers have grown up without regular and purposeful technology uses.

One professional learning model that has proven success is the Technology in Early Childhood (TEC) Mentor Program at the Erikson Institute, based on *Family Engagement in the Digital Age: Early Childhood Educators as Media Mentors* (Donohue, 2017). Mentors learn through a blended learning system of hands-on exploration in a tech "playground" of engaging tools, videos of model lessons, and online learning experiences that extend and provide for collaborative communications and reflections. While not yet the common professional development model, this model is being replicated as school districts and early learning centers realize its potential (Lieberman, Cook, & Jackson, 2018).

Two tools also provide comprehensive teacher guidance. The Pennsylvania Digital Media Literacy Project, comprised of respected leaders in the early childhood field from the Fred Rogers Center and the PA Office of Child Development and Early Learning, developed a *Checklist for Identifying Exemplary Uses of Technology and Interactive Media for Early Learning* (Robb et al., 2014). Another evaluation system that teachers can use to evaluate how technology tools are being used and what children are learning through play extended with technologies is the *Digital Play Framework* (Bird & Edwards, 2014).

The Technology and Young Children Interest Forum of NAEYC (2008) provided an example of technology best practices and shared a day in the life of a preschool that utilizes technology as powerful extenders to rich interactive materials. The class engages in *transmedia*, a constructivist learning technique in which students use multiple platforms (e.g., YouTube, Twitter, Instagram) to tell a story. Critical thinking supports students' viewpoints, and experiences bring resources and ideas together in ways that are enticing, engaging, and immersive. Children move fluidly and in a connected fashion with and across all types of media—digital, print, art, photography, video, music, dance—to create, express, play, and document their learning. Crossing mediums allows for greater exploration, perspective taking, and connections to new learning of content and skills (Hartle & Jaruszewicz, 2009; Herr-Stephenson, Alper, Reilly, & Jenkins, 2013). Children are working on a long-term investigation of fossils, bones and dinosaurs. The sand table has been turned into a dig site and children are using magnifying glasses and electronic microscopes to explore their excavations of bones which have been hidden by the teacher.

Children are not just considering local learning but also *global learning*. While young children may not be directly engaging in collaborative projects that have addressed worldwide issues through paleontology, learning about these issues through internet stories, PBS shows, or videos plants the seed for greater under-standing, and, hopefully eventual global issues participation. In another center, children, with the assistance of an adult, are emailing a local paleontologist who recently visited their classroom because they had a few more questions they wanted to ask. Technologies are seamlessly embedded as supports that are almost invisible within the other engaged practices. (See Simon, & Nemeth (2012), for more ways to embed technology seamlessly.)

Using *blended learning* (a mix of traditional classroom activities with online activities, readings, and assessment), children are also engaged in block building and using mobile devices similar to ones they use at home (e.g., tablets) to take digital photos of their structures so they can later reflect on the angles, lines, and building strength. Photos are stored in a *Learning Management System* (LMS) that provides accessible online organization for materials, lessons, and tests with ease and flexibility of access for both online and in-person learning experiences.

Some children are making digital books on their iPads, then printing the books to add paint, paper, or writing. The teachers help children select materials and organize their books. *Personalized learning* and giving each student a laptop (*1-to-1 computing*) is only the first step to improving student achievement; it depends on how the computer is used and how the student is supported. Zheng, Warschauer, Lin, and Chang (2016) in a meta-analysis of schools using 1-to-1 computing found that students expressed very positive attitudes about using the laptops, the ownership of their learning and problem solving skills increased, and, in some instances, project-based, student-centered, and individualized learning also increased.

These are only some of the appropriate practices teachers are using in public schools and community early learning settings. Two other resources are recommended: Chip Donohue's edited book: *Technology and Digital Media in the Early Years: Tools for Teaching and Learning* (2015) and Simon and Nemeth's book, *Digital Decisions: Choosing the Right Technology Tools for Early Childhood* (2012). Both resources follow the guidance of the Position Statement by NAYEC and Fred Rogers Center for Early Learning and Children's Media at Saint Vincent College (2012) and provide comprehensive guidance for practical, common-sense, technology-rich classrooms. With pictures, illustrations, charts, and explanations, these books guide teachers in appropriate practices to connect traditional play and learning materials with computers, software apps, interactive electronic whiteboards, mobile devices, e-books, e-readers, photos, videos, and tangible technologies.

Summary and Recommendations

New technologies have been emerging on the scene since the 1990s more rapidly than most early childhood teachers and parents can follow. Including digital media in early childhood programs may be one way to bridge the digital divide between families who can and who cannot afford technologies and high-speed internet at home. Most reports and research show that young children can be and should be engaged in interactive digital media, mentored by a knowledgeable adult. Teachers should follow the research and position statements when selecting, implementing, and monitoring children's uses of technology. High-quality books, websites, webinars, and other resources are emerging to guide teachers' best practices for young children; but these must be accompanied by investments in teacher preparation and ongoing, interactive professional learning to give teachers the knowledge and skills they need. Policies are needed for equitable access to technologies. This is an issue of social justice in a world where using technologies is a must in many careers; and communicating with technologies for collaborating and learning is essential. The early childhood communities need to advocate for more research funding to understand ways technologies can impact all aspects of children's development.

Best Practices Resources

- **Association of Library Service to Children,** "Media Mentorship in Libraries Serving Youth," list of resources. http://www.ala.org/alsc/publications-resources/white-papers
- **Common Sense Education, Scope and Sequence: Common Sense K–12 Digital Citizenship Curriculum**, https://www.commonsense.org/education/scope-and-sequencehttp://www.p21.org/
- **ISTE, International Society for Technology in Education**, www.iste.orghttp://www.iste.org/standards/for-students
- **KIBO**—Children ages 4–7 years old can playfully discover concepts by coding with wooden building blocks, creating sequences, and learning design processes. http://kinderlabrobotics.com/kibo/
- **Minecraft**—a sandbox (exploration) video game where you dig (mine) and build (craft) different kinds of 3-D blocks within a large world of varying terrains and habitats to explore. The game requires creativity from players. Other activities in the game include exploration, resource gathering, crafting, and combat https://minecraft.net/en-us/
- **National Library of Virtual Manipulatives,** Utah State University http://nlvm.usu.edu/en/nav/vlibrary.html
- **Pacific University Child Learning and Development Center** Best Practices and Tech Tools. http://fg.ed.pacificu.edu/cldc/bestpractices.html; http://fg.ed.pacificu.edu/cldc/techtools.html
- **Scratch Jr.**—Coding: young children (ages 5–7) can program their own interactive stories and games. In the process, they learn to solve problems, design projects, and express themselves creatively on the computer. http://scratchjr.org/
- **Technology in Early Childhood Center at Erikson Institute** resources for professional development and an online community for early childhood educators. http://teccenter.erikson.edu/
- **Transmedia**—Through transmedia play, children explore, enjoy, and remix elements from diverse media—for example, characters, settings, and plot elements taken from books, television, videos, toys, and current digital technologies, allowing children to tell new stories, work through problems, and share with others. http://joanganzcooneycenter.org/publication/t-is-for-transmedia/

References

American Academy of Pediatrics Council on Communications and Media. (2016). Media and young minds. *Pediatrics*, 138(5), 1–6. doi:10.1542/peds.2016–2591. Retrieved from http://pediatrics.aappublications.org/content/138/5/e20162591

Berkowitz, T., Schaeffer, M. W., Maloney, E. A., Peterson, L., Gregor, C., Levine, S. C., & Beilock, S.L. (2015). Math at home adds up to achievement at school. *Science*, 350 (6257), 196–198. doi:10.1126/science.aac7427

Bers, M. U. (2012). *Designing digital experiences for positive youth development: From playpen to playground.* Cary, NC: Oxford.

Bers, M. U. (2018). *Coding as a playground: Programming and computational thinking in the early childhood classroom.* New York, NY: Routledge.

Bird, J., & Edwards, S. (2014). Children learning to use technologies through play: A digital play framework. *British Journal of Educational Technology*, 46(6), 1149–1160. Retrieved from https://teccenter.erikson.edu/tec/the-digital-play-framework-a nd-the-exploration-of-technology-tools-guest-blog-by-jo-bird/

Bronfenbrenner, U. (1979). *The ecology of human development: Experiments by nature and design.* Cambridge, MA: Harvard University Press.

Bronfenbrenner, U. (1989). Ecological systems theory. In R. Vasta (Ed.), *Annals of child development: (Vol. 6) Six theories of child development: Revised formulations and current issues* (pp. 187–249). Greenwich, CT: JAI Press.

Bronfenbrenner, U., & Evans, G. (2000). Developmental science in the 21st century: Emerging questions, theoretical models, research design and empirical findings. *Social Development*, 9(1), 115–125.

Bronfenbrenner, U., & Morris, P. A. (2006). The bio-ecological model of human development. In W. Damon (Series Ed.) and R. M. Lerner (Vol. Ed.), *Handbook of child psychology: Theoretical models of human development* (pp. 793–828). New York, NY: Wiley.

Callaghan, M. N., & Reich, S. M. (2018) Are educational preschool apps designed to teach?: An analysis of the app market. *Learning, Media and Technology*, 43(3), 280–293. doi:10.1080/17439884.2018.1498355

Campbell, C., Haines, C., Koester, A., & Stoltz, D. (March 11, 2015). *Media mentorship in libraries serving youth.* Chicago, IL: Association for Library Service to Children (ALSC). http://www.ala.org/alsc/publications-resources/white-papers/mediamentorship

Care, E., Kim, H., Anderson, K., & Gustafsson-Wright, E. (March, 2017) *Skills for a changing world: National perspectives and the global movement.* Washington, DC: Brookings Institute. Retrieved from https://www.brookings.edu/research/skills-for-a-cha nging-world-2//

Cearley, D., Burke, B., Searle, S., & Walker, M. (2017,October 3). *Top 10 strategic technology trends for 2018: A Gartner trend insight report.* Stamford, CT: Gartner, Inc. Retrieved from https://www.gartner.com/doc/3811368

Common Sense Media. (2017). *Common Sense census: Media use by kids zero to eight.* San Francisco, CA: Author. Retrieved from https://www.commonsensemedia.org/research

Daugherty, L., Dossani, R., Johnson, E. E., & Oguz, M. (2014). *Using early childhood education to bridge the digital divide.* Santa Monica, CA: RAND Corporation, PE-119-PNC. Retrieved from https://www.rand.org/pubs/perspectives/PE119.html

Daugherty, L., Dossani, R., Johnson, E. E., & Wright, C. (2014). *Families, powered on: Improving family engagement in early childhood education through technology.* Santa Monica, CA: RAND Corporation, RR-673/5-PNC. Retrieved from https://www.rand.org/p ubs/research_reports/RR673z5.html

Davis, M. (2017, June 14). Five edtech experts weigh in on research needs, 1to1 computing, and "passive" vs. "active" learning. In *Technology counts 2017. Classroom tech: Where schools stand. EdWeek, 36*(35). Retrieved from https://www.edweek.org/ew/articles/2017/06/14/the-future-of-classroom-technology-5-experts.html

Dede, C. (2011) Emerging technologies, ubiquitous learning, and educational transformation. In C. D. Kloos, D. Gillet, R. M. Crespo García, F. Wild, & M. Wolpers (Eds). *Towards Ubiquitous Learning. EC-TEL 2011. Lecture Notes in Computer Science, Vol 6964.* Berlin, Heidelberg: Springer. Retrieved from https://doi.org/10.1007/978-3-642-23985-4_1

Dede, C. (2017, December 11). What will the job market look like in 2030? *Education Week, 37*(15), 32.

Donohue, C. (Ed.) (2015). *Technology and digital media in the early years: Tools for teaching and learning.* New York, NY: Routledge & Washington, DC: NAEYC.

Donohue, C. (Ed.) (2017). *Family engagement in the digital age: Early childhood educators as media mentors.* New York, NY: Routledge.

Donohue, C., & Schomburg, R. (2017). Technology and interactive media in early childhood programs: What we've learned from five years of research, policy, and practice. *Young Children, 72*(4), 72–78.

Early Childhood STEM Working Group. (2017, January). *Early STEM matters: Providing high-quality STEM experiences for all young learners.* Chicago, IL: Author. Retrieved from http://ecstem.uchicago.edu

Education Week Research Center. (2017, June 15). Data dive: devices and software flooding into classrooms: More access hasn't meant better use. In *Technology counts 2017: Classroom technology, where schools stand. Education Week, 36*(35), 16–17.

Epstein, A. S. (2015, February 3). Using technology appropriately in the preschool classroom. *Exchange Focus*, 1–12. Retrieved from https://www.childcareexchange.com/using-technology-appropriately-in-the-preschool

Freeman, A., Adams Becker, S., Cummins, M., Davis, A., & Hall Giesinger, C. (2017). *NMC/CoSN Horizon Report: 2017 K–12 Edition.* Austin, Texas: The New Media Consortium.

Guernsey, L., & Levine, M. (2017, April 25). *How to bring early learning and family engagement into the digital age: An action agenda for city and community leaders.* Washington, DC: New America's Education Policy Program & New York, NY: Joan Ganz Cooney Center at Sesame Workshop. Retrieved from https://www.newamerica.org/education-policy/policy-papers/how-bring-early-learning-and-family-engagement-digital-age/

Hartle, L. (2015). Technology and play. In D. L. Couchenour & J. K. Chrisman (Eds.). *Encyclopedia of contemporary early childhood education.* Thousand Oaks, CA: Sage Publications, Inc.

Hartle, L., & Berson, I. R. (2012). On our minds. NAEYC's technology and young children interest forum offers valuable resources for teachers and families. *Young Children, 67*(5), 62–64.

Hartle, L., & Jaruszewicz, C. (2009). Rewiring and networking language, literacy, and communication through the arts: Teachers' and young children's fluency to create with technology. In M. J. Narey (Ed.). *Making meaning: Constructing multimodal perspectives of language, literacy, and learning through arts-based early childhood education* (pp. 187–205). New York, NY: Springer Publishing Company.

Herr-Stephenson, B., Alper, M., Reilly, E., & Jenkins, H. (2013). *T is for transmedia: Learning through trans-media play.* Los Angeles and New York: USC Annenberg Innovation Lab and The Joan Ganz Cooney Center at Sesame Workshop. Retrieved from https://joanganzcooneycenter.org/wp-content/uploads/2013/03/t_is_for_transmedia.pdf

Hirsh-Pasek, K., Zosh, J. M., Golinkoff, R. M., Gray, J. H., Robb, M. B., & Kaufman, J. (2015). Putting education in "educational" apps: Lessons from the science of learning. *Psychological Science in the Public Interest, 16*(1), 3–34.

Institute of Medicine (IOM) & National Research Council (NRC). (2015). *Transforming the workforce for children birth through age 8: A unifying foundation.* Washington, DC: The National Academies Press. Retrieved from http://www.nap.edu/catalog/19401/tra nsforming-the-workforce-for-children-birth-through-age-8-a?utm_source=NAP

International Society for Technology in Education (ISTE). (2016). *ISTE standards for students: A practical guide for learning with technology* (ebook). Arlington, VA: Author.

Kinshuk Huang, H.-W., Sampson, D., & Chen, N.-S. (2013). Trends in educational technology through the lens of the highly cited articles published in the *Journal of Educational Technology and Society. Educational Technology and Society, 16*(2), 3–20.

Lerner, C., & Barr, R. (2014). *Screen sense, setting the record straight: Research-based guidelines for screen use for children under 3 years old.* Retrieved from https://www.zerotothree.org/ resources/series/screen-sense

Levay, K., Volmert, A., & Kendall-Taylor, N. (2018, April). *Crossing the boundaries: Mapping the gaps between expert and public understandings of bridging stem learning environments.* Retrieved from http://www.frameworksinstitute.org/stem-learning.html

Levin, D. (2013). *Beyond remote-controlled childhood: Teaching young children in the media age.* Washington, DC: National Association for the Education of Young Children.

Levine, M. H. (2018, April). What does the research say about tech and kids' learning? Part 1 & 2. [Web log post]. New York: NY: The Joan Ganz Cooney Center at Sesame Street Workshop. Retrieved from http://joanganzcooneycenter.org/blog

Lieberman, A., Cook, S., & Jackson, S. (2018). Building a cohort of early childhood technology leaders in Chicago, Illinois. In *Extracting success in Pre-K teaching: Approaches to effective professional learning across five states* (pp. 21–25). New York, NY: New America Foundation. Retrieved from https://www.newamerica.org/education-policy/reports/ extracting-success-pre-k-teaching/building-a-cohort-of-early-childhood-technology-lea ders-in-chicago-illinois/

Lim, C.-P., Zhao, Y., Tondeur, J., Chai, C.-S., & Tsai, C.-C. (2013). Bridging the gap: Technology trends and use of technology in schools. *Educational Technology and Society, 16*(2), 59–68.

McClure, E. R., Guernsey, L., Clements, D. H., Bales, S. N., Nichols, J., Kendall-Taylor, N., & Levine, M. H. (2017). *STEM starts early: Grounding science, technology, engineering, and math education in early childhood.* New York, NY: The Joan Ganz Cooney Center at Sesame Workshop. Retrieved from http://joanganzcooneycenter.org/publications/

NAEYC (1996). *Technology and young children—Ages 3 through 8: A position statement of the National Association for the Education of Young Children.* Washington, DC: Author.

National Association for the Education of Young Children (NAEYC) & Fred Rogers Center for Early Learning and Children's Media at Saint Vincent College. (2012). *Technology and interactive media as tools in early childhood programs serving children from birth through age 8.* Washington, DC: NAEYC; Latrobe, PA: Fred Rogers Center for Early Learning and Children's Media at Saint Vincent College.

National Association for the Education of Young Children (NAEYC). (2009). *NAEYC standards for early childhood professional preparation programs: A position statement of the national association for the education of young children.* Washington, DC: Author.

Paciga, K. A., & Donohue, C. (2017). *Technology and interactive media for young children: A whole child approach connecting the vision of Fred Rogers with research and practice.* Latrobe, PA:

Fred Rogers Center for Early Learning and Children's Media at Saint Vincent College. Retrieved from http://www.fredrogerscenter.org/frctecreport

Randles, J. (2018, April 25) *The 9 hottest topics in edtech.* Arlington, VA: International Society for Technology in Education (ISTE). Retrieved from https://www.iste.org/exp lore/articleDetail?articleid=674

Resnick, M. (2006). Computer as paintbrush: Technology, play, and the creative society. In D. Singer, R. Golikoff, & K. Hirsh-Pasek. (Eds.), *Play = Learning: How play motivates and enhances children's cognitive and social-emotional growth.* New York, NY: Oxford University Press, Inc.

Resnick, M. (2017). *Life long kindergarten: Cultivating creativity through projects, passion, peers, and play.* Cambridge, MA: MIT Press.

Rideout, V. (2014, January 24). *Learning at home: Families' educational media use in America.* New York, NY: Families and Media Project. The Joan Ganz Cooney Center. Retrieved from http://joanganzcooneycenter.org/publication/learning-at-home/

Robb, M., Catalano, R., Smith, T., Polojac, S., Figlar, M., Minzenberg, B., & Schomburg, R. (2014). *Checklist for identifying exemplary uses of technology and interactive media for early learning: The Pennsylvania digital media literacy project.* Retrieved from http://www. fredrogerscenter.org/2014/02/how-am-i-doing-checklist-exemplary-uses-of-technolo gy-early-learning/

Rogow, F. (2012). *The case for digital media literacy in early childhood education.* Ithaca, NY: Insighters Education Consulting.

Rogow, F. (2015). Media literacy in early childhood education: Inquiry-based technology integration. In C. Donohue, (Ed.) (2015). *Technology and digital media in the early years: Tools for teaching and learning* (pp. 91–103). New York, NY: Routledge & Washington, DC: NAEYC.

Rosa, E. M., & Tudge, J. R. H. (2013). Urie Bronfenbrenner's theory of human development: Its evolution from ecology to bio-ecology. *Journal of Family Theory and Review, 5*(4), 243–258.

Rosen, D. B., & Jaruszewicz, C. (2009). Developmentally appropriate technology use and early childhood teacher education. *Journal of Early Childhood Teacher Education, 30*(2), 162–171.

Roskos, K., Burstein, K., Shang, Y., & Gray, E. (2014, January–March). *Young children's engagement with e-books at school: Does device matter?* Retrieved from http://journals.sagep ub.com/doi/abs/10.1177/2158244013517244

Samuel, A. (2015, November 4). Parents: Reject technology shame, the advantages of helping kids learn to navigate the digital world, rather than shielding them from it. *The Atlantic.* Retrieved from https://www.theatlantic.com/technology/archive/2015/11/ why-parents-shouldnt-feel-technology-shame/414163/

Sarama, J., & Clements, D. H. (2013). Lessons learned in the implementation of the TRIAD scale-up model: Teaching early mathematics with trajectories and technologies. In T. Halle, A. Metz, & I. Martinez-Beck (Eds.), *Applying implementation science in early childhood programs and systems* (pp. 173–191). Baltimore, MD: Paul H. Brookes.

Shapiro, J. (2018, Winter). *Digital Play for global citizens. The Joan Ganz Cooney Center at Sesame Workshop,* New York: The Joan Ganz Cooney Center at Sesame Workshop, 1–37. Retrieved from http://joanganzcooneycenter.org/publication/digital-play-for-global-citizens/

Simon, F., & Nemeth, K. N. (2012). *Digital decisions: Choosing the right technology tools for early childhood.* Lewisville, NC: Gryphon House.

Simon, F., Nemeth, K. N., & McManis, D. (2013). Technology in ECE classrooms: Results of a new survey and implications for the field. *Exchange,* 68–75.

Technology and Young Children Interest Forum of NAEYC. (2008). On our minds. Meaningful technology integration in early learning environments. *Young Children, 63*(5), 48–50.

Tudge, J. R. H., Merçon-Vargas, E. A., Liang, Y., & Payir, A. (2017). The importance of Urie Bronfenbrenner's bioecological theory for early childhood education. In L. E. Cohen & S. Waite-Stupiansky, (Eds). *Theories of early childhood education: Developmental, behaviorist, and critical* (pp. 67–79). New York, NY: Routledge.

U.S. Department of Education, Office of Educational Technology. (October, 2016). *Early learning and educational technology policy brief.* Washington, DC: Author. Retrieved from https://tech.ed.gov/earlylearning/

Voogt, J., Erstad, O., Dede, C., & Mishra, P. (2013). Challenges to learning and schooling in the digital networked world of the 21st century. *Journal of Computer Assisted Learning, 29*(5), 403–413.

Wainwright, D. K., & Linebarger, D. L. (2006). *Ready to learn: Literature review, part I: Elements of effective educational TV.* Philadelphia, PA: University of Pennsylvania, Children's Media Lab. Retrieved from https://www.researchconnections.org/childcare/resources/16192

Wang, X. C., Berson, I., Jaruszewicz, C., Hartle, L., & Rosen, D. (2010). Young children's technology experiences in multiple contexts: Bronfenbrenner's ecological theory reconsidered. In I. Berson, & M. Berson. (Eds.). *Research in global child advocacy series volume 5: High-tech tots: Childhood in a digital world* (pp. 23–48). Charlotte, NC: Information Age Publishing, Inc.

Wartella, E., Blackwell, C. K., Lauricella, A. R., & Robb, M. B. (2013). *Technology in the lives of educators and early childhood programs.* Latrobe, PA: Fred Rogers Center for Early Learning and Children's Media at Saint Vincent College.

Zheng, B., Warschauer, M., Lin, C., & Chang, C. (2016). Learning in onetoone laptop environments: A metaanalysis and research synthesis. *Review of Educational Research, 86*(4), 1052–1084. Retrieved from https://doi.org/10.3102/0034654316628645

Zimmerman, E. (2018, July 27). The 4 C's of learning in a connected classroom. *Edtech Magazine.* Retrieved from https://edtechmagazine.com/k12/article/2018/07/4-cs-learning-connected-classroom

3

ENGINEERING IN EARLY LEARNING ENVIRONMENTS

Demetra Evangelou and Aikaterini Bagiati

Recent Innovations

The integration of engineering content in early childhood education (ECE) is taking place within the wider Science, Technology, Engineering and Mathematics (STEM) initiatives sweeping through contemporary education. In this chapter we will discuss recent developments on the integration of engineering in early learning environments.

We will present arguments as well as research findings in support of the idea that engineering is appropriate for early learning. We will comment on the nature of engineering activity and design as processes that lead to learning and share examples of programs and curricula already in existence. We conclude with highlighting selected early engineering activities and recommendations for next steps.

Putting the E in STEM took more than a village. A national community was mobilized to sound the alarm of the most convincing argument of all: The US was falling behind compared to other industrialized nations in the numbers and diversity of graduates in STEM (National Academy of Sciences, National Academy of Engineering, and Institute of Medicine, 2007). The report pointed to a need for novel ideas to address the problem of competitiveness in a globalized world.

While science, technology, and mathematics were considered key to educating a competitive workforce and an informed citizenry, inserting the E was a truly innovative idea. Traditional curricular practices demand theoretical underpinnings for any scientific field that enters mainstream school curriculum. Engineering, as a complete newcomer, was faced with the same request for compliance in terms of its value, rigor, and pedagogy in order to be considered appropriate for primary and secondary education. This was in addition to the most important question of all: *Who will teach it?*

From a different perspective, this is a case of a trickle-down effect where problems, in this instance, attracting and educating engineers at the college level, seek to overhaul the entire process beginning at square one. Overhauling the US educational system by identifying important themes as culprits happens systematically and appears to correspond to pendulum swings that follow a national agenda on questions of competitiveness and the overall standing of the US in a global economy (Spring, 1976).

In the current juncture, an advanced and technically sophisticated labor force dictates that additional attention and resources be placed at the disposal of schools for educating Americans in STEM. The competition this time is not Russia and Sputnik or poverty and the need for more social equality, but rather the economies of Asia, where high rates of economic development were achieved through technical advancements secured by a highly trained and very competitive workforce mostly through national education systems (Graham, 2018).

Two axis are identified: a) Altering the ways engineers are trained, and b) The need to insert E in STEM at the high school level for starters. In pursuing such a two-pronged agenda, the trickle-down effect began in earnest and the feeding ground of high school went all the way back to the preschool. Beginning with square one reveals a belief in the developmental value of education for the formation of character, personality, prosperity, and the future. When the system needs fixing, tweaking, or changing, start early and begin with the ECE classroom (National Research Council, 2011).

Questions of this nature were generally not considered until recently when a national and international conversation within the larger framework of STEM education started to take hold (Evangelou, 2010). This was particularly the case when evidence began to emerge that engineering could be regarded as a fundamental approach to learning and individual development (Brophy & Evangelou, 2007) and not, as conventional wisdom has it, a professional practice in which engineers engage.

In the past ten years, scholars have been examining whether introducing early childhood engineering is developmentally appropriate (Copple & Bredekamp, 2009). Several years of initial pilots followed by comprehensive-related research studies (Bagiati, 2011; Bagiati & Evangelou, 2015; Bagiati & Evangelou, 2016; Bagiati, Yoon, Evangelou, & Ngambeki, 2010; Bairaktarova, Evangelou, Bagiati, & Brophy, 2011; Brophy, Klein, Portsmore, & Rogers, 2008) have established our confidence in the inclusion of engineering in ECE. Observing human behavior reveals that engineering, expressed mainly by habitual altering of a surrounding environment as a way to solve a problem or serve a need, comes as a natural pre-wired human ability. In this sense, children can be seen as little engineers as they modify the world to satisfy their own needs and wants (Evangelou, Dobbs-Oates, Bagiati, Liang, & Choi, 2010; Meeteren & Zan, 2010). Recent developments have led to a rising number of practitioners and scholars examining different ways to introduce early engineering education (English & Moore, 2018). While many of these approaches follow a formal education path—universities, museums, governmental agencies, as well as the industry—an equally large effort is placed on creating informal education content and learning environments (Bagiati et al., 2010; Bagiati et al., 2015).

The Rationale for Early Engineering

R. J. Forbes (1958) prefaces his book, *Man the Maker: A History of Technology and Engineering*, by stating that Homo Faber differs from Homo Sapiens in that "his material achievements arose and became part of that complex of culture traits we call civilization" (preface p. 1). Evidence from discovery, invention, and engineering constitute a record of human activity that far precedes any written record. Taking this long view of the history of humans as *makers, builders,* and *creators* of our material world offers unequivocal justification for learning as a form of making and making as a way of learning (Evangelou, 2012). In contemporary early education settings, experiential pedagogies for young learners could be a sought solution to the problem.

Including Engineering in STEM has added a critical component mostly responsible for the renewed interest in the pedagogies of science, technology, and mathematics, subjects that have enjoyed a long presence in school curricula and the educational sciences. Engineering infused the debate with new insights and novel questions seeking new syntheses. Engineering is qualitatively different than its fellow neighbors in STEM in that it represents a way of thinking about the world with the intention of action; it is the par excellence activity learning occasion, an action as well as a way of thinking (Bairaktarova et al., 2011; Gold, Elicker, Choi, Anderson, & Brophy, 2015).

These unique elements are now the purview of a field called *early engineering,* and they are studied in the context of educational practice. We adopt the term early engineering as we first proposed it in our earlier publication (Brophy & Evangelou, 2007) to refer to the good fit between learning characteristics for young children and the mandates of early childhood curricula.

Early engineering combines two essential elements in our contemporary understanding of learning by *acting* and of *acting as a way to document learning.* Engineering employs tools and procedures, namely the design method, that correspond with our understanding of how people learn (National Research Council, 2000). Furthermore, engineering is a representation, a means as well as an outcome, of a world that is constructed with a purpose and is therefore worthy of our educational attention. Modern ECE as a developmental activity benefits from the possibility of including engineering methodology as a learning pedagogy. Early engineering education cultivates habits of mind and dispositions (Lucas, Claxton, & Hanson, 2014) intending to form thinking and acting akin to engineering as a universal human activity.

In order to introduce Engineering in Early Learning Environments the following questions are considered:

- What is engineering for the early years?
- Is engineering appropriate in developmental terms?
- Is engineering appropriate in cultural terms?
- Who should implement engineering in the early years classroom?

Next, we address these questions in order to shed light on the task at hand, that is, placing engineering in the world of early learning. It should be noted that the answers offered are not the result of a complete examination of the factors involved but are intended to contribute to a much-needed discussion on these issues.

What is Engineering for the Early Years?

Engineering for young children, called "*early engineering*," refers to curricular aspects and elements that are derived from the content and processes found within the scientific fields of engineering. While engineering relevant content can take many forms and represents many different aspects of knowledge, the fundamental underlying content refers to aspects of the human constructed world in which we live. It can be about clean water processes and prosthetic legs, as much as it can be about spaceships and food preservation. It is all encompassing and can be made relevant to local or global conditions depending on the interests and motivations of the learner. Early engineering can therefore mean content that is included in a curriculum at the appropriate level and complexity required to serve the need and ability of the learner (National Research Council, 2010). Engineering is, in this sense, an inexhaustible collection of interesting ideas and artifacts from prehistory to today (Pannell, 1964).

As it is a process, engineering is also a method (Koen, 1985; Petroski, 1996). Bringing about these ideas of connectivity, communication, computation, and material artifacts, structures, computers, and software that represent them is a fascinating universal human characteristic. The engineering method is called *design* and it is a way to tame/control/direct human imagination into material representation systematically through the intricate particularities and physical constrains of our finite natural world. Engineers call design the course of action by which an idea, born of necessity or desire, undergoes a transformative process of continuous negotiation and iteration to become a perceived corporality that is shareable: a thing to have, to use, to hold, to share. The engineering method as exemplified in the design process is an instance of constructionism, a "learning by making" event (Papert, 1980, 1993). Thus, to design is to create, proceeding from thought to action in a manner analogous to children's play and discovery of the world (Bruner, 1979).

Is Engineering Appropriate in Developmental Terms?

The criterion of developmental appropriateness has long been established in contemporary ECE. At this stage, knowledge from developmental science, primarily psychology, translates into educational practice in a series of normative assumptions about the order and sequence of developmental events in children's lives. Developmental approaches draw heavily on canonical notions of human evolution assuming a universal set of laws are in operation such as stages in the development of movement or speech or social interaction.

For over a century, the curriculum in ECE has been dominated by developmental psychology. Some see this as a "westernized" quality largely because it relegates a diversity of cultures and traditions to a rather unimportant status. As far as generating and implementing policy in this educational context ECE focuses on measures and outcomes from the social sciences justified in "scientific terms." Policies needed for regulation and coverage purposes increasingly demanded measurable outcomes. ECE was ascribed a preparatory role for responsible citizenship. At the same time this programmatic aspect of the curriculum limits its potential to reflect lived experiences and be a dynamic and flexible tool (Stacey, 2011; Wood & Hedges 2016).

Experiential Learning Context

Applying the aforementioned developmental framework to early engineering produces a number of insights:

As preeminent American pragmatist philosopher and educator John Dewey has pointed out, "tools are means and the consequences of action, adapted to each other" (Dewey, as cited in Hickman, 2009, p. 46). Tools are principal and enduring expressions of an interaction of humans with the environment. Tools allow children to interact creatively with nature as well as with each other and flourish as part of the experience (Resnick, Brennan, Cobo, & Schmidt, 2017). In a Deweyan sense of the curriculum, engineering as a form of inventing and reinventing aspects of a creative life is missing. Dewey's view is summarized in the following excerpt from his book, *Essays in Experimental Logic*:

> Hence, while all meanings are derived from things which antedate suggestion—or thinking or "consciousness"—not all qualities are equally fitted to be meanings of a wide efficiency, and it is a work of art to select the proper qualities for doing the work. This corresponds to the working over of raw material into an effective tool. A spade or a watchspring is made out of antecedent material but does not pre-exist as a ready-made tool; and, the more delicate and complicated the work which it has to do, the more art intervenes. (Dewey, 1954, p. 35)

Learning is creating; similarly, to building a house with blocks or building a cake, all cultural activity falls under the same premise of creative activity. Creative activity combined with learning generates developmentally appropriate opportunities.

Informal learning is at the core of contemporary early education, and play is at the heart of it. Thus, we argue that including engineering activities in the classroom will result in an enhancement of play. Play as well as engineering activities share a tantamount quality: recognizing that knowing the world requires a process of discovery and systematic understanding, constructed through a mental representation (Gold et al., 2015; Sutton, 2011).

Learning by Making

Engineering employs design method heuristics—a series of informal trial-and-error experiential approaches guided by a purpose—as opposed to strict algorithmic or logical calculations. The heuristic or informal, aspects of engineering design are mostly validated through a commitment to experiment with discovery, construction, and reconstruction (Ferguson, 1992) besides papers and worksheets. Engineering design heuristic practices are, in fact, quite proximal to ways children learn constructively (Papert, 1980, 1993).

The heuristic aspect of engineering reflects a commitment on behalf of the practitioner to "solving the problem" which makes engineering as a learning process fascinating and intriguing for young learners, especially when there is not a particular formal method, or plan, to follow. Similarly, most children, by the age of 3 years have already discovered a great variety of heuristics that they use as they work purposefully or incidentally to become adept users of technology and products (Fleer, 2014).

Taking such observations a step further into exploration and construction is essential in our effort to enhance, demystify, and introduce children properly to the human-made world.

Perhaps an important consideration in including engineering in ECE is the effect it can have on the cultivation of dispositions in young children. Engineering begins with a purposeful question (e.g., How we make this "object"?). Posing a question in the right way is significant to the outcome. And since engineering is synonymous to doing/acting/experiencing, as a learning process it cultivates a disposition to act and experiment, which is a significant life skill. Engineers keep an open mind while continuously trying to iterate and improve on their work. Last but not least, such aesthetic considerations as symmetry, harmony, and balance are adjacent to engineering heuristics and develop children's sense of beauty—not a least important aspect of life.

Is Engineering Appropriate in Cultural Terms?

Tinkering with toys and taking things apart in play-based approaches is very much valued and recognized as central to the early learning process. Tinkering practices recognize the social value of the activity and offer ways of structuring a curriculum that adhere to a significant aspect of human activity such as creating useful or ornamental objects. Engineering education, in more ways than one, offers similar opportunities. Creating opportunities for tinkering in the classroom is a continuation of the progressive educational tradition (Heroman, 2018).

Engineering is a way of learning about the world through the actual and virtual construction of the world. The world of engineering thinking continuously evolves as it adjusts to the needs of human activity in its various forms.

As a way of learning, engineering thinking is a solution-oriented activity driven by purpose. The process begins with a question and is seeded with constant improvement, practical and material, though iteration and refinement. In addition to the making aspect of the engineering method which includes the design adjusted to the life cycle of a product that has to be thought through upfront, running things, operating them, maintaining them, and even decommissioning them need be considered early on in the process as well. The whole procedure requires stewardship that is environmentally sensitive. In this sense, many, if not all of the environmental initiatives can be examined, and thus, enhanced under the lens of the maker/steward /custodian engineer and his or her object(s).

Furthermore, engineering is useful for teaching economic principles and fundamental social responsibilities on behalf of the individual. Since humans make useful objects as they interact with their environment, under specific financial and resource constraints, just to name a few, engineers become aware of the finite nature of the world, and their practice is marked by sensitivity and mindfulness. One can hardly think of more relevant practice in teaching human, environmental, and economic principles.

Who Should Implement Engineering in the Early Years Classroom?

ECE is broadly defined as the care and education of children from birth through age eight. This definition is widely accepted globally, and most modern systems design training processes for teachers on that premise. However, it is a well-known fact to anyone involved that human development and ensuing acculturation processes cannot be summarized in a simple chronological age.

In ECE, the age of the learner is not the only aspect that is significant and needs be taken into consideration. A host of parameters—psychological, social, socioeconomic, cultural, and political—come to bear on a growing human being in a true Borofenbrennerian sense. When a new proposal arrives that recommends a shift or an addition into the mix, the initial inertia is strong. In the conversation of STEM in education in general, we wish to shift the attention to ECE and engineering in particular. As with any request for change, there are key elements to success. Who adopts the change and how it spreads are critical questions. Of those two, the "who question" is important to us as it pertains to matters of training early childhood teachers and preparing them in ways that can respond openly, creatively, and constructively to such novel ideas as including engineering in their classrooms. Who should then implement the changes? The teacher should. The burden of educating future early childhood teachers always looms large because of our ambivalence about what this training should include. This ambivalence comes from our appreciation of the significance of human development in the early years.

Asking early childhood teachers to add more on their plates may not be the best approach for we have seen how only some early and talented adopters shine the way and take on the new challenge. The majority of teachers, confused or lost, gradually ascribe false meaning to the engineering practice. Past requests for ECE changes speak to this situation: the case of inquiry, the Reggio Emilia approach, documentation, assessment, and technology.

Perhaps a reconceptualization of the process of change is presenting itself in the case of the invitation to include engineering in the ECE experience. Engineering content and knowledge in education needs to be the outcome of collaboration. For example, inviting experts to become partners in classrooms should enhance the educational experience for teachers and engineers alike. As a universal human activity, engineering and design learning opens up opportunities for understanding child development in a deep sociocultural sense.

Selecting Content and Pedagogy

When bringing engineering into early education, there are two learning areas teachers can focus on: *learning about engineering* vs *learning how to practice engineering*, with the combination of both being the optimal and most holistic approach.

Learning About Engineering

Learning about engineering would consist of addressing the following topics in class:

a   What is an engineer?
b   What does an engineer do?
c   Who can be an engineer?
d   How does an engineer try to solve problems or design new things?
e   Who does an engineer work with?
f   How many types of engineering are there?

Depending on the classroom curriculum, the aforementioned topics can be addressed during small- or large-group discussion time, storytelling, free play time, role playing, or during various field trips. Table 3.1 provides specific suggestions on ways that these practices work.

TABLE 3.1 Suggestions for Learning about Engineering in Early Education

Classroom setting	Prompt questions and activities
Small / Large Group Discussion	• The teacher may use this time to discuss engineering-related topics with the kids, e.g., Hey kids I wonder if you know who designed my phone/car/house/school …—I wonder if anyone knows any famous engineers and what they have designed … • The teacher may invite parents who are engineers to discuss their work with the kids.
Storytelling	• The teacher may select a book where the hero is an engineer/inventor/designer as an opportunity to discuss what an engineer does, as well as to encourage gender and minority inclusiveness, e.g., *Eva the Engineer* by Yennie Solheim Fuller. • The teacher may select a book where the hero is facing a problem and needs to construct an artifact in order to come up with a solution, as an opportunity to discuss problem solving, the engineering design process, as well as engineering collaborations with other professionals, e.g., *Rosie Revere, Engineer* by Andrea Beaty.
Free Play Time	• Teachers may enhance the roleplaying activity space to support boys and girls adopting the role of an engineer. • Teachers may provide opportunities for block building or other construction-related activities and use children's constructions to initiate engineering-related discussions.
Field trips	• Teachers may take advantage of a field trip in order to initiate engineering-related discussions, e.g., Hey kids look at this building/bicycle/wheelchair/swimming pool… • Teachers may organize a field trip to an engineering work site e.g., a robotics lab, a toy factory, a makerspace… • Teachers may take advantage of the destination of the field trip to discuss other professions collaborating with engineers, e.g., During a field trip to a fire station the teacher can explain how firemen tell engineers how they want their new firetrucks to be; during a field trip to a pastry-store the teacher can explain how engineers help create edible color.

Practicing Engineering

Educators can consider the Fundamental Design Process (Figure 3.1), common across all engineering disciplines, to be the core of the engineering process that also connects science, math, and technology. Due to its very nature, as presented in Figure 3.2, engineering can either be taught as a stand-alone topic through integration with other subjects within the STEM field, the arts, and beyond; or it can be used as a pedagogical tool for science, math, and technology classes.

When choosing, a design project can either be suggested by the teacher upfront (Figures 3.3 and 3.4) or emerge through discussion (Figure 3.5). Furthermore, not all children need to work on the same project. It is critical, however, that all groups of children follow the Fundamental Design Process or an adaptation.

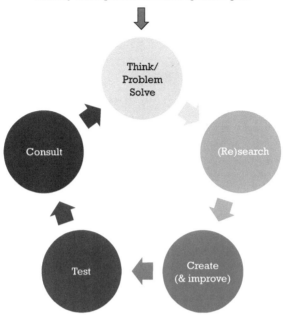

FIGURE 3.1 The Fundamental Design Process
Source: adapted from Bagiati & Evangelou, 2018

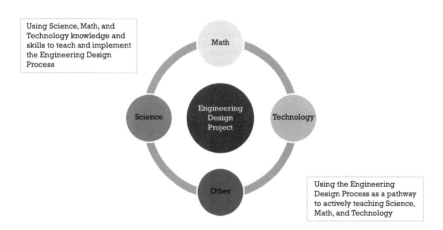

FIGURE 3.2 Pathways to Engineering

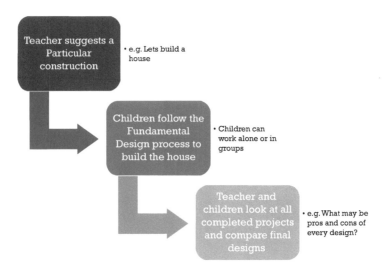

FIGURE 3.3 Implementation Model for a Project where a Construction is Presented by the Teacher

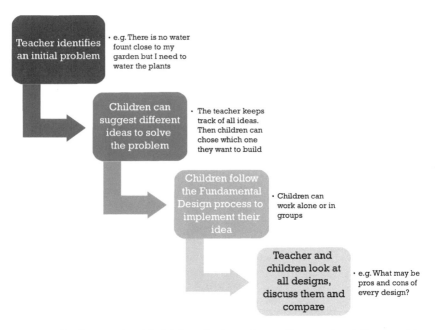

FIGURE 3.4 Implementation Model for a Project where a Construction is Presented by the Teacher and Solutions are Identified by the Children

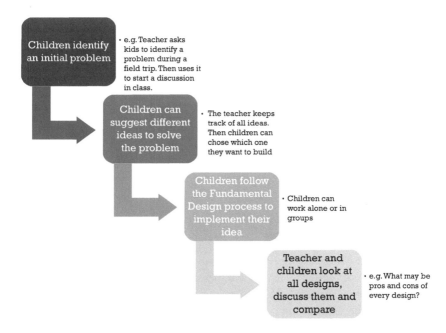

FIGURE 3.5 Implementation Model for a Project where Both the Problem and Solutions are Identified by the Children

To choose the most appropriate class approach, teachers can select, or be inspired by, a large variety of small-scale activities and lesson plans that have already been developed, as well as explore a small number of long-term implemented and evaluated early engineering curricula. At this point it should be noted that despite the short life of early engineering, a large number of scattered lesson plans and activities can be found on the web; however, most of them have never been evaluated, and they also fail to present appropriate assessment tools (Bagiati et al., 2010; Bagiati et al., 2015; Bagiati & Evangelou, 2018). It is therefore highly recommended that teachers should examine the developers' credentials when choosing class resources. The following paragraphs present resources recommended by the authors as state-of-the-art early engineering resources.

Engineering is Elementary—Boston Museum of Science

The Engineering is Elementary (EiE) curriculum has been developed by the Boston Museum of Science. The goal of this project is to support educators with curricula and professional development for engineering literacy. EiE consists of 20 flexible and fun units for grades 1–5. Every unit uses a unifying theme from the engineering field. Each curriculum unit integrates materials from Life, Earth and Space, and Physical Sciences, which are taught in elementary school. Research-based, teacher-tested activities have been designed to develop creativity, critical thinking, and problem-solving skills. Every unit consists of three components: a teacher guide, a storybook, and a kit that contains the materials to be used. Teacher guides include four detailed lesson plans, one context-setting storybook, background content, teacher tips, suggestions for English Learner differentiation and grade level adaptation, and duplication masters for student handouts and assessments. Units can be taught separately or as a series of classes. Furthermore, they can be incorporated into a science or technology class or taught independently.

Complimentary to the EiE curriculum, the Boston Museum of Science is currently developing *Wee Engineer*, a curriculum for the PreK level, and *EiE for Kindergarten*. More information regarding the aforementioned curricula can be found at www.eie.org.

Puppeteering to Engineering

Puppeteering to Engineering (P2E) is a semester-long, age-appropriate, design-based curriculum, designed by the authors of this book chapter. P2E aims to achieve higher integration of STEM in the preschool classroom, with primary emphasis on the engineering component. P2E was carefully designed based on four years of preliminary observations in various PreK classrooms, after careful consideration of several early engineering-related research studies conducted through the School of Engineering Education at Purdue University (Bagiati et al., 2010; Bagiati & Evangelou, 2016; Bagiati & Evangelou, 2018; Bairaktarova et al., 2011; Brophy et al., 2008). Following development, P2E was implemented in classrooms, where it was further researched and evaluated in regard to student-learning outcomes (Bagiati, 2011; Bagiati & Evangelou, 2011), as well as regarding the transitional experience of a teacher who decides to bring such a new content into class (Bagiati & Evangelou, 2015). Complementary to the P2E curriculum, and based on all prior research findings, an observation protocol was designed by the authors to support engineering-related guided project-based instruction (Bagiati & Evangelou, 2018). Teachers can visit www.puppetengineering.com to download the P2E curriculum, as well as find information regarding early engineering-related publications.

Novel Engineering

Novel Engineering is an innovative approach to integrate engineering and literacy.

> In Novel Engineering students use literature as the basis for engineering design challenges, drawing information from the text to identify engineering problems, consider characters as clients, and using details from the story to impose constraints as they build functional solutions in their classroom to the characters' problems.... As students work on text-based engineering projects, they also engage in productive and self-directed literacy practices, including noting key

details in text, making inferences, and writing lists and notes that support their design process. (Portsmore & Milto, 2018, p. 204)

Novel Engineering was developed by the Center for Engineering Education and Outreach at Tufts University, and although it was mainly developed for elementary and middle school students, texts for early education have also been explored by teachers. More information regarding the program as well as suggested resources can be found at www.novelengineering.org.

PictureSTEM

"The PictureSTEM project consists of instructional units for grades K-2 that employ engineering and literacy contexts to integrate science, technology, engineering, mathematics, and computational thinking (STEM +C) content instruction" (Tank et al., 2018, p. 175). Three units have been developed through the PictureSTEM project so far, *Designing Paper Baskets* for Kindergarten; *Designing Hamster Habitats* for First Grade; and *Designing Toy Box Organizers* for second grade. In these units, PictureSTEM "utilized picture books and an engineering design challenge to provide students with authentic, contextual activities that engage learners in specific STEM content" (Tank et al., 2018, p. 175). More information regarding the PictureSTEM project can be found at www.picturestem.org.

Complimentary Tools

In addition to curricula, a large number of complimentary tools are being developed with engineering and design concepts in mind. These tools that can be used in classrooms, during afterschool activities, or at home, and consist of particularly designed construction kits and toys, 3-D puzzles, robots, as well as engineering focused books, games, and digital apps. In an attempt to summarize all these tools, the INSPIRE Institute at Purdue University worked on developing a catalogue named *Engineering Gift Guide*. According to the project website, the guide includes fun toys, games, books, and applications to engage girls and boys ages 3–18 in engineering thinking and design. "Items included in the guide have gone through an extensive review process. Researchers looked for toys that would promote engineering practices ranging from coding and spatial reasoning to problem solving and critical thinking." (INSPIRE, 2017, para. 1)

Conclusion

We have presented a brief history of how the national STEM initiatives that swept through the US education conversation of the recent decade have altered the terrain of traditional curricula from early childhood to college. In that context, Engineering has offered the greatest opportunity for reexamination of practices and content as well as teacher training because of its distinctly different nature compared to science, technology, and mathematics. In the early years, engineering appears to offer a number of interesting opportunities to move closer to otherwise well accepted pedagogies of experiential learning, hands-on learning of the constructivist tradition, as well as the more recent constructionism ideas. The proximal relation between thought and action found in engineering also lies at the heart of early development. The current consensus of this new field is producing a number of programs and curricula as well as research-based practices.

In our understanding, the critical question centers around developing methods of research and evidence gathering that would add strength to the current arguments and bolster ongoing practices. Overall, this is a positive step in advancing a conversation on content and method in ECE with promise of renewed interest and creativity.

References

Bagiati, A. (2011). *Early engineering: A developmentally appropriate curriculum for young children.* Doctoral Dissertation. Retrieved from Proquest Dissertations (Accession Order No. 3512219). Purdue University.

Bagiati, A., & Evangelou, D. (2011, October). *Starting young: Outcomes of a developmentally appropriate PreK engineering curriculum,* Research Paper in Engineering Education Symposium, Madrid, Spain.

Bagiati, A., & Evangelou, D. (2015). Engineering curriculum in the preschool classroom: The teacher's experience. *European Early Childhood Education Research Journal, 23*(1), 112–128. Retrieved from http://dx.doi.org/10.1080/1350293X.2014.991099

Bagiati, A., & Evangelou, D. (2016). Practicing engineering while building with blocks: Identifying engineering thinking. *European Early Childhood Education Research Journal, 24*(1), 67–85. Retrieved from http://1dx.doi.org/10.1080/1350293X.2015.1120521

Bagiati, A., & Evangelou, D. (2018). Identifying engineering in a PreK classroom: An observation protocol to support guided project-based instruction. In L. English, & T. Moore (Eds.) *Early engineering learning* (pp. 83–111). Singapore: Springer.

Bagiati, A., Yoon, S. Y., Evangelou, D., & Ngambeki, I. (2010). Engineering curricula in early education: Describing the landscape of open resources. *Early Childhood Research & Practice, 12*(2).

Bagiati, A., Yoon, S. Y., Evangelou, D., Magana, A., Kaloustian, G., & Zhu, J. (2015). The landscape of PreK-12 engineering online resources for teachers: Global trends. *International Journal of STEM Education, 2*(1). doi:10.1186/s40594–40014–0015–0013

Bairaktarova, D., Evangelou, D., Bagiati, A., & Brophy, S. (2011). Engineering in young children's exploratory play with tangible materials. *Children, Youth and Environments, 21* (2), 212–235.

Brophy, S., & Evangelou, D. (2007). Precursors to engineering thinking (PET) project: Intentional designs with experimental artifacts (IDEA). In *Proceedings of the 2007 Annual Conference of the American Society for Engineering Education Conference and Exposition* (pp. 12.1169.1–12.1169.11).

Brophy, S., Klein, S., Portsmore, M., & Rogers, C. (2008). Advancing engineering education in P-12 classrooms. *Journal of Engineering Education, 97*(3), 369–387.

Bruner, J. S. (1979). *On knowing: Essays for the left hand*. Cambridge, MA and London: Harvard University Press.

Copple, C., & Bredekamp, S. (2009). *Developmentally appropriate practice in early childhood programs serving children from birth through age 8*. (3rd ed.). Washington, DC: NAEYC.

Dewey, J. (1954). *Essays in experimental logic*. Mineola, NY: Dover Publications.

Evangelou, D. (2010). Why STEM now? Guest editorial: Child development perspectives in engineering education. *Early Childhood Research and Practice, 12*(2), 1–4.

Evangelou, D. (2012). *Homo fabiens redux: Engineering education in the 21st century*. Keynote Address. Annual SEFI Conference, Thessaloniki, Greece.

Evangelou, D., Dobbs-Oates, J., Bagiati, A., Liang, S., & Choi, J. Y. (2010). Talking about artifacts: Preschool children's explorations with sketches, stories, and tangible objects. *Early Childhood Research & Practice, 12*(2).

English, L., & Moore, T. (2018). *Early engineering learning*. Singapore: Springer,.

Ferguson, E. S. (1992). *Engineering and the mind's eye*. Cambridge, MA: The MIT Press.

Fleer, M. (2014). The demands and motives afforded through digital play in early childhood activity settings. *Learning, Culture and Social Interaction, 3*(3), 202–209.

Forbes, R. J. (1958). *Man the maker: A history of technology and engineering*. Abelard-Schuman Limited: London and New York.

Gold, Z. S., Elicker, J., Choi, J. Y., Anderson, T., & Brophy, S. P. (2015). Preschoolers' engineering play behaviors: Differences in gender and play context. *Children, Youth and Environments, 25*(3), 1–21.

Graham, R. H. (2018). *The global state of the art in engineering education*. Cambridge, MA: Massachusetts Institute of Technology.

Heroman, C. (2018). *Making and tinkering with STEM: Solving design challenges with young children*. Washington, DC: NAEYC.

Hickman, L. (2009). John Dewey as a philosopher of technology. *Readings in the Philosophy of Technology, 43*, 43–55.

INSPIRE (2017). *Engineering Gift Guide Archive*. Retrieved from https://engineering.purdue.edu/INSPIRE/EngineeringGiftGuide

Koen, B. V. (1985). *Definition of the engineering method*. Washington, DC: ASEE Publications.

Lucas, B., Claxton, G., & Hanson, J. (2014). *Thinking like an engineer: Implications for the education system*. London: Royal Academy of Engineering.

Meeteren, B., & Zan, B. (2010). Revealing the work of young engineers in early childhood education. *Early Childhood Research & Practice, SEED Papers*: Fall.

National Academy of Sciences, National Academy of Engineering, and Institute of Medicine. (2007). *Rising above the gathering storm: Energizing and employing America for a brighter economic future*. Washington, DC: The National Academies Press. Retrieved from https://doi.org/10.17226/11463

National Research Council. (2000). *How people learn: Brain, mind, experience, and school*: Washington, DC: The National Academies Press. Retrieved from https://doi.org/10.17226/9853

National Research Council. (2010). *Standards for K-12 engineering education*. Washington, DC: National Academies Press.

National Research Council. (2011). *Successful K-12 STEM education: Identifying effective approaches in science, technology, engineering, and mathematics*. Washington, DC: National Academies Press.

Pannell, J. P. M. (1964). *Man the builder: An illustrated history of engineering*. Crescent Books: New York.

Papert, S. (1980). *Mindstorms: children, computers, and powerful ideas.* New York: Basic Books.

Papert, S. (1993). *The children's machine: Rethinking school in the age of the computer.* New York: Basic Books.

Petroski, H. (1996). *Invention by design: How engineers get form thought to thing.* Cambridge, MA: Harvard University Press.

Portsmore, M., & Milto, E. (2018). Novel engineering in early education classrooms. In L. English & T. Moore (Eds.) *Early engineering learning* (pp. 83–111). Singapore: Springer.

Resnick, M., Brennan, K., Cobo, C., & Schmidt, P. (April, 2017). Creative Learning@ Scale. In *Proceedings of the Fourth ACM Conference on Learning@ Scale* (pp. 99–100). ACM.

Spring, J. (1976) *The sorting machine: National educational policy since 1945.* New York, NY: McKay.

Stacey, S. (2011). *The unscripted classroom: Emergent curriculum in action.* St Paul, MN: Redleaf Press.

Sutton, M. J. (2011). In the hand and mind: The intersection of loose parts and imagination in evocative settings for young children. *Children Youth and Environments, 21*(2), 408–424.

TankK. M., Moore, T. J., Dorie, B. L., Gajdzik, E., Sanger, M. T., Rynearson, A. M., & Mann, E. F. (2018). Engineering in early elementary classrooms through the integration of high-quality literature, design, and STEM+C content. In L. English & T. Moore (Eds). *Early engineering learning* (pp. 175–201). Singapore: Springer.

Wood, E., & Hedges, H. (2016). Curriculum in early childhood education: Critical questions about content, coherence, and control, *The Curriculum Journal, 27*(3), 387–405. doi:10.1080/09585176.2015.1129981

4

MATHEMATICS IN EARLY-LEARNING ENVIRONMENTS

Douglas H. Clements and Julie Sarama

Integration of science, technology, engineering, and mathematics, carefully guided, can show the relations among these STEM subjects in the context of real-world issues, which makes them more relevant to students and teachers (Committee on Integrated STEM Education, 2014). This can enhance motivation for learning and improve student interest, achievement, and persistence (Committee on Integrated STEM Education, 2014). However, although examples of contexts in which abstract mathematics is applied can be particularly useful, it is also important to ensure that learning in mathematics itself is supported for three reasons. First, mathematics is, as Carl Friedrich Gauss claimed, the "queen of the sciences" and a deep understanding of it is important for all subjects. Second, learning mathematics is more sequential and hierarchical than the learning of other subjects. Third, possibly due to this, integration of STEM benefits science but not necessarily math (Committee on Integrated STEM Education, 2014), so attention to mathematics itself is important.

Math is arguably the most abstract of the STEM domains. Along with memories of their own classroom experiences with math, this can lead teachers of young children to be cautious about doing "too much math," especially before first grade, or resigned to submit their students to the type of joyless skill work they remember.

Fortunately, recent research and educational innovations provide positive pathways to mathematics education in the early years. To do so, we have to clear up some myths and misconceptions about mathematics and young children and then learn how to guide children down the pathways that we call *learning trajectories*.

Clearing up Myths and Misconceptions

People in and out of schools hold beliefs about early math that are false and misleading. These myths and misconceptions persist, and many harm children. We adapt and modify these from a previous publication (Clements & Sarama, 2018).

Myth/Misconception 1: Math is Developmentally Inappropriate for Young Children

For reasons described in the first paragraph, many view mathematics as too abstract for the very young and an imposition of a bleak learning environment on any children birth to age 8 years. This opinion has a long history, but it emerges from serious misconceptions. Consider the behaviorist Edward Thorndike. Misunderstanding the remarkable mathematical "gifts and occupations" created by the inventor of kindergarten, Frederick Froebel, Thorndike promoted "health" instead of math by replacing the first gift of Froebel's gifts (manipulatives), which were small spheres, with a toothbrush and the first occupation (a mathematical activity) with "sleep" (Brosterman, 1997).

In a similar vein, for decades some have argued that children should be playing with building blocks, rather than learning mathematics. However, the original inventor of those blocks, Caroline Pratt (1948), created these unit blocks to teach mathematics! In her book, she tells of a teacher who told her student Diana that she would give her a toy horse when she had made a stable for it. Diana and her friend Elizabeth did so, but the horse did not fit. They had made a stable with a large area but a low roof. After several unsuccessful attempts to get the horse in, Diana removed the roof, added blocks to the walls to make the roof higher, and replaced the roof. She then tried to put into words what she had done. "Roof too small." The teacher gave her new words such as "high" and "low," and Diana later gave a more mathematical explanation to the other children. Just building with blocks, children have important foundational experiences. However, teachers such as Diana's help children mathematize those experiences, further developing these intuitive ideas by extending them, discussing them, and connecting the language of mathematics to their actions. Like Pratt, we believe that "doing mathematics" is natural and appropriate for children of all ages—if done well. We know young children can learn mathematics more deeply than many assume (Clements, Fuson, & Sarama, 2017b). Clearing up myths and misconceptions, and using research-based learning and teaching approaches, can help all of us do just that.

Myth/Misconception 2: Early Math is Rote Counting and Naming Four Shapes

Counting is important, but it should include verbal counting, object counting, and the use of counting strategies to solve problems. And from their earliest years, children in rich environments can think mathematically in creative ways with counting…and beyond (e.g., Clements & Sarama, 2014; Rittle-Johnson, Fyfe, & Zippert, 2018). They can learn foundations of arithmetic, geometry and spatial reasoning, measurement, and patterning. They can engage in mathematical processes, such as persevering in solving problems, reasoning, and communicating about their reasoning, and they can search for and understand different kinds of patterns and structures (Mulligan, Mitchelmore, & Crevesten, 2013; NCTM, 2006; NGA/CCSSO, 2010). They can build on what they know and invent ways to solve problems, even challenging arithmetic. A preschooler might put up four fingers on one hand, two on the other, then count them all. Jose, a kindergartner in Angela Andrew's class counted on starting at four, counting five, then six. These children are powerful problem solvers (Andrews & Trafton, 2002). They model problem—another mathematical process—and use what they know to solve them.

Myth/Misconception 3: Time Spent on Math is Time Taken Away from Play and from Social-emotional Development and Literacy

Children engage in spontaneous mathematics during almost half of every minute of free play (Seo & Ginsburg, 2004; see also van Oers, 1994), including toddlers (Reikerås, Løge, & Knivsberg, 2012). Teachers can build on such experiences. One teacher engaged in parallel play with children with playdough and raised questions regarding shapes and amount of dough. She told two boys she was "going to hide the ball" made of play dough, covered it with a flat piece, and pressed down. The boys said the ball was still there, but when she lifted the piece, the ball was "gone." This delighted them and they copied her actions and discussed that the ball was "in" the "circle" (Forman & Hill, 1984, pp. 31–32).

Even intentional, structured mathematics activities take a playful approach. Importantly, children who learn math with such intentional activities are more likely to engage in higher-quality socio-dramatic play during free-choice play time (Aydogan et al., 2005). In this richer environment, individual children find more opportunities for meaningful engagement in free play. Thus, preventing children from experiencing planned, structured mathematical experiences may actually deprive them not only of the joy and fascination of mathematics (Balfanz, 1999; Clements & Sarama, 2014; Fuligni, Howes, Huang, Hong, & Lara-Cinisomo, 2012; Stipek, 2013) but also of higher-quality play resulting from their increased mathematical knowledge. In other studies, preschool mathematics programs promoted children's language, literacy, and social-emotional development as much as literacy- or socially-focused programs did (Preschool Curriculum Evaluation Research Consortium, 2008; Sarama, Lange, Clements, & Wolfe, 2012). Everybody wins in every domain with more and better STEM.

Myth/Misconception 4: The Only Good Way to Teach Math is Through Teachable Moments

As our examples show, teachable moments can be wondrous and satisfying (e.g., Davis, 1984; van Oers, 2010). However, as our comments on intentional teaching argue, teachable moments alone are inadequate (Ginsburg, Lee, & Stevenson-Boyd, 2008). Teachers find it difficult to find, much less engage in, these moments and it is unrealistic for any teacher to see opportunities for multiple children to build multiple concepts consistently over the year (Ginsburg, Lee, & Stevenson-Boyd, 2008; Lee, 2004).

Myth/Misconception 5: Math Centers Are All You Need

Good centers, with teacher and peer interactions, can be positive learning environments. But, like teachable moments, centers are insufficient by themselves (Clements & Sarama, 2018). Centers as usually implemented promote incidental learning at best and rarely build one mathematical idea on the next. Mathematics is a sequential and hierarchical subject—each idea builds on the previous ideas and skills. Research agrees: intentional activities focused on mathematics appear to make by far the most significant contributions to children's learning (Fuligni et al., 2012; Klein, Starkey, Clements, Sarama, & Iyer, 2008).

Myth/Misconception 6: Young Children Must Sit Down and Learn Math. Sometimes You Just Have to Do Worksheets

As mentioned in our introduction, our memories of learning mathematics often are filled with images of workbooks and seat work—a very different notion than myths 4 and 5. In contrast to this dull image—for all ages, but especially for young children, good mathematics is about engagement and interest, not drudgery and drill (Clements & Sarama, 2014; Stipek, 2017; van Oers, 2010). High-quality early mathematics includes debating which child is bigger and drawing maps to a playhouse. It is about building with unit blocks and estimating and checking how many steps it is to the playground. It involves playing games, counting the dots on dice and moving a game piece that many spaces (Clements & Sarama, 2007/2013; Ginsburg, Greenes, & Balfanz, 2003).

Myth/Misconception 7: Young Children Must Do Mathematics Concretely.

Concrete objects, manipulatives, and narratives can be essential in some situations and helpful in others (Sarama & Clements, 2009a; Sowell, 1989; Thompson, 2012). In early phases of learning, without objects to count, children cannot understand or work with quantities. Les Steffe covered six of nine marbles with his hand and asked first grader Brenda to count them all. She counted all of Les' five fingers then the three visible marbles. Les pointed out he had six marbles beneath his hand and Brenda replied, "I don't see no six!"(Steffe & Cobb, 1988, p. 23).

However, it is a misconception to believe manipulatives "carry" mathematical ideas (Clements & McMillen, 1996; Sarama & Clements, 2016). Without concepts and strategies, manipulatives are no help. Deborah Ball put it this way: "… understanding does not travel through the fingertips and up the arm" (1992, p. 47). Children may require concrete materials to build meaning initially, but they need teachers to help them reflect on their actions with manipulatives to do so (Ball, 1992; Clements & McMillen, 1996; Sarama & Clements, 2016).

Contrary to this myth, it is often best to move away from manipulatives as soon as possible (Clements & McMillen, 1996; Sarama & Clements, 2016). In number work, although modeling necessitates manipulatives at some early levels of thinking, even preschoolers and kindergartners can use other representations, such as drawings and verbal or written symbols (Carpenter, Ansell, Franke, Fennema, & Weisbeck; Outhred & Sardelich, 1997; van Oers, 1994). For example, in one study kindergartners performed just as well without as with manipulatives in both accuracy or in their discovery of arithmetic strategies (Grupe & Bray, 1999). Third-grader Emily explains: "I find it easier not to do it [simple addition] with my fingers because sometimes I get into a big muddle with them [and] I find it much harder to add up because I am not concentrating on the sum. I am concentrating on getting my fingers right … which takes a while. It can take longer to work out the sum than it does to work out the sum in my head" (Gray & Pitta, 1997, p. 35).

This has another counterintuitive implication: Educational technology can provide useful manipulatives and representations, even if they are not physically concrete (Foster, Anthony, Clements, & Sarama, 2016; Foster, Anthony, Clements, Sarama, & Williams, 2018; National Mathematics Advisory Panel, 2008; Sarama & Clements, in press). Computers can provide representations that are just as personally meaningful to students as physical objects and, paradoxically, research indicates that computer representations may even be more manageable, "clean," flexible, and extensible than their physical counterparts (Sarama & Clements, 2016). Children who use physical and software manipulatives demonstrate a much greater sophistication in classification and logical thinking than do children that used physical manipulatives only (Olson, 1988).

Beyond Myths and Misconceptions

Teachers matter more than other factors, and teachers in the early years matter the most (Tymms, Jones, Albone, & Henderson, 2009). So, teachers of early mathematics have to use the best research and wisdom of expert practice to design their classroom environments, plan activities, and teach. Myths and misconceptions limit teachers' visions of the breadth of such pedagogical strategies (Clements & Sarama, 2018). A broader and more positive vision serves teachers, parents, and their children well.

Moreover, such a vision serves vulnerable children the most, as they benefit most from a comprehensive, research-based approach to early mathematics education, as a challenge and a joy (Clements & Sarama, 2014; Raudenbush, 2009). This is critical: Children in some communities are provided more opportunities to learn mathematics than children in others (e.g., Baroody & Purpura, 2017; Clements, Fuson, & Sarama, 2017a). This gap hurts children who live in poverty and who are members of linguistic and ethnic minority groups (Clements, Fuson, & Sarama, 2017a; National Research Council, 2009).

Awareness of these issues led to the appointment of a National Research Council Committee that issued a report in 2009 entitled: Mathematics learning in early childhood: Paths toward excellence and equity (National Research Council, 2009). This report summarized research-based foundational, challenging-but-achievable goals for children in preschool through grade 2 based on learning trajectories. What learning trajectories are and how they support teachers, parents, and children—especially those with a history of limited opportunities to learn—is the subject of the second section of this chapter.

Learning Trajectories: Paths for Successful Learning

Why Learning Trajectories?

We have referred to positive pathways for children learning mathematics several times. Research from many fields shows that there are certain natural developmental paths, or progressions—levels of thinking through which most children develop as they learn a particular topic in math. When teachers understand the progression of levels of thinking along these paths, and sequence and individualize activities based on them, they can build effective early-learning environments. Learning trajectories help early childhood educators respect both children's developmental processes and constraints and their potential for thinking about and understanding mathematical ideas (Clements & Sarama, 2009; Sarama & Clements, 2009b).

Each learning trajectory has three parts: a goal, a developmental progression, and instructional activities (Sarama & Clements, 2009b). To develop a certain mathematical competence (the goal), children construct each level of thinking in turn (the developmental progression), aided by tasks (instructional activities) and teaching strategies designed to help build the mental actions-on-objects that enable thinking at each level (Clements & Sarama, 2009; Sarama & Clements, 2009b). The developmental progressions ensure that math education is developmentally appropriate (recall myth/misconception 1). And so does the instruction: Our approach is finding the mathematics in, and developing mathematics from, children's activity, helping children extend and mathematize their everyday activities, from building blocks to art to songs to puzzles (Clements & Sarama, 2007/2013; Clements, Sarama, Spitler, Lange, & Wolfe, 2011). We avoid inappropriate and potentially harmful routines, such as flash cards and timed tests to promote memorization of basic facts (especially before thinking strategies are well established) (Henry & Brown, 2008) or dull calendar exercises in which one child performs routine actions while the other passively wait for it to be over.

An Example of a Learning Trajectory: Geometry

There are learning trajectories for most topics in early math, and most people are comfortable with the notion that number topics progress. However, they may not similarly see progressions for other topics. Therefore, our first example will involve geometric shapes. The goal of the learning trajectory is the ability to name, describe, analyze, and classify geometric shapes. Combined with other geometric and spatial reasoning competencies, the larger domain is second in importance only to numerical goals.

Although the research is not as well developed as in domains of number and operation, it has been used to produce a developmental progression—the core of a learning trajectory—for young children's learning of two-dimensional geometric figures (Sarama & Clements, 2009b). Grounded in Piagetian (Piaget & Inhelder, 1967) and Van Hielian (1986) theories, this developmental progression was structured to establish more fine-grain levels than those frameworks (Clements, 1992). The progression for knowledge of geometric figures moves from increasingly sophisticated comparing (matching) through levels of recognizing and naming geometric shapes, then identification of the components of these shapes, to the understanding of properties of shapes. Table 4.1 shows the "forest and the trees"—the broad categories and the fine-tuned levels of the learning trajectory that supports teaching day by day.

Next, we will briefly discuss several levels of this learning trajectory, both the developmental progression level and an instructional activity that helps children attain that level of thinking. But first, we will introduce you to a tool that will allow you to see children and teachers in action.

The Learning and Teaching with Learning Trajectories (LTLT, OR [LT]^2) website at www.LearningTrajectories.org is a professional development tool for teachers and caregivers to support early math instruction. It provides resources to learn about the development of mathematics and how to teach mathematics to young children. There you can review short video clips of children's development and related instructional activities (documents can also be downloaded, from a guide to [LT]^2 to full lesson plans). As we present example levels of two learning trajectories, please visit [LT]^2 to see children in action, as well as teachers working with children, for both those levels…and all the other levels and topics we could not discuss here.

TABLE 4.1 Categories of Development, Levels of the Developmental Progression, and Example Behaviors from the Trajectory for 2-D Geometric Figures

Category	Developmental progression levels	Example child behaviors
Foundations	Same Thing Comparer Shape Matcher—Identical	Says two pictures of houses are the same or different
Visual Thinker	Shape Matcher (all other) Shape Recognizer—Typical Shape Matcher—More Shapes Shape Recognizer—Circles, Squares, and Triangles +	"It's a rectangle because it looks like a door"
Parts	Constructor from Parts Shape Recognizer—All Rectangles Side Recognizer…Corner (Angle)	Correctly identifying and counting parts of shape. "It has four sides"
Property	Angle Representer Shape Class Identifier Shape Property Identifier Property Class Identifier	"It's a rectangle because the four sides are parallel and there are 4 right angles"

Returning to the shape learning trajectory, children at the *Shape Recognizer—Typical* level can names circles, as well as squares and triangles—as long as they look familiar (see the typical triangles in Figure 4.1). Instructional activities to develop this level include matching and naming physical shapes in large and small groups (see Circle Time!, Find the twin, and True or False in $[LT]^2$). Also effective is a suite of software activities *Mystery Pictures*, in which children build pictures by matching or identifying shapes that are named by the Building Blocks software program (Clements & Sarama, 2007/2018). *Mystery Pictures 1* and *2* address typical shapes, and *3* and *4* include a wider variety, including rhombuses, hexagons, and trapezoids. In the first of each of these pairs, *1* and *3*, children see an outline and have to choose that shape, whereupon they hear the shape name. So, they are doing the matching, but being taught the shape names. See Figure 4.2a for an example of *Mystery Pictures 1*. When they finish, they see an animation (Figure 4.2b). In the second of each of these pairs, *Mystery Pictures 2 and 4*, children are not given an outline, so they have to *recognize* the shape name pronounced by the software (Figure 4.2c shows *Mystery Pictures 4*) and select the named shapes to finish the picture (resulting in Figure 4.2d).

When children progress to the *Shape Recognizer—Circles, Squares, and Triangles* level, they can name less typical squares and triangles (see variations of triangles in Figure 4.1) and may recognize typical rectangles. They learn about these variations, enriching their visual images of each shape class, in corresponding activities in $[LT]^2$ (see many there, such as Is it or not? (Triangles), Feely Box, and True or False) as well as *Mystery Pictures 3 and 4*.

At the level *Constructor from Parts*, children draw or build shapes that fit the shape class. Thus, they have to think about the *parts* of shapes and how to put

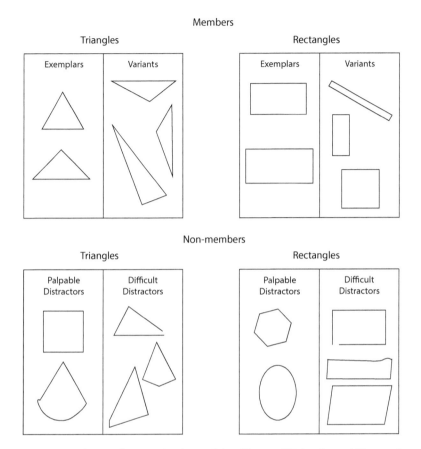

FIGURE 4.1 Members and Non-Members of the Classes of Triangles and Rectangles

them together to make a shape. In the instructional activity *Build Shapes*, children use plastic stirrers cut to various lengths to make shapes as well as to create pictures and designs that include these shapes (see Build Shapes/Straw Shapes in [LT]²). To make a square, for example, children have to select four sides of equal length and put them together to create (approximately) right angles.

Jumping up to the *Shape Property Identifier*, children understand, discuss, and use properties of geometric shapes. An instructional activity could be *Guess My Rule* in which children watch as you sort several shapes into piles based on a secret rule (a property, such as, "has at least one right angle"—see [LT]²). Ask children to silently guess your sorting rule. Sort shapes one at a time, continuing until there are at least three shapes in each of the two piles. Pick up a new shape, holding it between the two piles. With a look of confusion, gesture to children to encourage all of them to point to which pile the shape belongs. Place the shape in its correct pile. After all shapes are sorted, ask children to think-pair-share and tell their partner what the sorting rule is.

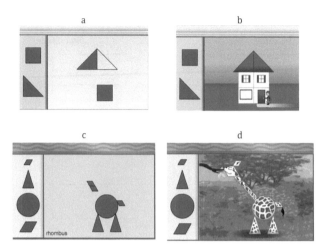

FIGURE 4.2 Mystery Pictures

Teaching Using Learning Trajectories: Early Arithmetic

Learning trajectories' instructional tasks might offer a sketch of a curriculum—a sequence of activities, which is essential as too many preschoolers experience no such sequence. However, research suggests that they can offer more. They should support teachers' use of formative assessment—the ongoing monitoring of student learning to inform and guide instruction. Several reviews indicate that formative assessment is an effective teaching strategy (National Mathematics Advisory Panel, 2008). However, the strategy is of no use to teachers unless they can accurately assess where students are in learning a mathematical topic and know how to support them in learning the following level of thinking. The goal of a learning trajectory helps define the mathematical content that teachers have to teaching and know well themselves. The developmental progression gives teachers a tool to understand the levels of thinking at which their students are operating, along with the next level of thinking that each student should learn. Finally, the matched instructional tasks provide guidance as to the type of educational activity that would support that learning and help explain why those activities would be particularly effective. Such knowledge helps teachers be more effective professionals.

Our second example illustrates ways to put this all into practice, focusing on the learning trajectory for early addition and subtraction. A study of textbooks in California showed the importance of teaching core concepts and meaningful strategies for arithmetic, not simply facts (Henry & Brown, 2008). The learning trajectory therefore should include core knowledge, strategies, and skills.

1. The Goal

Doing formative assessment well requires answering three key questions. The first is: Where are you trying to go? That is the learning trajectory's goal. Mathematically, whole-number addition can be viewed as an extension of counting (National Research Council, 2009; Wu, 2011). The sum 7 + 5 is the whole number that results from counting up 5 numbers starting at 7; that is, 7, 8, 9, 10, 11, 12. Using counting strategies such as counting on and other approaches (see Composing Numbers in [LT]^2) flexibly to solve different kinds of problems is this learning trajectory's goal. Of course, some problems are more difficult, simply because they involve larger (even larger single-digit) numbers, and this is an important consideration. This difficulty is, unfortunately, often much greater than it should be because too many curricula and teachers provide far more practice on problems with smaller digits and neglect the larger single-digit numbers (Hamann & Ashcraft, 1986). Teachers should ensure students receive more balanced experiences.

Beyond the size of the number, however, it is the type, or structure of the word problem that determines its difficulty. Type depends on the situation and the unknown. The situation can be a Join problem (have two apples, got four more) or Separate problem (had two applies, ate one); a Part-Part-Whole problem (three are girls and four are boys—no action is involved); or compare (John has four, Emily has six). For each of these categories, there are three quantities that play different roles in the problem, any one of which could be the unknown. For join problems, the differences in difficulty are significant. Easiest is result unknown, the most familiar type (have two apples, got four more, how many in all). More difficult is the change unknown (had two, got some more, now has six, how many got) and the most difficult are the start unknown (had some, got four more, now has six, how many started with). This is due in large part to the increasing difficulty children have in modeling, or acting out, each type.

In summary, a main goal of the addition and subtraction learning trajectory is that children learn to solve many types of arithmetic problems with flexible strategies. Addition and subtraction can be understood though counting, and that is one way children come to learn more about these arithmetic operations that we focus on here.

2. The Developmental Progression

The second key question for doing formative assessment is: Where are you now, and what is the next step? That is answered by the learning trajectory's developmental progression (remember, see LearningTrajectories.org). For counting-based arithmetic, children develop increasingly sophisticated counting strategies to solve increasingly difficult problem types. For example, most initially use a counting-all procedure. At the Find Result +/- level, given a join, result-unknown problem such as 7 + 2, such children count out objects to form a set of seven items, then count out two more items, and finally count all those and say "nine." At the following Find

Change +/- level, children solve join, change unknown (5 + _ = 7) problems by adding on objects. For example, asked, "You have 5 balls and then get some more. Now you have seven in all. How many did you get?" the child counts out 5, then counts those 5 again starting at 1, then adds more, counting "6, 7," then counts the balls added to find the answer, "two." Children use such counting methods to solve story situations if they understand the language in the story.

After children develop such methods, they eventually curtail them at the Counting Strategies +/- level. Often independently, children as young as 4 or 5 years invent counting on, solving the previous problem by counting, "Seven… eight, nine. Nine!" The elongated pronunciation may be substituting for counting the initial set one-by-one, as if they counted a set of seven items.

Children then move to the counting-on-from-larger strategy, which is preferred by most children once they invent it. Presenting problems such as 4 + 25, where the most counting on work is saved by reversing the order of the addends, often prompts children to start counting with the 25. Counting-on for increasing collections and the corresponding counting-back-from for decreasing collections are important numerical strategies for students to learn. However, they are only beginning strategies. In the case where the amount of increase is unknown, children use counting-up-to to find the unknown amount. If six items are increased so that there are now nine items, children may find the amount of increase by counting and keeping track of the number of counts, as in "Siiiix…7, 8, 9. 3!" And if nine items are decreased so that six remain, children may count from nine down to five to find the unknown decrease, as follows: "Nine; 8, 7, 6. 3!" However, counting backwards, especially more than two or three counts, is difficult for most children unless they have consistent instruction. Instead, children might learn counting-up-to the total to solve a subtraction situation. For example, "I took away 6 from those 9, so 7, 8, 9 (raising a finger with each count)—that's 3 more left in the 9."

Many additional levels and the types of problems children can solve (and how—using what strategy) can be found at [LT]². For formative assessment, teachers can pose problems for these levels to students and see if they can answer them correctly and especially what strategies they use.

3. The Instructional Tasks

The third key question for doing formative assessment is: How can you get there? That is answered by the learning trajectory's instructional tasks. As stated, instructional tasks in most resources (such as Clements & Sarama, 2014, or [LT]²) are not the only ones, but rather are illustrative examples. Thus, teachers implement them, adapt them, or use them as a template to gauge the appropriateness and expected effectiveness of other lessons, including those in published curricula.

In some cases, though, there is evidence that certain aspects of the instructional tasks are especially effective. For example, if students need extra help in learning counting on skills, there is theory and empirical work (El'konin & Davydov,

1975) that provide specific instructional strategies. After setting up the problem situation with objects (say, 5 + 3), the teacher guides children to connect the numeral signifying the first addend to the objects in the first set. Students then learn to recognize that the last object of that set is assigned the counting word ("five"). Next, the teacher helps the children understand that the first object in the second set will always be assigned the next counting number ("six"). Students learn that they can start with the five immediately and count on. These understandings and skills are reinforced with additional problems and a variety of specific, focused questions.

A second example of instructional activities supported by specific research evidence is found in the next level, Deriver +/-. Teaching Break-Apart-to-Make-Ten (BAMT) is an extended process that shows the interrelated nature of the learning trajectories. Initially, children develop solid knowledge of numerals and counting (i.e., move along the counting learning trajectory). This includes the number structure for teen numbers as 10 + another number. They learn to solve addition and subtraction of numbers with totals less than 10, often chunking numbers into 5 (e.g., 3 as 5-plus-3) and using visual models. With these levels of thinking established, children develop several levels of thinking within the composition/decomposition developmental progression. For example, they work on break-apart partners of numbers less than or equal to 10. They solve addition and subtraction problems involving teen numbers using the 10s structure ($10 + 5 = 15$), and addition and subtraction with three addends using 10s (e.g., $6 + 4 + 7 = 10 + 7 = 17$).

Teachers then introduce problems such as 9 + 6. They elicit, value, and discuss child-invented strategies and encourage children to use these strategies to solve a variety of problems. Only then do they proceed to the use of BAMT. They provide supports to connect visual and symbolic representations of quantities. In the example 9 + 6, they show nine counters (or fingers) and six counters, then move one counter from the group of six to join the nine, making a group of ten. Next, they highlight the five left in the group. Last, children see 10 counters and 5 counters and think 10-and-5, or 15.

Conclusion

Young students can learn more mathematics than many current programs provide. Policy makers, practitioners, and parents can replace negative myths and misconceptions with a vision of capable, engaged young children.

Learning trajectories can help policy makers, professional development experts, and teachers across age/grade levels share a common positive vision. Learning trajectories also provide a common language and understanding of mathematics and children's thinking and learning of mathematics. In these ways, learning trajectories support students' learning of more profound ideas in mathematics. Current research in learning trajectories points the way toward more effective and efficient, yet creative and enjoyable mathematics.

Research indicates that to make such teaching a reality, professional development of all teachers is critical (Sarama & Clements, 2013). A total of 50 to 70 hours of professional development appears necessary to achieve measurable effectiveness (Yoon, Duncan, Lee, Scarloss, & Shapley, 2007). Situating the materials not just in the classroom but also each school is important because it establishes a cultural practice and provides peer support. Having in-house leaders (e.g., early childhood and mathematics supervisors or coordinators) organize and lead study teams is not only logistically important, but promotes positive spread and shift in ownership to school personnel.

There is much to gain and little to lose by divesting ourselves of pernicious myths and misconceptions and using learning trajectories and other research-based guides to give all children equal opportunity to experience engaging, effective mathematics education. Integration mathematics with other STEM subjects can provide meaningful and motivating contexts for the application of mathematics, but frequently the mathematics used in STEM projects is mostly application of procedures already learned. Therefore, careful consideration of how to build new mathematical understandings in STEM projects, along with a focus on children's sequential and hierarchical learning of mathematical topics by themselves, will support successful learning of all STEM subjects. This approach gives all children equal opportunity to experience engaging, successful school careers but is especially critical for those who have not had rich opportunities to learn mathematics and other STEM subjects (National Research Council, 2009).

Authors' Note: This research was supported by the Institute of Education Sciences, U.S. Department of Education, through grants R305K05157 and R305A110188 and also by the National Science Foundation, through grants ESI-9730804 and REC-0228440. The opinions expressed are those of the authors and do not represent views of the IES or NSF. Address correspondence to Douglas H. Clements, University of Denver, Kennedy Institute and Educational Research, Policy & Practice, Katherine A. Ruffatto Hall 224 1999 East Evans Avenue Denver CO 80208–1700. Douglas.Clements@du.edu.

References

Andrews, A., & Trafton, P. R. (2002). *Little kids—Powerful problem solvers: Math stories from a Kindergarten classroom*. Portsmouth, NH: Heinemann.

Aydogan, C., Plummer, C., Kang, S. J., Bilbrey, C., Farran, D. C., & Lipsey, M. W. (2005, June 5–8). *An investigation of prekindergarten curricula: Influences on classroom characteristics and child engagement*. Paper presented at the NAEYC, Washington, DC.

Balfanz, R. (1999). Why do we teach young children so little mathematics? Some historical considerations. In J. V. Copley (Ed.), *Mathematics in the early years* (pp. 3–10). Reston, VA: National Council of Teachers of Mathematics.

Ball, D. L. (1992). Magical hopes: Manipulatives and the reform of math education. *American Educator, 16*(2), 14;16–18;46–47.

Baroody, A. J., & Purpura, D. J. (2017). Number and operations. In J. Cai (Ed.), *Handbook for research in mathematics education* (pp. 308–354). Reston, VA: National Council of Teachers of Mathematics (NCTM).

Brosterman, N. (1997). *Inventing kindergarten.* New York, NY: Harry N. Abrams.

Carpenter, T. P., Ansell, E., Franke, M. L., Fennema, E. H., & Weisbeck, L. (1993). Models of problem solving: A study of kindergarten children's problem-solving processes. *Journal for Research in Mathematics Education, 24*(5), 428–441. doi:10.2307/749152

Clements, D. H. (1992). Elaboraciones sobre los niveles de pensamiento geometrico [Elaborations on the levels of geometric thinking]. In A. Gutiérrez (Ed.), *Memorias del Tercer Simposio Internacional Sobre Investigatcion en Educacion Matematica* (pp. 16–43). València: Universitat De València.

Clements, D. H., Fuson, K. C., & Sarama, J. (2017a). The research-based balance in early childhood mathematics: A response to Common Core criticisms. *Early Childhood Research Quarterly, 40,* 150–162.

Clements, D. H., Fuson, K. C., & Sarama, J. (2017b). What is developmentally appropriate teaching? *Teaching Children Mathematics, 24*(3), 179–188. doi:10.5951/teacchilmath.24. 3. 01doi:78

Clements, D. H., & McMillen, S. (1996). Rethinking "concrete" manipulatives. *Teaching Children Mathematics, 2*(5), 270–279.

Clements, D. H., & Sarama, J. (2007/2013). *Building blocks,* Volumes 1 and 2. Columbus, OH: McGraw-Hill Education.

Clements, D. H., & Sarama, J. (2007/2018). *Building blocks software* [Computer software]. Columbus, OH: McGraw-Hill Education.

Clements, D. H., & Sarama, J. (2009). *Learning and teaching early math: The learning trajectories approach.* New York, NY: Routledge.

Clements, D. H., & Sarama, J. (2014). *Learning and teaching early math: The learning trajectories approach* (2nd ed.). New York, NY: Routledge.

Clements, D. H., & Sarama, J. (2018). Myths of early math. *Education Sciences, 8*(71), 1–8. doi:10.3390/educsci8020071

Clements, D. H., Sarama, J., Spitler, M. E., Lange, A. A., & Wolfe, C. B. (2011). Mathematics learned by young children in an intervention based on learning trajectories: A large-scale cluster randomized trial. *Journal for Research in Mathematics Education, 42*(2), 127–166. doi:10.5951/jresematheduc.42. 2. 01doi:27

Committee on Integrated STEM Education. (2014). *STEM integration in K-12 education: Status, prospects, and an agenda for research.* Washington, DC: The National Academies Press.

Davis, R. B. (1984). *Learning mathematics: The cognitive science approach to mathematics education.* Norwood, NJ: Ablex.

El'konin, D. B., & Davydov, V. V. (1975). Children's capacity for learning mathematics. In L. P. Steffe (Ed.), *Soviet studies in the psychology of learning and teaching mathematics* (Vol. 7, pp. 1–11). Chicago: University of Chicago Press.

Forman, G.E., & Hill, F. (1984). *Constructive play: Applying Piaget in the preschool.* Menlo Park, CA: Addison-Wesley Pub. Co.

Foster, M. E., Anthony, J. L., Clements, D. H., & Sarama, J. (2016). Improving mathematics learning of kindergarten students through computer assisted instruction. *Journal for Research in Mathematics Education, 47*(3), 206–232. Retrieved from https://doi.org/10. 5951/jresematheduc.47.3.0206

Foster, M. E., Anthony, J. L., Clements, D. H., Sarama, J., & Williams, J. J. (2018). Hispanic dual language learning kindergarten students' response to a numeracy intervention: A randomized control trial. *Early Childhood Research Quarterly, 43*, 83–95. doi:10.1016/j. ecresq.2018. 01. 00doi:9

Fuligni, A. S., Howes, C., Huang, Y. D., Hong, S. S., & Lara-Cinisomo, S. (2012). Activity settings and daily routines in preschool classrooms: Diverse experiences in early learning settings for low-income children. *Early Childhood Research Quarterly, 27*(2), 198–209. doi:10.1016/j.ecresq.2011. 10. 00doi:1

Ginsburg, H. P., Greenes, C., & Balfanz, R. (2003). *Big math for little kids*. Parsippany, NJ: Dale Seymour.

Ginsburg, H. P., Lee, J. S., & Stevenson-Boyd, J. (2008). Mathematics education for young children: What it is and how to promote it. *Social Policy Report, 22*(1), 1–24.

Gray, E. M., & Pitta, D. (1997). Number processing: Qualitative differences in thinking and the role of imagery. In L. Puig & A. Gutiérrez (Eds.), *Proceedings of the 20th Annual Conference of the Mathematics Education Research Group of Australasia* (Vol. 3, pp. 35–42). Rotorua, New Zealand: Mathematics Education Research Group of Australasia.

Grupe, L. A., & Bray, N. W. (1999, April). What role do manipulatives play in kindergartners' accuracy and strategy use when solving simple addition problems? Paper presented at the Society for Research in Child Development, Albuquerque, NM.

Hamann, M. S., & Ashcraft, M. H. (1986). Textbook presentations of the basic addition facts. *Cognition and Instruction, 3*, 173–192.

Henry, V. J., & Brown, R. S. (2008). First-grade basic facts: An investigation into teaching and learning of an accelerated, high-demand memorization standard. *Journal for Research in Mathematics Education, 39*(2), 153–183.

Klein, A., Starkey, P., Clements, D. H., Sarama, J., & Iyer, R. (2008). Effects of a pre-kindergarten mathematics intervention: A randomized experiment. *Journal of Research on Educational Effectiveness, 1*(2), 155–178. doi:10.1080/19345740802114533

Lee, J. (2004). Correlations between kindergarten teachers' attitudes toward mathematics and teaching practice. *Journal of Early Childhood Teacher Education, 25*(2), 173–184.

Mulligan, J. T., Mitchelmore, M. C., & Crevesten, N. (2013). Reconceptualising early mathematics learning: The fundamental role of pattern and structure. In L.D. English & J.T. Mulligan (Eds), *Reconceptualizing early mathematics learning* (pp. 47–66). Dordrecht: Springer. doi:10.1007/978-94-007-6440-8_7

National Mathematics Advisory Panel. (2008). *Foundations for success: The final report of the National Mathematics Advisory Panel*. Washington, DC: U.S. Department of Education, Office of Planning, Evaluation and Policy Development.

National Research Council. (2009). *Mathematics learning in early childhood: Paths toward excellence and equity*. Washington, DC: National Academy Press. doi:10.17226/12519

NCTM. (2006). *Curriculum focal points for prekindergarten through grade 8 mathematics: A quest for coherence*. Reston, VA: National Council of Teachers of Mathematics.

NGA/CCSSO. (2010). *Common core state standards*. Washington, DC: National Governors Association Center for Best Practices, Council of Chief State School Officers.

Olson, J. K. (1988, August). Microcomputers make manipulatives meaningful. Paper presented at the International Congress of Mathematics Education, Budapest, Hungary.

Outhred, L. N., & Sardelich, S. (1997). Problem solving in kindergarten: The development of representations. In F. Biddulph & K. Carr (Eds.), *People in Mathematics Education. Proceedings of the 20th Annual Conference of the Mathematics Education Research Group of Australasia* (Vol. 2, pp. 376–383). Rotorua, New Zealand: Mathematics Education Research Group of Australasia.

Piaget, J., & Inhelder, B. (1967). The child's conception of space (F. J. Langdon, & J. L. Lunzer, Trans.). New York, NY: W. W. Norton.

Pratt, C. (1948). *I learn from children*. New York, NY: Simon and Schuster.

Preschool Curriculum Evaluation Research Consortium. (2008). *Effects of preschool curriculum programs on school readiness (NCER 2008–2009)*. Retrieved from Government Printing Office: http://ncer.ed.gov

Raudenbush, S. W. (2009). The Brown legacy and the O'Connor challenge: Transforming schools in the images of children's potential. *Educational Researcher, 38*(3), 169–180. doi:10.3102/0013189X09334840

Reikerås, E., Løge, I. K., & Knivsberg, A.-M. (2012). The mathematical competencies of toddlers expressed in their play and daily life activities in Norwegian kindergartens. *International Journal of Early Childhood, 44*, 91–114. doi:10.1007/s13158-011-0050-x

Rittle-Johnson, B., Fyfe, E.R., & Zippert, E. (2018). The roles of patterning and spatial skills in early mathematics development. *Early Childhood Research Quarterly*. doi:10.1016/j.ecresq.2018. 03. 00doi:6

Sarama, J., & Clements, D. H. (2009a). "Concrete" computer manipulatives in mathematics education. *Child Development Perspectives, 3*(3), 145–150.

Sarama, J., & Clements, D. H. (2009b). *Early childhood mathematics education research: Learning trajectories for young children*. New York, NY: Routledge.

Sarama, J., & Clements, D. H. (2013). Lessons learned in the implementation of the TRIAD scale-up model: Teaching early mathematics with trajectories and technologies. In T. G. Halle, A. J., Metz & I. Martinez-Beck (Eds.), *Applying implementation science in early childhood programs and systems* (pp. 173–191). Baltimore, MD: Brookes.

Sarama, J., & Clements, D. H. (2016). Physical and virtual manipulatives: What is "concrete"? In P. S. Moyer-Packenham (Ed.), *International perspectives on teaching and learning mathematics with virtual manipulatives* (Vol. 3, pp. 71–93). Switzerland: Springer International Publishing. doi:10.1007/978-3-319-32718-1_4

Sarama, J., & Clements, D. H. (in press). Promoting a good start: Technology in early childhood mathematics. In E. Arias, J. Cristia & S. Cueto (Eds.), *Promising models to improve primary mathematics learning in Latin America and the Caribbean using technology*. Washington, DC: Inter-American Development Bank.

Sarama, J., Lange, A., Clements, D. H., & Wolfe, C. B. (2012). The impacts of an early mathematics curriculum on emerging literacy and language. *Early Childhood Research Quarterly, 27*(3), 489–502. doi:10.1016/j.ecresq.2011. 12. 00doi:2

Seo, K.-H., & Ginsburg, H. P. (2004). What is developmentally appropriate in early childhood mathematics education? In D. H. Clements, J. Sarama & A.-M. DiBiase (Eds), *Engaging young children in mathematics: Standards for early childhood mathematics education* (pp. 91–104). Mahwah, NJ: Erlbaum.

Sowell, E. J. (1989). Effects of manipulative materials in mathematics instruction. *Journal for Research in Mathematics Education, 20*, 498–505.

Steffe, L. P., & Cobb, P. (1988). *Construction of arithmetical meanings and strategies*. New York, NY: Springer-Verlag.

Stipek, D. (2013). Mathematics in early childhood education: Revolution or evolution? *Early Education and Development, 24*(4), 431–435. doi:10.1080/10409289.2013.777285

Stipek, D. (2017). Playful math instruction in the context of standards and accountability. *Young Children, 72*(3), 8–12.

Thompson, A. C. (2012). *The effect of enhanced visualization instruction on first grade students' scores on the North Carolina standard course assessment*. (Dissertation), Liberty University, Lynchburg, VA.

Tymms, P., Jones, P., Albone, S., & Henderson, B. (2009). The first seven years at school. *Educational Assessment and Evaluation Accountability*, *21*, 67–80. doi:10.1007/s11092-008-9066-7

van Hiele, P. M. (1986). *Structure and insight: A theory of mathematics education*. Orlando, FL: Academic Press.

van Oers, B. (1994). Semiotic activity of young children in play: The construction and use of schematic representations. *European Early Childhood Education Research Journal*, *2*, 19–33.

van Oers, B. (2010). Emergent mathematical thinking in the context of play. *Educational Studies in Mathematics*, *74*(1), 23–37. doi:10.1007/s10649-009-9225-x

Wu, H.-H. (2011). *Understanding numbers in elementary school mathematics*. Providence, RI: American Mathematical Society.

Yoon, K. S., Duncan, T., Lee, S. W.-Y., Scarloss, B., & Shapley, K. L. (2007). *Reviewing the evidence on how teacher professional development affects student achievement (Issues & Answers Report, REL 2007–No. 033)*. Retrieved from U.S. Department of Education, Institute of Education Sciences, National Center for Education Evaluation and Regional Assistance, Regional Educational Laboratory Southwest: http://ies.ed.gov/ncee/edlabs

PART II

STEM and Higher Order Thinking Skills

5

DESIGNING AN ASSESSMENT OF COMPUTATIONAL THINKING ABILITIES FOR YOUNG CHILDREN

Emily Relkin and Marina Umaschi Bers

What is Computational Thinking (CT)?

In 1963, computer scientist Alan Perlis observed that computer programming required exercising special classes of logical and creative thought processes. Perlis saw value in developing these thinking abilities early in life and recommended that computer programming become part of everyone's education (Grover & Pea, 2013; Perlis, 1963). Two decades later, mathematician, computer scientist and educational innovator Seymour Papert briefly mentioned the term "Computational Thinking" (CT) in his foundational book *Mindstorms: Children, Computers, and Powerful Ideas* (Papert, 1980). Later in his career, Papert became convinced that the acquisition of CT skills empowered children and adults to process and create knowledge of their world (Papert, 1996).

In the early 2000s, Jeanette Wing popularized the term CT in an article in which she defined it as solving problems, designing systems, and understanding behavior by drawing upon the concepts of Computer Science (Wing, 2006). Wing viewed CT as a vital and universal skill set that should be acquired by everyone (Wing, 2008). According to Wing, CT was not only of value in computer science but provided opportunities to succeed in the arts, humanities, and everyday life (Wing, 2008). Hemmendinger, (2010) stated that the goal of CT education should not be to have everyone thinking like a computer scientist but to facilitate real-world problem solving. Past studies have shown that children as young as 4 years old can begin to acquire CT skills (Bers, 2018; Bers, 2008; Leidl, Bers, & Mihm, 2017; Sullivan, Bers, & Mihm, 2017).

There is a paucity of information about the development of CT abilities in young children. The term is still evolving and there is currently no agreed upon age or stage of development at which children should be introduced to CT.

There are also no universally agreed upon curricula for CT (Lockwood & Mooney, 2018). Researchers and educators still debate whether CT is its own category of thought or if it relies on other areas of thought such as mathematical thinking (Gadanidis, 2017; Pei, Weintrop, & Wilensky, 2018). For present purposes, we will define CT as the set of thought processes that allows framing and solving problems using computers, robots, and other computational devices (Sullivan, Bers, & Mihm, 2017). Mastery of CT requires a broad set of cognitive abilities, including but not limited to elements of pattern recognition, conceptualization, sequencing, planning, and problem solving.

Despite the uncertainty behind CT, there is an increasing use of this term in education and in various national and state wide Computer Science frameworks (K–12 Computer Science Framework Steering Committee, 2016; National Research Council, 2010; Massachusetts Digital Literacy and Computer Science (DLCS) Curriculum Framework, 2016). This chapter seeks to help operationalize "Computational Thinking" in such a way that it becomes possible to assess.

CT Assessment in Young Children

Despite the recent proliferation of programming languages, educational apps, and robotics platforms designed to teach coding to young children, there are currently no well-validated assessment tools designed for measuring CT abilities in young children.

Assessing CT is a recognized challenge for educators, researchers, and technology specialists who work with young children. As one set of authors pointed out, "Because CT is not evaluated by standardized testing, it is difficult in the current educational climate for teachers to teach CT concepts directly… the field requires systematic assessment procedures…" (Lee et al., 2011, p. 36). Without a means of measuring baseline abilities or gauging progress, PreK and elementary school teachers are limited in their ability to document individual progress and to assess the effectiveness of the curricula designed to teach computer and robotic programming.

Since computer science (CS) has only recently been taught in preschool and early elementary schools, most prior studies of CT assessment were carried out with older children and in a research rather than classroom setting. Werner, Denner, and Campe (2014) examined children ages 11 and 12 as they created their own computer games using the program Alice 2.2 or the story-telling Alice programming environment. The researchers categorized the development of programming skills in terms of a three-level hierarchy and noted that students sometimes generated code mechanically without showing full understanding of their own work.

Some past studies that attempted to assess proficiency in CT skills used informal methods of collecting data such as interviews and free-form observations. Wang, Wang, and Liu (2014) observed children using a tangible programming tool.

After they completed two tasks the researchers interviewed them. This was said to provide the researchers with a broad qualitative assessment of abstraction, automation, and creativity, as well as decomposition and analysis. An exploratory case study by Portelance and Bers (2015) recorded students three times during a 13-day coding curriculum with the ScratchJr application. Students were asked questions about their individual projects and results indicated that qualitative clinical interviews can be an effective way to assess CT. However, the interview approach employed by both of these studies is challenging to conduct and not readily adapted to a classroom setting. Additionally, it does not provide a basis for categorizing younger children's abilities in terms of stages of CT competency.

Other relevant work on the assessment of CT in young children using robots was carried out by Mioduser, Levy, and Talis in Israel. In their initial study, they tested a group of six kindergarten students using a LEGO robot that employed on-screen programming (Mioduser, Levy, & Talis, 2009). This study focused on learning and changes in thinking rather than project-based assessment or programming outcomes. They observed the children in 5 30–40-minute sessions over the span of one week. There were two parts to this study: description and construction. The tasks for this study ranged from low difficulty to high difficulty. All of these tasks and descriptions were videotaped and coded. Children's responses were coded as "spontaneous" or "supported" depending on the amount of help a researcher had to give (Mioduser et al., 2009). Supported answers involved probing from a researcher in order to help bring the child to Vygotsky's "Zone of Proximal Development."

Vygotsky's cognitive theories emphasize that children's social interactions with others is vital for development. Vygotsky defined the term, "Zone of Proximal Development" (ZPD) as the potential for performance at a higher level of ability attainable through the guidance from others (Vygotsky, 1978). He pointed out the value of ZPD in predicting development by saying children who first work with an adult or peer will be able to work independently in the future (Vygotsky, 1987). In regard to assessment involving a child's development, Vygotsky believed that children should be assessed in a way that is not static, but which is dynamic and interactive. This type of assessment as now called DA (Dynamic Assessment). Vygotsky stressed the importance of testing children outside of expectations for their mental age in order to bring them out of their typical comfort zone (Vygotsky, 1998; Vygotsky, 1978).

Based on their observations in this study, Mioduser and colleagues (Mioduser et al., 2009) proposed three constructs relevant to assessment of CT using robots. The first construct is the *episode*, which is the observation of a specific action or sequence of actions taken by the robot that leads to the formation of a literal mental representation. The second construct is the *script*, which is the child's recognition of repetitive actions as a pattern. The third construct is *rules*, which are sequences and repetitions of actions from which the child forms an abstract representation.

Mioduser and Levy (2010) further studied the effect of acquiring programming skills on the explanations that children give when they observe the behavior of robots. They found that as children gained experience in programming robots, they applied different descriptions to the robotic behaviors they observed. When the robot's behaviors were simple, the children with less experience in programming tended to ascribe human or animal-like motivations to the robot while those who were more experienced gave more mechanistic explanations. When children observed more complex programs, they typically give a combination of both types of explanations. In this study, construction tasks were designed to increase in complexity as the child learned. In addition, the researchers did not help the child beyond prompting, such as, "Why do you think that happened?" The researchers recorded the amount of prompting the children required (Mioduser & Levy, 2010).

Using children's explanations of robotic behaviors as a measure of CT has some assets but also limitations. The K-12 Computer Science Framework suggests that assessments of programming should involve not only the students' ability to write a program but also their ability to explain the significance of it (K-12 Computer Science Framework Steering Committee, 2016). Braitenberg (1984) argued that it is more difficult to understand a robot's behavior through observing a program than it is to understand the behavior by creating a program. Young children's expressive language skills may also limit the nature of the explanations they provide for the behaviors they observe. Mioduser and colleagues critiqued their study by stating, "While deepening how we understand young children's evolving knowledge of autonomous artificial behaviors, it is limited in its small sample and disconnect from classroom situations" (Mioduser et al., 2009, p. 19). They also observed that combining the task of robot construction and explanations in the same subjects introduced a potential confound and recommended that future studies examine these separately.

Design Considerations for a CT Assessment Tool

Based on the work in this area carried out by past investigators, various considerations for the design of a valuable CT assessment tool for young children can be identified:

1. **Age appropriateness:** In order to optimally impact the acquisition of CT abilities, interventions need to target preschool and early elementary school levels. At this age, children are in the process of developing representational and abstract thinking and have sufficient linguistic skills to perform basic programing. An assessment tool for this age group must use age-appropriate language and tasks to assure that abilities and factors such as manual dexterity and attention span and the use of jargon (Sattler, Dumon, & Coalson 2016) are not the limiting factors in measurements.

2. **Authentic interaction:** To place young children at ease and avoid stress that can be associated with formal standardized testing, a CT assessment tool should be structured as authentically as possible, ideally capturing the dynamics of play and familiar teacher-child, parent-child, and/or peer to peer interactions. Authentic assessment should be something that is worthwhile for the child (Dewey, 1938). Shaffer and Resnick (1999) describe authenticity in assessment as relevant to the learning process. They also argue that computers and technologies can lead to new types of authentic assessment and learning if used correctly. The assessment should not be intrusive or disruptive and should include context specific prompts (Ming, Ming, & Bumbacher, 2014).

3. **Ease of administration:** Past researchers studied children's CT over long periods of time requiring three or more hours of time per child (Mioduser & Levy, 2010; Mioduser et al., 2009; Werner et al., 2014). Many educational assessments currently are too lengthy and/or complex for teachers to give effectively. Teachers continue to feel unprepared to conduct high-level assessments and many have a low assessment literacy despite educational efforts (DeLuca & Bellara, 2013). The National Research Council indicates that it is difficult to assess CT and recommends that teachers must be extremely skilled in coding through professional development in order to properly assess children (National Research Council, 2010). Ideally, teachers who are not particularly skilled at coding and assessments should be able to administer CT assessments.

4. **Time constraints:** The duration of testing sessions should be kept relatively short in light of the limited attention spans of children in this age group and the limitations on time available to teachers for individualized assessments (Moyer & Gilmer, 1953). To be of practical value for preschool and early elementary school use, the instrument should require no longer than 15–30 minutes for a single assessment.

5. **Sensitivity:** Following the "low floor, high ceiling" model (Papert, 1980), an ideal assessment tool should be equally useful for assessing novices as well as experts (Sattler, 2014).

6. **Scoring:** To create an assessment tool that does not require an expert to administer or score, the ratings system employed should use simple outcome categories and/or numeric scores that are straightforward to calculate (Koretz, McCaffrey, Klein, Bell, & Stecher, 1992).

7. **Communication of results:** While numeric scores are suitable for rating the level of CT proficiency, descriptive names (e.g., "Early Programmer") based on the score may better convey the meaning. It is important to present results in a fashion that is easy for people unfamiliar with CS concepts but can still give quality technical data (Sattler, Dumont, & Coalson, 2016).

Development of a Pilot CT Assessment Tool for Young Children

To address the above criteria, we set out to create a pilot CT assessment tool that permits standardization and increased sensitivity, by presenting children with specific structured scenarios rather than simply observing free play with the robot. Structured scenarios permit assessments to be carried out in children who have only rudimentary understanding of the robot's operation and limited manual dexterity. To capture the full range of CT abilities, the scenarios are presented in gradually increasing complexity, from simplest to most complex. The assessment includes a combination of questions and simple coding tasks designed to create a balance between the need for well-developed language skills and non-verbal communication. Scoring and categorizations are sufficiently flexible so that missing one question or failing to complete one task does not disqualify the child from achieving a rating appropriate to their skill level.

We based our assessment on the "Seven Powerful Ideas" of CS that according to Bers (2018) inform curriculum that can promote CT in early childhood and that are developmentally appropriate. These are further described in Table 5.1.

TABLE 5.1 Seven Powerful Ideas of Computer Science (Based on Bers, 2018)

Powerful Idea	Definition	Example
Algorithms	Sequencing/order, logical organization	Child understands that KIBO blocks must be scanned in a specific order
Modularity	Breaking up larger task into smaller parts, instructions	Child uses repeat blocks in order to accomplish a goal rather than scanning a large number of blocks
Control Structures	Recognizing patterns and repetition, cause and effect	Child recognizes that he or she must use a beginning and an end when making a program and are able to use If Blocks and Repeat Blocks
Representation	Symbolic representation, models	Child sees the difference between the blue motion blocks and the orange sound blocks
Hardware/ Software	Smart objects are not magical, objects are human engineered	Child describes what the function of KIBOs electronics do. Child understands that one must give the robot a program in order for it to work
Design Process	Problem solving, perseverance, editing/ revision	Child has the capability to plan and test an idea in order to improve a project
Debugging	Identifying problems, problem solving, perseverance	Child identifies a bug in either hardware or software and is able to fix the problem

Past researchers empirically identified stages in the development of programming skills and related those to acquisition of CT skills (Jenkins, 2002; Rogalski & Samurçay, 1990). For this purpose, we chose the Developmental Model of Programming proposed by Vizner (2017). One advantage that this model offered for our prototype assessment was it was developed using the KIBO robot platform based on observation of children 4–7 years old with various levels of skill and exposure to the platform. This model consists of four stages of programing and provides some parameters for assessing children's coding proficiency.

The four levels of proficiency specified in Vizner's Developmental Model of Programming are as follows:

1. **Proto-Programmer:** Child has little to no understanding of what a program is; child does not create his or her own code and may press the "On" button repeatedly without first programming the robot.
2. **Early Programmer:** Child is capable of creating programs with the Begin and End blocks. The child may try to use as many blocks as possible and may scan blocks that are not part of a meaningful program sequence.
3. **Programmer:** Can use 3–6 instructions without using complex blocks such as Repeat. This child may debug a program using trial and error but needs assistance from others when creating programs that are complex.
4. **Fluent Programmer:** Solves 6+ instructional tasks and uses advanced debugging techniques.

A Prototype Early Childhood CT Assessment: TACTIC-KIBO

Our pilot CT assessment tool called TACTIC-KIBO (**T**ufts **A**ssessment of **C**omputational **T**hinking **i**n **C**hildren—**KIBO** robot version) is specific to the KIBO robotics platform which was designed to teach coding to children ages 4–7. The KIBO robotics platform was chosen because it is time-tested and developmentally appropriate. However, it is our hope that this approach may be applicable to many other programming and robotic technologies. The KIBO robotic platform is used widely in 54 countries throughout the world as a means of teaching CT and coding skills to young children. KIBO was developed under a grant from the National Science Foundation (NSF Grant No. DRL-1118897) as a developmentally appropriate tool for teaching the basics of computer programing to neurotypical children aged 4–7 (Sullivan, Elkin, & Bers, 2015).

To use the KIBO robot, children must align and scan barcodes on programming blocks representing steps in a program that guides the robot's actions (See Figure 5.1a). The child then presses a green flashing button to make the robot perform the program. Every program must have a "Begin" and "End" block. Other examples of programming blocks are "Spin," "Sing," "Turn Right," and "Shake." By virtue of resembling building blocks, programming blocks are in a

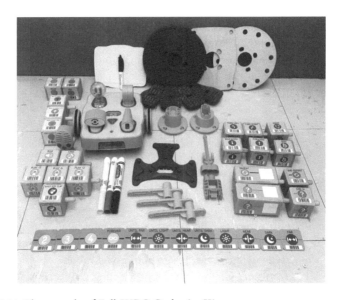

FIGURE 5.1A Photograph of Full KIBO Robotics Kit

format that is familiar to young children and arguably more manageable than computer screens that have only two dimensions.

The KIBO robotics kit is an exemplary educational robotics platform designed with a "low floor and high ceiling" (Papert & Harel, 1991) The programs that KIBO performs can be as simple as a three-block program and as complex as a program featuring conditional blocks, repeat blocks and nested statements. The more complex blocks (repeats and ifs) require "parameter" stickers which include "if near" "repeat until dark." (See Figure 5.1b) KIBO was designed to make young children producers of technology, not consumers. Children can have fun and express themselves as they make personally meaningful projects with KIBO.

The KIBO robot also has four openings on its upper surface for sensors that can detect light, sound, and proximity, as well as modules that can flash a light or record/play sounds. In addition, KIBO contains attachable art and building platforms compatible with LEGO bricks that allows children to use various materials to decorate their robot. There is also an attachable expression module that allows children to attach drawing using a dry erase board and marker extensions so that they can draw as KIBO moves, and a free throw extension to aid children in learning concepts of physics and math. This robot has been shown to help children learn technological literacy as well as other curriculum such as math, science, art, and language (Bers, 2018; Sullivan et al., 2015; Sullivan et al., 2017).

KIBO robot was selected as the initial robotics platform for CT assessment in children for several reasons. It is a time-tested, award-winning robotics platform designed for preschool to elementary school age children. It has an existing user

FIGURE 5.1B KIBO Robot Sensors

base that spans multiple continents and languages, making it available to a large number of children and teachers. Its use of tangible programming blocks is not only advantageous for children but can help to create a more user-friendly environment for teachers or other evaluators to interact with the children they are assessing. KIBO uses programming principles that are analogous to those used in other robotic platforms for young children as well as platforms developed for older children and adults. It is hoped this will facilitate creation of versions of the assessment instrument that are applicable to other coding platforms in the future.

Bers' Seven Powerful Ideas were adapted as the domains for our prototype CT assessment tool and combined with Vizner's Developmental Model of Programming, which were adapted for use as a hierarchical scoring system. The design foundations of the TACTIC assessment tool are summarized in Figure 5.2.

The TACTIC assessment tool involves pre-programmed KIBO robot activities of escalating complexity which serve as the framework for asking questions and posing tasks for the child to complete. Figure 5.3 shows the block sequences and commands for all levels.

The examiner programs the KIBO in front of the child using the specified program and add-ons. This assessment can be done on a tablet or computer for automatic scoring or by paper for manual scoring. The examiner takes the child through the series of questions and tasks for each level. The test continues until the children reach a level that they get three or more questions or tasks incorrect, or until all four levels have been completed.

To help characterize TACTIC-KIBO in terms of its age appropriateness and face validity, a pilot study was carried out with participants from the Boston area. Fifteen kindergarten and early elementary school children between the ages of 5 and 7 with

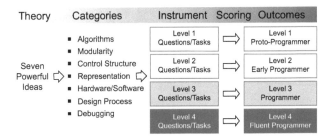

FIGURE 5.2 The Design Foundations of the TACTIC-KIBO CT Assessment Tool

Action	Blocks and parameter cards	Add-ons
LEVEL 1 BEGIN - FORWARD - END		
LEVEL 2 BEGIN - FORWARD - WHITE LIGHT ON - END		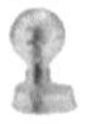
LEVEL 3 BEGIN - REPEAT TWO TIMES - FORWARD - WHITE LIGHT ON - END REPEAT - END		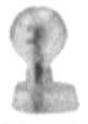
LEVEL 4 BEGIN - REPEAT UNTIL NEAR - FORWARD - WHITE LIGHT ON - END REPEAT - END		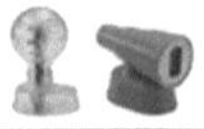
FINAL PROGRAM BEGIN - REPEAT IF NEAR - FORWARD - WHITE LIGHT ON - END IF - END		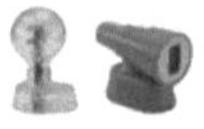

FIGURE 5.3 The Set of Robotic Activities Used in the Pilot TACTIC-KIBO CT Assessment

past exposure to the KIBO robot were recruited and consented using an Institutional Review Board approved protocol. The children were videotaped during the TACTIC-KIBO assessment and again as they engaged in structured interactive play sessions (IPS) with the KIBO. This IPS sessions allowed an independent assessment of CT skills to be assessed by expert raters.

The IPS was created as a means of measuring the validity of TACTIC-KIBO based on its correlation to expert assessments. The IPS had three parts, the first being a confrontational naming game used to test the child's knowledge of KIBO hardware. Then, a free-play construction session in which the child was encouraged to program a project of their own choice. Finally, the IPS included a construction challenge in which the child was asked to augment a program using higher level skills. The challenge was designed to bring the children to their ZPDs as described by Vygotsky.

A simple curriculum was created to guide the IPS with the goal of collecting sufficient information to permit an assessment of CT ability based on review of the IPS by independent expert raters. A scoring sheet for the IPS was developed to help standardize scoring by the outside raters. Experts rated 25% of the students using the same four-level classification system used for the CT assessment tool but based exclusively on the behaviors observed during the IPSs. The expert ratings of the IPS and the ratings based on the CT assessment tool were used to establish the inter-rater reliability. Demographic data (date of birth, gender, hours of experience with KIBO, experience with other robotics platforms, experience with programmable robots) were collected from the parent/legal guardian after the consent was signed.

Pilot Study Outcomes

The primary outcome measure of the TACTIC-KIBO pilot study was the correlation between the TACTIC-KIBO ratings and IPS ratings by the primary examiner. Fourteen out of 15 children completed TACTIC-KIBO as well as IPS. Among the children who completed both assessments, there was a highly significant correlation between the total TACTIC scores and the expert rating of the IPS ($r= 0.895$, $p< 0.001$). Discrepant ratings occurred exclusively among four children rated as Level 4 Fluent Programmers by TACTIC who were judged to be Level 3 by IPS. The average administration time for TACTIC-KIBO was 16 minutes compared to 19 minutes for the IPS. The IPS, however, required an additional 15–30 minutes for scoring, while TACTIC-KIBO was scored as it was administered.

Using pre-specified criteria for administration and scoring, TACTIC-KIBO identified four levels of CT abilities ranging from novice to fluent in kindergarten and first-grade children. TACTIC-KIBO scores correlated significantly with expert assessments based on observation of KIBO IPSs (See Figure 5.4). According to past research and recommendations, administration time and ease of scoring were suitable for use in classroom and research settings (Moyer & Gilmer, 1953; Ruff & Lawson, 1990). These results suggest that TACTIC-KIBO is a promising means of assessing CT abilities in young children. Limitations to this study include the sample size, biases in subject selection, biases in test administration and ratings, context, and issues relating to the lack of availability of a true gold standard for measuring CT in young children.

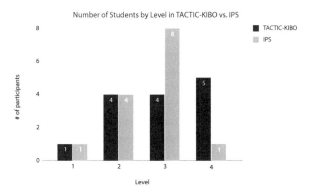

FIGURE 5.4 Comparison between TACTIC-KIBO Level Scores and Expert Rating Scores from KIBO Interactive Play Sessions

We observed that TACTIC-KIBO was engaging and enjoyable for the majority of children tested. This included students who were not yet fully literate, and for whom English was a second language. TACTIC-KIBO duration proved suitable for 5–7-year old children despite the relatively short attention spans of children in this age group.

A caveat in the interpretation of the data on mean number of correct responses per level is that the method of administration used in this pilot allowed children to advance to the next level of questions only if they successfully responded in three or more categories on the preceding level. The assumption in the analysis of correct responses is that children would not be able to respond correctly on higher levels if they did not meet the three-correct response criterion on the lowest levels. It is possible that this approach underestimated the total number of correct responses children may have provided in a given category.

Future Directions

TACTIC-KIBO requires further testing and validation before it can be recommended for use in schools and research studies. This should include testing a broader range of ages (4–7 years), experienced and inexperienced robot programmers, all genders, and children of different socioeconomic backgrounds and nationalities.

In the next phase of development, we anticipate testing will include administration by elementary school teachers. This will require the creation of a training program for educators and a certification process to assure that they meet acceptable standards of inter-rater reliability. A training curriculum along with annotated videos of TACTIC-KIBO being administered can be used for these purposes. A software application to help in the administration and scoring of TACTIC-KIBO has been developed. This will allow for easier administration by employing automated prompts, feedback, and permitting remote data collection.

In its current form, TACTIC-KIBO requires a child be taken out of class to be tested individually. Although individual assessments out of the classroom are currently a common practice in preschool and elementary school classrooms, it may be more beneficial and less disruptive to adapt this study design so that it could be given to an entire class at one time. A version of TACTIC suitable for in-classroom is currently under development.

In a recent pilot study, TACTIC-KIBO was applied to assessing CT in young children longitudinally before and after a KIBO robotics coding enrichment program. Results indicate that after the program, most children increased in their level by at least a level. In the future, repeated administrations could help to establish the reproducibility of the CT assessment. If repeated administration results in stable scores, TACTIC-KIBO may prove useful for longitudinal assessment. However, if repeated administration is associated with a learning effect that causes scores to drift between testing session, it may be necessary to create alternative forms with equivalent questions.

TACTIC-KIBO was designed around the KIBO robotic platform. However, there are many other robotic toys and programming games existing and under development for young children as well as adolescents. The question of the generalizability of methods used to assess CT in this study may be best addressed by developing alternative forms of TACTIC that are applicable to other platforms. Creating alternative forms for other platforms would be useful in developing intuitions about lines of questioning that are more or less universal across platforms.

To date research has focused on CT assessments for young children who are neurotypical. It is important to understand typical development of CT abilities to obtain normative data on CT assessment. Once sufficient normative data are obtained, it is important to extend the application to a more diverse population, including children with Autism Spectrum Disorder (ASD). There is evidence that children with severe ASD are engaged by the KIBO robot and that they may become more communicative with their teachers as a consequence of playing with and programming the robot (Albo-Canals et al., 2018). In light of this, it would be interesting to study the acquisition of CT abilities in such children and compare their development with that of neurotypical children.

Our initial experience with TACTIC-KIBO leads us to conclude that assessment of CT abilities in young children is a viable and promising area of future research. It is critical to continue to develop appropriate CT instruments for use in classroom and research settings in order to move CT educational initiatives forward. Through assessment, researchers can understand the development and acquisition of CT abilities, which in turn help in the creation of better technology platforms for young children. By bringing validated assessment tools to the classroom, early childhood educators can be empowered to implement developmentally appropriate CS curricula that help children to learn to code and reason in ways that can have lifelong benefits.

Acknowledgments

The KIBO robotics kit was created under a grant from the National Science Foundation (NSF Grant No. DRL-1118897). A very special thank you to the members of the DevTech Research Group at Tufts University, Dr. Martha Pott, and Dr. Brian Gravel, as well as the teachers and children that made this research possible.

References

Albo-Canals, J., Martelo, A. B., Relkin, E., Hannon, D., Heerink, M., Heinemann, M., … Bers, M. U. (2018). A Pilot Study of the KIBO Robot in Children with Severe ASD. *International Journal of Social Robotics*, *10*(3), 371–383. http://dx.doi.org/10.1007/s12369-018-0479-2

Bers, M. (2008). *Blocks to robots: Learning with technology in the early childhood classroom*. New York, NY: Teachers College Press.

Bers, M. U. (2018). *Coding as a playground: Programming and computational thinking in the early childhood classroom.* New York, NY: Routledge.

Braitenberg, V. (1984). *Vehicles: Experiments in synthetic psychology.* Cambridge, Massachusetts: The MIT Press.

DeLuca, C., & Bellara, A. (2013). The current state of assessment education: Aligning policy, standards, and teacher education curriculum. *Journal of Teacher Education, 64*(4), 356–372. http://dx.doi.org/10.1177/0022487113488144

Dewey, J. (1938). *Experience and education.* New York, NY: Collier Books.

Gadanidis, G. (2017). Five affordances of computational thinking to support elementary mathematics education. *Journal of Computers in Mathematics and Science Teaching, 36*(2), 143–151.

Grover, S., & Pea, R. (2013). Computational thinking in K–12: A review of the state of the field. *Educational Researcher, 42*(1), 38–43. http://dx.doi.org/10.3102/0013189X12463051

Hemmendinger, D. (2010). A please for modesty. *ACM Inroads,* 1(2), 4–7. http:/dx.doi.org/ 10.1145/1805724.1805725

Jenkins, T. (2002). *On the difficulty of learning to program. Proceedings of the 3rd Annual. Conference of the LTSN Centre for Information and Computer Sciences,* 53–58. Leeds. Retrieved from http://www.psy.gla.ac.uk/~steve/localed/jenkins.html

K-12 Computer Science Framework Steering Committee. (2016). *K–12 computer science framework.* Retrieved from https://k12cs.org

Koretz, D., McCaffrey, D. F., Klein, S. P., Bell, R. M., & Stecher, B. M. (1992). *The Reliability of scores from the 1992 Vermont portfolio assessment program: Interim report.* Santa Monica, CA: RAND Corporation.

Lee, I., Martin, F., Denner, J., Coulter, B., Allan, W., Erickson, J. … . Werner, L. (2011). *Computational thinking for youth in practice. ACM Inroads,* 2, 32–37.

Leidl, K., Bers, M. U., & Mihm, C. (2017). Programming with ScratchJr: A review of the first year of user analytics. *In the proceedings of the International Conference on Computational Thinking Education,* Wanchai, Hong Kong, 116–125.

Lockwood, J., & Mooney, A. (2018). Computational thinking in education: Where does it fit? A systematic literary review. *International Journal of Computer Science Education in Schools, 2*(1) 41–60. https://doi.org/10.21585/ijcses.v2i1.26

Massachusetts Digital Literacy and Computer Science (DLCS) Curriculum Framework. (2016). *Massachusetts Department of Elementary and Secondary Education.* Retrieved from http://www.doe.mass.edu/frameworks/dlcs.pdf

Ming, V., Ming, N., & Bumbacher, E. (2014) Aligning learning with life outcomes through naturalistic assessment. *Socos LLC white paper.* Retrieved from http://about.socoslearning.com/socoswhitepaper.pdf

Mioduser, D., & Levy, S. T. (2010). Making sense by building sense: Kindergarten children's construction and understanding of adaptive robot behaviors. *International Journal of Computers for Mathematical Learning, 15*(2), 99–127. https://doi.org/10.1007/s10758-010-9163-9

Mioduser, D., Levy, S. T., & Talis, V. (2009). Episodes to scripts to rules: Concrete-abstractions in kindergarten children's explanations of a robot's behavior. *International Journal of Technology and Design Education, 19*(1), 15–36. https://doi.org/10.1007/s10798-007-9040-6

Moyer, K., & Gilmer, B. V. H. (1953). The concept of attention spans in children. *Elementary School Journal, 54*(1), 464–466.

National Research Council. (2010). Report of a workshop on the scope and nature of computational thinking. *The National Academies Press*. Washington, DC: Joseph Henry Press.

Papert, S. (1980). *Mindstorms: Children, computers, and powerful ideas*. New York, NY: Basic Books.

Papert, S. (1996). An exploration in the space of mathematics educations. *International Journal of Computers for Mathematical Learning, 1*(1), 95–123.

Papert, S., & Harel, I. (1991). *Situating constructionism. Constructionism*. New York, NY: Ablex Publishing.

Pei, C. (Yu), Weintrop, D., & Wilensky, U. (2018). Cultivating computational thinking practices and mathematical habits of mind in lattice land. *Mathematical Thinking and Learning, 20*(1), 75–89. https://doi.org/10.1080/10986065.2018.1403543

Perlis, A. J. (1963). The computer in the university. In M. Greenberger (Ed.). *Computers and the world of the future* (pp. 180–219). Cambridge, MA: MIT Press.

Portelance, D. J., & Bers, M. U. (2015). Code and tell: Assessing young children's learning of computational thinking using peer video interviews with ScratchJr. *In Proceedings of the 14th International Conference on Interaction Design and Children (IDC '15)*. Boston, MA: ACM.

Rogalski, J., & Samurçay, R. (1990) Acquisition of programming knowledge and skills. In J-M. Hoc, T. R. G.Green, D. J.Gilmore and R. Samurçay (Eds.) *Psychology of programming* (pp. 157–174). London: Academic Press.

Ruff, H. A., & Lawson, K. R. (1990). Development of sustained, focused attention in young children during free play. *Developmental Psychology, 26*(1), 85–93.

Sattler, J. M. (2014). *Foundations of behavioral, social, and clinical assessment of children*. La Mesa, CA: J.M. Sattler Publishers.

Sattler, J. M.Dumont, R., & Coalson, D. (2016) *Assessment of Children WISC-V and WPPSI-VI*. La Mesa, CA: J.M. Sattler Publishers.

Shaffer, D. W., & Resnick, M. (1999). "Thick" authenticity: New media and authentic learning. *Journal of Interactive Learning Research, 10*(2), 195–215.

Sullivan, A., Bers, M. U., & Mihm, C. (2017). Imagining, playing, & coding with KIBO: Using KIBO robotics to foster computational thinking in young children. *In the proceedings of the International Conference on Computational Thinking Education*, Wanchai, Hong Kong.

Sullivan, A., Elkin, M., & Bers, M. U. (2015). KIBO robot demo: engaging young children in programming and engineering. *Proceedings of the 14th International Conference on Interaction Design and Children (IDC'15)*. Boston, MA: ACM. http://doi.org/10.1145/2771839.2771868

Vizner, M. Z. (2017). *Big robots for little kids: Investigating the role of sale in early childhood robotics kits* (Master's thesis). Available from ProQuest Dissertations and Theses database (UMI No. 10622097).

Vygotsky, L. S. (1978). *Mind in society: The development of higher psychological processes*. Cambridge, MA: Harvard University Press.

Vygotsky, L. S. (1987). Thinking and speech. (N. Minick, Trans.). In R. W. Rieber & A. S. Carton (Eds.), *The collected works of L. S. Vygotsky* (Vol. 1., pp. 39–285). *Problems of general psychology*. New York: Plenum Press. (Original work published 1934).

Vygotsky, L. S. (1998). Infancy (M. Hall, Trans.). In R. W. Rieber (Ed.), *The collected works of L. S. Vygotsky: Child psychology* (Vol. 5., pp. 207–241). New York: Plenum Press. (Original work written 1933–1934).

Wang, D., Wang, T., & Liu, Z. (2014). A tangible programming tool for children to cultivate computational thinking. *The Scientific World Journal, 2014*(3). https://doi.org/10.1155/2014/428080

Werner, L., Denner, J., & Campe, S. (2014). Using computer game programming to teach computational thinking skills. In K. Schrier. (Ed.), *Learning, education and games: Curricular and design considerations* (Vol. 1) (pp. 37–53). Pittsburgh, PA: ETC Press. Retrieved from https://dl.acm.org/citation.cfm?id=2811150

Wing, J. (2006). Computational thinking. *Communications of Advancing Computing Machinery*, *49*(3), 33–36. New York, NY: Association for Computing Machinery. http://doi.org/10.1145/1118178.1118215

Wing, J. M. (2008). Computational thinking and thinking about computing. *Philosophical transactions of the royal society of London. Mathematical, physical and engineering sciences*, 366 (1881), 3717–3725. http://doi.org/10.1098/rsta.2008

6

ENGAGING YOUNG CHILDREN IN ENGINEERING DESIGN

Encouraging Them to Think, Create, Try and Try Again

Pamela S. Lottero-Perdue

Molly was focused. She was thinking and her hands were moving, placing wooden and foam building blocks deliberately on the table in front of her. When her hands stopped moving, she seemed satisfied, looked at me, and said: "There." Molly had just finished her first try at an engineering design challenge to create a fence to contain Henrietta, a Hexbug Nano® robot about the size of a toothbrush head. Earlier, Molly and her kindergarten classmates giggled when they felt Henrietta vibrate and watched the robot move haphazardly on the classroom's linoleum floor. After explaining to me why she made the fence the way that she did, Molly was eager to test it out. We turned Henrietta on, lowered her inside the fence, and within about 10 seconds, Henrietta escaped. Molly caught Henrietta as the little robot left the fenced-in area. "What happened?" I asked, prompting Molly to analyze what happened. Her analysis was excellent and rooted in her earlier understanding of science concepts. I then asked: "So do you have any ideas about how you can make your fence a little better for Henrietta?" Molly-the-kindergarten-engineer shared her ideas—which were based on fixing where the fence had failed the first time—and without hesitation began to reconstruct the fence.

Molly (a pseudonym) was one of 53 kindergartners who participated in a research study about their engagement in an engineering design challenge with opportunities to integrate scientific and mathematical knowledge as they engineered (see Lottero-Perdue, Sandifer, & Grabia, 2017 for the science and engineering lesson). As the sole data collector on the project and co-teacher for the science and engineering instruction that went along with it, I was able to get an in-depth look at individual children's thinking as they engineered. Normally, my observations of young children, a term I will use in this chapter for children in grades pre-kindergarten through grade two (PreK-2), doing engineering have been of students working in teams within their classrooms to solve engineering design challenges. For many years, I have had the privilege to work with pre-service and in-service educators, bringing engineering curricula that I have used or helped to develop to young learners.

In this chapter, I aim to address some big ideas about teaching engineering through play and more scaffolded instructional practices. These ideas come from the nascent but growing body of research and curriculum development efforts in early childhood engineering education, from my own experiences as a science and engineering teacher educator, and from the voices of teachers who have taught engineering to young children and who have seen its value in early childhood education. Regarding the latter point, I have included three vignettes written by four educators who teach young learners to engineer. Before getting into the context of early childhood engineering, I will review some fundamental ideas about engineering design.

Engineering Design and Habits of Mind

Engineering is the E in STEM but does more than provide a vowel in this acronym. It has its own unique characteristics that distinguish it from the S, T, and M and make it a useful in partnership with these subjects. The National Academy of Engineering (NAE) and National Research Council (NRC) define engineering as follows:

> Engineering is both a body of knowledge – about the design and creation of human-made products – and a process for solving problems. This process is design under constraint. One constraint in engineering design is the laws of nature, or science. Other constraints include such things as time, money, available materials, ergonomics, environmental regulations, manufacturability, and reparability. Engineering utilizes concepts in science and mathematics as well as technological tools. (2009, p. 17)

There are different fields of engineering that focus on solving specialized types of problems. While biomedical engineers may use their knowledge of the human body to design artificial limbs, civil engineers may apply what they know about transportation systems and structures to design new highways and bridges.

One word used in both of these examples of engineering work is "design." The fundamental work of engineering, regardless of field, is the design of technologies (Petroski, 2011). Design is an intentional, thoughtful, and creative process. Technologies are objects, systems, or processes that are designed by people to solve problems or meet needs (EiE, 2018c). Engineers implement design processes to solve problems by creating technologies (Cunningham, 2018). In so doing, they strive to understand those technologies—and the technologies they improve—thoroughly. There are many engineering design processes (EDPs), but there are some common features across them including identifying and researching the problem; brainstorming ideas to solve the problem; deciding which of those ideas to choose and making a detailed plan to represent that design idea; creating and testing the design; analyzing test results; and iterating and improving (i.e., repeating previous parts of the process leading to subsequent designs) (Moore et al., 2014). Engineers may attend to some of these steps out of order (e.g., returning to re-research the problem after working on a plan). This process is complete when a design is able to meet or exceed the criteria—or requirements—for the problem or challenge.

There are certain habits of mind that are central to engineering design. These habits of mind are not only ways of thinking, they are also deeply embedded values and dispositions within a community. Some of these are unique to engineering, while others are shared with other disciplines. There is no one agreed upon list of engineering habits of mind, there are many (e.g., Cunningham & Kelly, 2017; Lottero-Perdue, 2018; NAE & NRC, 2009) Here, I will share a representative sample of engineering habits of mind that translate well to the early childhood setting and are captured in one or more of these references. Engineers …

- Are creative and innovative
- Work in a team and value teamwork
- Are persistent even when designs fail
- Make decisions based on evidence

In summary, engineers use these and other engineering habits of mind as they design solutions to problems.

Engineering Design and Habits of Mind in Early Childhood

Engineering, once the exclusive domain of colleges and universities, has been a part of K-12 education for about 20 years, with most of the curricular and research emphasis since this time at the high school level (NAE & NRC, 2009). Curriculum development and research on elementary-level engineering education has expanded since the mid-2000s, and early childhood education has been a small but growing effort for approximately the last five or more years. It is safe to say that the emphasis of engineering education throughout K-12 is on engaging students in developmentally appropriate EDPs and developing students' engineering habits of mind. Aside from these goals to immerse students in the major activities and dispositions of engineering, there are multiple reasons to include it in the curriculum. Christine Cunningham, a national leader in elementary engineering education, summarized the following reasons why engineering should be included in elementary education. Engineering can …

- Help children understand and consider how to improve their world;
- Foster problem-solving skills and dispositions [including perseverance];

- Increase motivation, engagement, responsibility and agency for learning;
- Improve math and science achievement;
- Increase access to STEM careers for all students;
- Promote educational equity [by teaching all students habits of mind that are valuable in engineering and beyond];
- Transform instruction [within and beyond engineering to be more open-ended, hands-on and student-centered]. (Cunningham, 2018, pp. 14–19 with some paraphrasing).

And finally, engineering is included in state and national standards, including within the Next Generation Science Standards, which address K-12 education (NGSS Lead States, 2013). These reasons to include engineering in elementary education are consistent with those identified by the NAE and NRC (2009) and in my writing about engineering for pre-service K-8 teachers (Lottero-Perdue, 2018). For young learners, engineering offers opportunities for students to: develop social-emotional skills while working in teams, use fine and gross motor skills while engaging in hands-on creation, employ executive functioning while moving through the EDP and reflecting on their designs, and acquire and use language relevant to the problem and solution (EiE, 2018b, 2018d).

Engineering Design During Play

It is often said that young children are natural engineers. By "natural," the implication is that this occurs without scholastic intervention or adult guidance. In other words, engineering is a part of human nature (Petroski, 1992). "Children naturally engineer. Watch young children at play and you'll see them engage in engineering behaviors" (Cunningham, 2018, p. 19). In this section, I will borrow the term, "engineering play" from Gold and colleagues to mean play that includes some aspects of engineering design and habits of mind (Gold, Elicker, Choi, Anderson, & Brophy, 2015).

Researchers have observed this empirically. For example, Bagiati and Evangelou observed preschoolers' (3–5-year-olds') open-ended block play for four months and observed the children's engagement in an iterative design process, e.g., identifying problems, setting goals, testing solutions, iterating, and collaborative teamwork (2016). An earlier study explored preschoolers' engineering play during open play activities including puzzles, drawing, painting, sandboxes, water tables, and snap circuits; blocks were not included in this study (Bairaktarova, Evangelou, Bagiati, & Brophy, 2011). They regularly observed children asking questions, stating goals, explaining how things work, making things, solving problems, and evaluating what they created.

Engineering play is inspired by some contexts more than others. In the study by Bairaktarova and colleagues (2011), some activities (e.g., snap circuits) elicited more engineering play than did others (e.g., sandbox). Gold and colleagues observed that when compared to play in a traditional playground and dramatic play area, the large block area encouraged more engineering play by preschoolers (Gold et al., 2015). An unsurprising finding regarding context is the importance of students' play with real tangible artifacts (or what engineer would call technologies) (Evangelou, Dobbs-Oates, Bagiati, Liang, & Choi, 2010; Lippard, Lamm, & Riley, 2017). Engagement with real, 3-D artifacts (not sketches of them or their presence in storybooks) enabled 4- to 5-year-olds to explore how those artifacts worked, another aspect of engineering play (Evangelou et al., 2010).

Play is an essential part of learning within early childhood education for a multitude of reasons. For engineering education, the importance of play is that it can be a catalyst for children's construction—and often co-construction with peers—of ideas about problems and their solutions and simple technologies in their worlds. Play is also a means to practice habits of mind such as learning how to work with others and being creative or imaginative. These ideas about the power of play are supported by both Piagetian and Vygotskian theory. Piagetian theory supports the notions that play helps children co-construct ideas and that play is an essential mechanism for young children to learn "about reciprocity or mutuality in their play interactions with peers" (Waite-Stupiansky, 2017, p. 12). According to Vygotsky and his followers, imagination is not only used during play, it is "an outgrowth of play" (Bodrova & Leong, 2017, p. 65). Furthermore, Bodrova and Leong (2017) explain that in the course of this imaginative play, children take on roles, use props, and establish "rules they need to follow when playing these roles and using these props" (p. 65). In this way, children design play experiences under particular sets of constraints they construct.

Including and beyond preschool, early childhood educators can create learning centers to encourage engineering play (Moomaw, 2013). A common example is a block center where children can construct towers, houses, and other structures. Another example is the "Child-Designed Inclines" center as described by Moomaw (2013, pp. 20–21). In this center, children manipulate multiple ramps that connect to a vertical board in order to design creative ways for a ball (e.g., a table tennis ball) to move from the top to the bottom of the board, rolling down ramps and hopping from one ramp to another.

Scaffolded Engineering Design

There is, however, evidence to suggest that open-ended play is not enough to engage young learners fully in engineering design and habits of mind. Not all children will choose to engage in open-ended play that is most likely to engage them in engineering. Also, "different children spontaneously exhibit elements of engineering-relevant dispositions" (Bairaktarova et al., 2011, p. 229). In other words, instruction should be scaffolded to support young children's full participation in engineering design and habits of mind. This notion of scaffolding was introduced by Wood, Bruner, and Ross (1976) to describe the assistance that children need from teachers and others to move through the Vygotskian Zone of Proximal Development and towards their independent understanding of concepts and application of skills (Bodrova & Leong, 2017; Vygotsky, 1978).

A recent systematic literature review aimed to explore what interactions, materials, or activities promoted engineering thinking and play among children ages 3 to 5 (Lippard et al., 2017). Ultimately locating just 27 articles pertaining to these subjects in this young field of early childhood engineering education, they shared the following assertion:

> **Intentionality is key**. [Emphasis in text] Although we have identified challenges to drawing implications from these [27] papers, one clear conclusion is that intentionality is crucial in promoting children's engineering thinking. (Lippard et al., 2017, p. 465)

Intentionality here includes adults, be they parents or teachers, providing guidance and asking questions to promote engineering thinking in children. In grades PreK-2 and beyond, the way to make engineering activities more intentional includes the following: 1) the use of design challenges that are defined by a problem and/or goal, constraints (e.g., material limitations), and criteria (i.e., sharing design requirements and how they will be tested); and 2) the use of an EDP. Each of these intentional aspects support the aforementioned idea of the importance of scaffolding children's engineering design experiences.

VOICES FROM THE FIELD

A Bit of Structure Encourages Design-based Play

by Sioux Wereska, Early Special Educator, Marshfield Public Schools, Massachusetts

I've been working in the field of Early Education for 23 years. I've worked in home settings, center-based programs and, for the last 17 years, within the Marshfield Public School system as an Early Special Educator in an integrated preschool program. As an educator, my goal has always been to create environments where young children are encouraged to explore, experiment, discover, feed their curiosity and develop a love for learning and a confidence in themselves as learners that lasts a lifetime. If my students cannot identify letters or differentiate rhyming words when they transition to kindergarten, I'm okay with that as long as they feel confident in their ability to try and their belief that they will figure it out if they keep trying. I have always rebelled against the idea of structured curriculum for early childhood programs. When young children are given the space, materials and opportunities to engage in open-ended play, they drive their own learning and their discoveries become more meaningful because it came from them.

Despite my skepticism of structured curricula, I became excited to implement a new preschool engineering program in my classroom. The program seemed to embrace what is intrinsic to preschool-aged children: the need to explore, solve problems and figure things out. When I implemented the engineering challenges in the program, I noticed that my students developed stronger problem solving and critical thinking skills. Because they were given a specific problem to solve and a process to follow, they explored materials and experimented in a more targeted manner. They also reflected on their observations more critically because they were looking for specific qualities and results. They were not simply experimenting to see what items would sink or float in water; rather, they were looking for materials that would be able to keep a weighted raft afloat. Solving the problem amplified the meaningfulness of their learning and they became engineers. I still believe in the benefits of open-ended play, but I have come to appreciate that design-based play needs a bit of structure to help my students grow as problem solvers, critical thinkers, and young engineers.

EDPs for Early Childhood

Different EDPs have been used for early childhood. I will share four of those here. Sioux Wereska, who wrote the "Bit of Structure" vignette, used a three-step EDP in the Engineering is Elementary (EiE) program's Wee Engineer preschool curriculum with her students (EiE, 2018d). These three steps and their descriptions are as follows:

- **Explore:** Find out more. Children learn about the problem they need to solve and explore the available materials to find out more about them.
- **Create:** Try an idea. Children work in small groups with an adult to create their first design. They then test their design to determine how well it meets the goal.
- **Improve:** Make it better. Children improve their designs, then come together to share what they've found out with the group. (EiE, 2018d, p. ix).

This preschool EDP is depicted in Figure 6.1.

The EiE program uses a five-step EDP in its "EiE for Kindergarten" (2018b) and in its Grades 1–5 elementary curriculum (2018a): Ask, Imagine, Plan, Create, Improve. These five steps are the following:

FIGURE 6.1 Wee Engineer—Engineer Design Process
Source: Reprinted with permission, *Wee Engineer Challenges for Pre-K/Preschool* (2018)
Museum of Science, Boston, MA

- **Ask**: What is the problem? What are the constraints and criteria? What do we know that can help us solve the problem?
- **Imagine**: What are some solutions? Brainstorm ideas. Choose the best one.
- **Plan**: Draw a diagram. Make lists of what you need.
- **Create**: Follow your plan and create something. Test it out!
- **Improve**: What works? What doesn't? What could work better? Modify your design. Test it out! (EiE, 2018a, n.p.)

Figure 6.2 shows the image the EiE program uses to denote the iterative nature of this EDP.

Another EDP is a four-step EDP that I developed with colleagues that is a modification of the EiE EDP: Ask, Imagine, Try and Try Again (Lottero-Perdue et al., 2016). The Ask step in our EDP is communicated via rhyme, and replaces "constraints" and "criteria" with an encompassing word, "rules":

What is the problem?
What is the goal?
What are the rules?
What do we know?

EiE's "Plan and Create" step is replaced by "Try" and EiE's "Improve Step" is replaced by "Try Again." Try includes show-and-tell type planning rather than a drawn plan. The vignette by Michelle Bowditch and Michelle Kagan, "Practicing Perseverance …," describes how using this EDP has helped their students try and try again in engineering and beyond and to address an engineering habit of mind: persistence. Yet another EDP for early childhood is from the PictureSTEM curriculum, which has six steps: Define and Learn (parts of defining the problem); and Plan, Try, Test, and Decide (parts of solving the problem) (PictureSTEM, 2018).

There are common threads across these and other EDPs used for young children. There are six or fewer steps for simplicity; they are iterative, suggesting that the child could repeat steps or even go "backwards" to a previous step if necessary; and they all

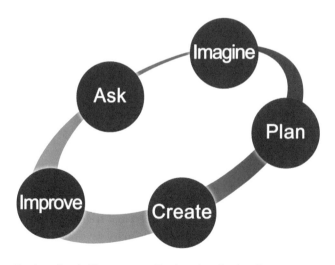

FIGURE 6.2 Engineering is Elementary—Engineering Design Process
Source: Reprinted with permission, *Engineering is Elementary* (2018) Museum of Science, Boston, MA

include work to understand the problem, brainstorm and plan, create and test a solution, and improve. Also, all of the developers of these design processes aim to make design process steps explicit to students. This is not so that children memorize a list of steps, but rather, to help young learners do the following: 1) take care to address each important aspect of engineering design (e.g., attending to understanding the problem before rushing in to try to solve it); and 2) during each of the steps, to use the EDP as a sort of roadmap, reminding them of where they have been, what they are doing now, and what they are likely to do next (e.g., including that they will have a chance to improve or try again).

VOICES FROM THE FIELD

Practicing Perseverance in Engineering and Beyond

by Michelle Bowditch and Michelle Kagan, Kindergarten Teachers, Hall's Cross Roads Elementary School, Harford County Public Schools, Maryland

We are kindergarten teachers in a Title One School which has a population of 515 students and where we have worked for 7 and 8 years, respectively. Our students are 5 and 6 years old, come from diverse backgrounds, and present with varying abilities. For several years, we have been using an EDP that encourages our students to "try" and "try again." These are two of four explicit steps in this EDP, and these simple words – try and try again – make sense to our young learners. Since implementing this EDP, we have seen benefits within and beyond teaching our students to engineer.

The biggest growth that we have witnessed is in our students' perseverance and stamina when solving problems or approaching a difficult task. Our students also demonstrate understanding that there can be more than one way to solve a problem and have come to see us more like coaches than as sources for answers, especially since there is no one right answer or solution to an engineering problem. Students have a greater awareness that problems sometimes require multiple strategies and it is okay to fail on the first (or even second!) attempt to solve the problem. Before introducing the EDP, students would become frustrated and we would frequently see tears when they were not successful at solving problems on the first try. The overwhelming majority of our students understand that sometimes it takes multiple attempts in order to be successful and continue their efforts without tears.

We have seen the perseverance our students developed in engineering carry over to other subjects like writing, where students are more willing to revise and edit their work because they know the first draft does not have to be perfect. In math, we often hear students coach each other to "keep trying" or suggest an alternate strategy when faced with a new task. These are skills

> they have learned from their work with EDP which have had a positive and direct impact in other subject areas. We hope, too, that our students apply the idea of trying again to their lives outside of school, practicing perseverance not only as young engineers but also as people.

Finally, regardless of the particular EDP, the intent is for the *children* to make the design decisions through the process and it is *their* habits of mind that we wish to develop. Teachers are facilitators of learning throughout the EDP: checking for understanding about the problem, constraints, criteria, and testing process; posing questions to stimulate children's application of prior knowledge to understanding the problem; creating prompts or questions to stimulate the idea generation process during brainstorming; helping students understand the intent of each step; encouraging students to work together as a team; guiding post-testing discussions to help students evaluate their own and learn from one another's test results; and posing questions to help students think about how to improve their designs.

Engineering Design Curricula

Each of the above EDPs are associated with engineering or integrated STEM curricula for PreK-2 classrooms. Table 6.1 is a summary of some commercially available (WeeEngineer, EiE for Kindergarten, EiE) and free downloadable

TABLE 6.1 Summary of Available STEM Curricula for PreK-2 Engineering Design Curricula

Curricula	Grade levels	Number of units	Integration	Approximate duration of a unit	Problem/goal statement from an example unit
WeeEngineer (by EiE)	Preschool/ PreK	4	E, T	1 hour	Puppet needs a loud noisemaker!
EiE for Kindergarten	K	4	S, T, E, M with L (literacy)	6 hours	Penny, the dog, needs a shelter that protects her from the sunlight
PictureSTEM	K, 1, and 2	3	S, T, E, M + C (computational thinking) + L	11–14 hours	Perri's Pet Palace wants to offer its customers an enlarged hamster habitat that meets all of the basic needs of a hamster. (First Grade)
EiE	Grades 1–5	20	S, T, E, M with L	8–10 hours	Design a hand pollinator to pollinate a model flower. (Second Grade)

(PictureSTEM) curricula; it is not an exhaustive summary. The listed programs are well-tested curricula: field tested by teachers and studied by researchers. Included in the table are the following for each curriculum: grade levels, number of units, with a unit including one engineering design challenge, not including an introductory challenge; integration with STEM, literacy (e.g., through storybooks or trade books), and/or computational thinking; the approximate duration of the unit (including the design challenge and other unit activities); and a problem or goal statement for the engineering challenge within a sample unit. Other features of the EiE-produced curricula include tips for differentiating instruction for English Language Learners and children with special needs, as well as lessons written in Spanish.

In addition, engineering lessons that connect to the NGSS can be found in the National Science Teachers Association (NSTA) journal, *Science and Children*. This teachers' journal is a resource for early childhood through elementary science and engineering lessons that have been developed and classroom-tested by educators. Engineering lessons can also be found online on a variety of websites including www.TeachEngineering.org.

Regardless of where lessons are found—in commercial curriculum, in journals, online, or from school-system-created materials—educators should consider the following questions when evaluating engineering design challenges and STEM units that include engineering:

1. Does this engineering design challenge help students identify and restate the problem and/or goal, constraints, and criteria for the challenge (e.g., through a design brief, an email to the children, or a storybook)?
2. Does the main challenge of the unit utilize an EDP? (Note that some units use a less structured design challenge prior to conducting a larger design challenge that utilizes an EDP.)
3. Is the challenge at an appropriate level for students, such that it is neither too easy nor too difficult?

Beyond the design challenge, teachers who wish to have students apply, develop, or reinforce practices and content from other areas (e.g., Science, Technology, Math, Literacy, Computational Thinking) may look for those integrative unit features.

Trade Books

Teachers can reinforce engineering learning through the use of trade books that feature engineering design and habits of mind. The NSTA Best STEM Books K–12 list was started in 2017 and identifies books that invite "STEM thinking," which includes engineering design thinking. In the 2017 and 2018 lists there are a few books where the EDP and engineering habits of mind are addressed and accessible to young learners (NSTA, 2017, 2018). For example, *The Most Magnificent Thing*, a 2017 winner, is about creativity and persistence in design, and has a touch of humor (Spires, 2014). From the 2018 list, *John Deere, That's Who!* tells the true story of John Deere's design of a steel plow (Nelson Maurer & Zeltner, 2017), while *The Music of Life: Bartolomeo Cristofori & the Invention of the Piano* artfully describes the design of the piano(forte) (Rusch & Priceman, 2017).

Outcomes of Engineering Design in PreK-2 Childhood

The engineering education and early childhood education communities are still learning how these young learners engage in aspects of the EDP, develop engineering habits of mind, and do so perhaps differently from PreK to grade 2. Natalie Whitney's vignette offers some insight about this from the field in her vignette, "Growing Young Engineers."

VOICES FROM THE FIELD

Growing Young Engineers

by Natalie Whitney, K-2 STEM Teacher Specialist, Brentwood Elementary School, North Carolina

Brentwood Elementary is a school of about 400 students with a free and reduced lunch population of 76%, many first- or second-generation Americans, and many who are new to the English language. We use engineering design challenges in grades K-5 and use the EiE EDP as a way to solve problems across the curriculum. As the K-2 STEM coordinator for the last four years, I have worked with teachers to co-design, co-plan and co-teach K-2 engineering design challenges. In this role, I have noticed growth in K-2 learners with respect to how they work in a team, plan, and use tools.

Working in a Team: At the beginning of the K year, many students prefer to work alone, finding it difficult to share ideas and take suggestions. Still, we put kindergartners in teams of three from the start and encourage respect for others' ideas (e.g., by having students celebrate what they like about other teams' ideas). By the end of the year, students seek peers' ideas as they move through the EDP together. In first and second grades, students are excited for engineering and welcome the teamwork that comes with it. Students are better able to distribute team roles—often using rock-paper-scissors to do so—and communicate ideas within the team.

Planning: Plans in K are simple and quick, consisting of pictures with some labeling and taking 10 minutes or less to complete. K students typically plan to use as many materials as possible (especially tape!). In first and second grades, students are expected to take more time – about 30 minutes in first and more than an hour in second—on detailed plans that are a part of their engineering notebooks, labeling all materials and including a title. Their material choices in their plans are increasingly more purposeful, selective, and creative.

Using Tools: K students' developing fine motor skills are strengthened during engineering design challenges as they tear paper, bend chenille stems, and so on. With time and experience, they can use scissors to cut thin materials. Beyond K, students can tear or cut an adequate amount of tape and can use scissors to cut stiffer materials and to cut accurately. While in first grade, students use everyday objects for nonstandard measurements or as straight edges, second graders learn to use tools like rulers or stopwatches for more precise measurements.

Our students show tremendous growth in their early years at Brentwood, and, by the end of second grade, are ready for the even more challenging problems to solve in upper elementary school!

Although a great deal of engineering education research has been done on or by the EiE program, published research by and about EiE has focused largely on upper elementary students. Research on young learners' engagement in engineering design will undoubtedly grow with EiE's publications of *WeeEngineer* and *Engineer for Kindergarten* curricula (EiE, 2018b, 2018d).

Recent research has examined younger children's problem scoping, troubleshooting, evidence-based reasoning, and iteration practices—all aspects of engineering design—and outcomes for their spatial reasoning, literacy and engagement. While the first two of the following studies includes students in first or second grade (7 to 8 years old), most focus on kindergarten.

Problem Scoping

Some insight about growth across these grade levels is in some recent work by Haluschak and colleagues, who investigated how kindergartners, first graders, and second graders who learned three different PictureSTEM units, respectively, engaged in "problem scoping" (Haluschak et al., 2018). Problem scoping is about how students make sense of and ask questions about the problem, constraints and criteria. It occurs during and throughout an EDP when students are first introduced to the problem and later as they simultaneously gain deeper understanding of the problem as they try to solve it. Haluschak and colleagues' work focused on problem scoping when the problem was introduced via an "email" to the students; the email contained the problem statement, why it was a problem, constraints and criteria, but they were not named as such. The researchers found that while all students engaged in problem scoping to some degree, kindergartners and first graders needed more scaffolding from their teachers than did the second graders in order to pull out key pieces of information.

Troubleshooting

A study on 7–11-year-olds and their parents engaged in an engineering design challenge (without an explicit EDP) examined the troubleshooting processes in which the children and their parents engaged (Ehsan, Rush Leeker, Cardella, & Svarovsky, 2018). In some cases, the children troubleshot like informed designers, i.e., expert engineers engaging in a design process as articulated by Crismond and Adams (2012). In other cases, they performed like beginning or novice designers. Ehsan and colleagues suggested that scaffolding, in this case from parents, may encourage more informed troubleshooting performances by the students. A study on kindergartners and third-graders experiences with iteration yielded similar results for the kindergarten group, who had difficulty troubleshooting their designs and identifying sources of failure (Kendall, 2015). They also "need[ed] more scaffolding in recognizing variables, constraints and specifications within designs" (p. 12), which is consistent with the problem scoping findings from Haluchak et al., 2018, albeit for problem scoping during the design process.

Evidence-Based Reasoning

Rynearson and colleagues collected evidence that kindergartners can and do engage in evidence-based reasoning—making design decisions based upon evidence—motivated by their participation in a PictureSTEM unit (Rynearson, Moore, Tank, & Gajdzik, 2017). While children readily shared claims, prompting (e.g., "Why?") was required to push students to support their claims with reasons. My own ongoing work, related to the opening vignette about Molly, is supportive of the idea that kindergartners can engage evidence-based reasoning during an engineering design challenge and that prompting is often required to elicit students' reasons.

Spatial Reasoning

A study by Casey and colleagues (2008) examined growth in visual-spatial thinking after children engaged in either open-ended block play or a design-based block activity in which children were asked to solve a problem using the blocks. Although an EDP was not used, the second condition was akin to an engineering design challenge with a well-defined problem, constraints, and criteria. The authors found that visual-spatial scores did not change post-instruction for the open-ended block play group, but increased for the design-based block activity. This is consistent with Lippard and colleagues' (2017) aforementioned big idea that "intentionality is key" (p. 465) and an additional tentative finding that engineering experience may promote early mathematics skills in preschool children.

Discussion and Engagement

Aguirre-Muños and Pantoya conducted a case study of six academically diverse female kindergarten students whose first language was not English to investigate the relationship between engagement and discussion (Aguirre-Muñoz & Pantoya, 2016). The children learned the EiE Pollination unit (briefly described in Table 6.1). Student discussion increased with engagement level, and engagement level was highest during the engineering design challenge for the unit.

Professional Learning for Early Childhood Educators

Lippard and colleagues' review of preschool engineering literature suggested that "some direct instruction for adults on engineering topics is beneficial to their interactions with children" (2017, p. 461). Dorie and Cardella (2015) found that even parents who are engineers were uncertain about how to teach engineering skills to their preschool children. It is no surprise, then, that multiple researchers suggest the importance of professional learning in engineering for early childhood educators (Bagiati & Evangelou, 2015; Glen, 2018; Park, Dimitrov, Patterson, & Park, 2016). One study used a survey of 830 preschool through third grade educators in rural Kentucky to explore beliefs about early childhood STEM education (Park et al., 2016). Roughly 70% had lower-level beliefs about readiness for teaching STEM; the remainder had higher-level beliefs about their STEM-teaching readiness. Those in the second group were "more likely to be aware of the importance of teaching STEM and of the difficulties that they may encounter in teaching STEM" (p. 282). This suggests the need for professional learning experiences to address these topics. Work by Glen (2018) and Bagiati and Evangelou (2015) suggests the importance of professional learning that addresses the affordances and challenges of early childhood engineering as expressed by early childhood experts and engineering education experts. For example, teachers in Bagiati and Evangelou's study (2016) identified a lack of evidence for students' STEM learning as a barrier, while researchers had concerns about lackluster parental involvement; both groups were concerned about time constraints. All of these concerns should be addressed for the benefit of early childhood educators and their students.

Future Directions

There is much to be done to grow resources and research to support engineering design learning experiences in early childhood. While there are many gaps in what we know, there are enough signs from practice and research to know that *it is a good thing* for young children to engage in engineering design challenges—to think, create, try and try again—and for Molly from the opening vignette to give the fence another try. It is a good thing to provide students with opportunities for engineering play, implement high-quality engineering design challenges and integrated STEM units, guide students through simple EDPs as they engage in those challenges, and add engineering to their reading lists. And it is a good thing for teachers and parents alike to learn how to facilitate the engineering design education of young children. As the field grows and learns in the years to come, we educators will adjust our practice accordingly. That is okay in this work. That is improvement. That is trying again in a design process, yet in a smarter way and based on evidence.

References

Aguirre-Muñoz, Z., & Pantoya, M. L. (2016). Engineering literacy and engagement in kindergarten classrooms. *Journal of Engineering Education, 105*(4), 630–654. doi:10.1002/jee.20151

Bagiati, A., & Evangelou, D. (2015). Engineering curriculum in the preschool classroom: The teacher's experience. *European Early Childhood Education Research Journal, 23*(1), 112–128. doi:10.1080/1350293X.2014.991099

Bagiati, A., & Evangelou, D. (2016). Practicing engineering while building blocks: Identifying engineering thinking. *European Early Childhood Education Research Journal, 24*(1), 67–85. doi:10.1080/1350293X.2015.1120521

Bairaktarova, D., Evangelou, D., Bagiati, A., & Brophy, S. (2011). Early engineering in young children's exploratory play with tangible materials. *Children, Youth and Environments, 21*(2), 212–235. doi:10.7721/chilyoutenvi.21. 2. 02doi:12

Bodrova, E., & Leong, D. J. (2017). The Vygotskian and Post-Vygotskian Approach. In L. E. Cohen & S. Waite-Stupiansky (Eds.), *Theories of early childhood education: Developmental, behaviorist, and critical* (pp. 58–70). New York, NY: Routledge.

Casey, B. M., Andrews, N., Schindler, H., Kersh, J. E., Samper, A., & Copley, J. (2008). The development of spatial skills through interventions involving block building activities. *Cognition and Instruction, 26*(3), 269–309. doi:10.1080/073700008021771777

Crismond, D. P., & Adams, R. S. (2012). The Informed Design Teaching and Learning Matrix. *Journal of Engineering Education, 101*(4), 738–797.

Cunningham, C. (2018). *Engineering in elementary STEM education: Curriculum design, instruction, learning and assessment.* New York, NY: Teachers College Press.

Cunningham, C., & Kelly, G. (2017). Epistemic practices of engineering for education. *Science Education, 101*(3), 486–505. doi:10.1002/sce.21271

Dorie, B., & Cardella, M. E. (2015). *An Engineering Tale: Using storybooks to analyze parent-child conversations about engineering.* Paper presented at the 2015 American Society for Engineering Education Annual Conference and Exposition, Seattle, WA.

Ehsan, H., Rush Leeker, J., Cardella, M. E., & Svarovsky, G. N. (2018). *Examining children's engineering practices during an engineering activity in a designed learning setting: A focus on troubleshooting.* Paper presented at the 2018 American Society for Engineering Education Annual Conference and Exposition, Salt Lake City, UT.

Engineering is Elementary (EiE). (2018a). *The engineering design process.* Retrieved from https://www.eie.org/overview/engineering-design-process

Engineering is Elementary (EiE). (2018b). *EiE for Kindergarten.* Boston, MA: Museum of Science. https://info.eie.org/eie-k

Engineering is Elementary. (2018c). *Science, technology and engineering: Distinct but interconnected.* Retrieved from https://www.eie.org/overview/science-engineering-technology

Engineering is Elementary (EiE). (2018d). *WeeEngineer: Engineering challenges for Pre-K/ Preschool*. Boston, MA: Museum of Science.

Evangelou, D., Dobbs-Oates, J., Bagiati, A., Liang, S., & Choi, J. Y. (2010). Talking about artifacts: Preschool children's explorations with sketches, stories, and tangible objects. *Early Childhood Research & Practice, 12*(2), 1–16.

Glen, N. J. (2018). *Preschool teachers learn to teach the engineering design process*. Paper presented at the 2018 American Society for Engineering Education Annual Conference & Exposition, Salt Lake City, UT.

Gold, Z. S., Elicker, J., Choi, J. Y., Anderson, T., & Brophy, S. P. (2015). Preschoolers' engineering play behaviors: Differences in gender and play context. *Children, Youth and Environments, 25*(3), 1–21.

Haluschak, E. M., Stevens, M. L., Moore, T. J., Tank, K. M., Cardella, M. E., Hynes, M. M., & Gajdzik, E. (2018). *Initial problem scoping in K-2 classrooms*. Paper presented at the 2018 American Society for Engineering Education Annual Conference and Exposition, Salt Lake City, UT.

Kendall, A. L. M. (2015). *Evaluate-and-redesign tasks: Using interviews to investigate how elementary students iterate*. Paper presented at the 2015 American Society for Engineering Education Annual Conference and Exposition, Seattle, Washington.

Lippard, C. N., Lamm, M. H., & Riley, K. L. (2017). Engineering thinking in Pre-kindergarten children: A systematic literature review. *Journal of Engineering Education, 106*(3), 454–474. doi:10.1002/jee.20174

Lottero-Perdue, P. S. (2018). Engineering design into science classrooms. In J. Settlage, S. A. Southerland, L. S. Smetana, & P. S. Lottero-Perdue (Eds.), *Teaching science to every child: Using culture as a starting point*. New York, NY: Routledge.

Lottero-Perdue, P. S., Bowditch, M., Kagan, M., Robinson-Cheek, L., Webb, T., Meller, M., & Nosek, T. (2016). An engineering design process for early childhood: Trying (again) to engineer an egg package. *Science and Children, 54*(3), 70–76.

Lottero-Perdue, P. S., Sandifer, C., & Grabia, K. (2017). Oh No! Henrietta got out! Kindergarteners investigate forces and use engineering to corral an unpredictable robot. *Science and Children, 55*(4), 46–53.

Moomaw, S. (2013). *Teaching STEM in the early years: Activities for integrating science, technology, engineering and mathematics*. St. Paul, MN: Red Leaf Press.

Moore, T. J., Glancy, A. W., Tank, K. M., Kersten, J. A., Smith, K. A., & Stohlmann, M. S. (2014). A framework for quality K-12 engineering education: Research and development. *Journal of Pre-College Engineering Education Research, 4*(1). doi:10.7771/2157-9288.1069

National Academy of Engineering (NAE) & National Research Council (NRC). (2009). *Engineering in K-12 Education: Understanding the status and improving the prospects*. Washington, DC: The National Academies Press.

Nelson Maurer, T., & Zeltner, T. (2017). *John Deere, that's who!* New York, NY: Macmillan Children's Publishing Group, Henry Holt and Co.

NGSS Lead States. (2013). *The Next Generation Science Standards: For States, By States*. Washington, DC: The National Academies Press. doi:10.17226/18290

National Science Teachers Association (NSTA). (2017). Best STEM Books. *Science and Children, 54*(6), 71–78.

National Science Teachers Association (NSTA). (2018). Best STEM Books. *Science and Children, 55*(7), 87–94.

Park, M.-H., Dimitrov, D. M., Patterson, L. G., & Park, D.-Y. (2016). Early childhood teachers' beliefs about readiness for teaching Science, Technology, Engineering, and

Mathematics. *Journal of Early Childhood Research, 15*(3), 275–291. doi:10.1177/ 1476718X15614040

Petroski, H. (1992). *To engineer is human: The role of failure in design.* New York, NY: Vintage.

Petroski, H. (2011). *An engineer's alphabet: Gleanings from the softer side of a profession.* New York, NY: Cambridge University Press.

PictureSTEM. (2018). *Engineering design process.* Retrieved from http://picturestem.org/ engineering-design-process/

Rusch, E., & Priceman, M. (2017). *The music of life: Bartolomeo Cristofori & the invention of the piano.* New York, NY: Simon & Schuster, Atheneum Books for Young Readers.

Rynearson, A. M., Moore, T. J., Tank, K. M., & Gajdzik, E. (2017). *Evidence-based reasoning in a kindergarten classroom through an integrated STEM curriculum.* Paper presented at the 2017 American Society for Engineering Education Annual Conference and Exposition, Columbus, OH.

Spires, A. (2014). *The most magnificent thing.* Tonawanda, NY: Kids Can Press.

Vygotsky, L. S. (1978). *Mind in society: The development of higher mental processes.* Cambridge, MA: Harvard University Press.

Waite-Stupiansky, S. (2017). Jean Piaget's constructivist theory of learning. In L. E. Cohen & S. Waite-Stupiansky (Eds.), *Theories of early childhood education: Developmental, behaviorist, and critical* (pp. 3–17). New York, NY: Routledge.

Wood, D., Bruner, J. C., & Ross, G. (1976). The role of tutoring in problem solving. *Journal of Child Psychology and Psychiatry, 17*, 89–100.

7

TINKERING/MAKING

Playful Roots of Interest in STEM

Olga S. Jarrett and Aliya Jafri

Homo Sapiens and pre-Homo Sapiens have been tinkering and making ever since they have been on this planet. The oldest stone tools yet discovered are around 3.3 million years old, well before the Homo genus evolved (Morelle, 2015). The invention of tools by these folks was undoubtedly driven by the necessity of killing animals for protection or food. Approximately 20,000 years ago, the cave painters of Lascaux, France, engaged in inventing that was not needed for their survival. They invented paints, ways to apply the paint to cave walls, and a way to make enough light in dark caves so that they could see to paint (Gurstelle, 2016a). These inventions could not have appeared ready-made. They required a lot of tinkering until the people *got it right*.

What is tinkering? *Merriam Webster* says to *tinker is to repair, adjust, or work with something in an unskilled or experimental manner. Fiddle* (www.merriam-webster. com). Microsoft Word's thesaurus synonyms for tinkering include *fiddling, playing, toying, mending, repairing, fixing, messing around*, and *putting right*. Given these definitions, my family has done a lot of tinkering. As a child, I built dollhouse furniture, made doll clothes, raided my mother's spice shelf for spices to turn into sachets, made up exams and puzzles for playing school, put on puppet shows, and created a museum for my rock and fossil collection. A Gilbert chemical magic booklet that came with my brother's chemistry set inspired and sparked my interest in chemistry as well as magic. As a teenager, I made a model Roman house from wood for my Latin teacher and designed my own tricks for my magic show performances. My brother made a crystal radio, built a working Ferris wheel model from Erector Set pieces, had his own radio station (I was co-opted as his assistant) that broadcast his programs around the immediate neighborhood, and assembled his own meteorology station where he collected weather data for years. My husband repaired his own bicycle, built a derby car from a board and baby carriage wheels, created an intercom from old phone parts and batteries, and made several kinds of model boats that ran by rubber band, candle, or battery power. Our three sons made boat and airplane models, drew pictures and diagrams, took things apart, and built and rebuilt with LEGOs. For all of us, there are important connections between the way we played and tinkered as children and our career choices. I became an educator. My brother, husband, and one son became engineers, and our other sons majored in architecture and industrial design. We were all lucky to have access to tools, parental expertise, and time for tinkering. The next story shows that the drive to solve problems and tinker with solutions is not dependent upon ready access to tools and materials or parental expertise.

The Boy who Harnessed the Wind: A Modern Tinkerer

William Kamkwamba grew up in a village without electricity in Malawi, in East Africa. Drought brought famine, and his poverty-stricken family could not afford his secondary schooling. Instead, William requested use of the school library where he discovered physics. There he learned about generators and decided to build a windmill that would generate enough electricity to light his house. At age 14, with a lot of experimentation and trips to a dump, he combined bicycle parts and other scrap metal into a windmill generator that lit not only lights but also operated two radios. With a car battery to store electricity, he was able to charge village cell phones. His story, (Kamkwamba & Mealer, 2010) is an inspiration [see the Children's literature list for their books written for children of various ages]. A story in a Malawi newspaper led to a TED Talk and eventually a scholarship to Dartmouth College where he graduated in 2014. William now works with WiderNet "to develop appropriate technology curriculum that will allow people to bridge the gap between *knowing* and *doing*" (About William, n.d., para.6). William was unusual in that he had to assemble his materials and tools from trash heaps. Other inventors also began their life interests at an early age.

Theoretical Framework

Constructivism and Constructionism

Two theories of learning and understanding have influenced interest in tinkering and making, constructivism and constructionism. Both involve the brain and hands. Jean Piaget (1970) referred to his theory as *constructivism*, meaning that children construct their understandings through interaction with materials in their environment. Although children pick up social knowledge through adults and other children, their understanding of mathematics and the physical world must be learned through action with the objects, rather than verbally, as they manipulate objects in various ways. According to Piaget (1976), knowledge acquired through "free investigation and spontaneous effort" (p. 93) will be acquired along with a methodology that is useful over the lifetime. Vygotsky (1980), also a constructivist, added the importance of community in helping children build their understandings. Vygotsky's theory speaks to the value of having children work in groups where they can share ideas and understandings.

Seymour Papert, who worked with Piaget at the University of Geneva, was profoundly influenced by Piaget. Without rejecting his mentor's ideas, Papert adapted *constructivism* to a theory he called *constructionism*. Papert believed that children understood best when they could actually construct, whether physical structures or computer programs. Papert's book *Mindstorms, Children, Computers, and Powerful Ideas* (1993) gave its name to LEGO robotics; and Papert and his mentee, Mitchel Resnick, worked at MIT with LEGO sponsorship to develop creative materials that lend themselves to tinkering. LEGO has a foundation whose aim is to "raise awareness of the role of play for creativity, learning and development and to build and share knowledge about how to engage children in learning-rich play activities" (Gauntlett & Thomsen, 2013, p. 2). I heard Resnick speak at a conference on his MIT *Lifelong Kindergarten* program (Resnick, 2017), an allusion to the traditional kindergarten based on play, making, and fun stuff to build. During the discussion period, I pointed out that kindergarten is not play-based and more like a first grade class. The addition of tinkering to elementary school could help bring back joy to kindergarten and make other grades more like the lifelong kindergarten that Resnick described. Besides building understanding through constructivism and constructionism, tinkering has the potential to build interest in STEM careers and bring about positive changes in the brain through increased use of the hands.

The Hand and the Brain

Two physicians, American neurologist Frank R. Wilson and Swedish hand surgeon Göran Lundborg, have written books about the critical relationship between the hand and the brain. According to Lundborg (2014),

> a very active hand results in increased activation of the nerve cells in the sensory and motor hand representational areas....Thus, the hand can 'shape' the brain: the brain is functionally shaped based on the hand's experiences.... Quite simply, the hand has to be active to maintain its representation in the brain—use it or lose it. (p. 94)

Similarly, Wilson (1998) concludes...:

> The interaction of brain and hand, and the growth of their collaborative relationship throughout a life of successive relationships with all manner of other selves—musical, building, playing, hiking, cooking, juggling, riding, artistic selves—not only signifies but proves that what we call learning is a

quintessential mystery of human life....The desire to learn is reshaped continuously as brain and hand vitalize one another, and the capacity to learn grows continuously as we fashion our own personal laboratory for making things. (p. 295)

Wilson and Lundborg raise a critical question for educators: Are children's brains being limited by not making things, by not learning to write in cursive, by swiping screens, and by hours of filling in blanks on tests?

Why Tinker?

Tinkering Background of Scientists, Inventors, and Engineers

Studies of scientists and inventors strongly suggest that childhood experiences of tinkering and play, involving construction and experimentation, developed their interest in science (e.g., Lonnie G. Johnson, n.d.; Feynman, 1985; Goertzel & Goertzel, 1962; Johnson, 2016; Thackray & Myers, Jr., 2000). Two of America's most famous inventors, Benjamin Franklin and Thomas Edison, started tinkering early. Franklin, inventor of the lightning rod, bifocals, the Franklin Stove, and the glass "armonica" (a musical instrument), invented swim fins at age 11 (Franklin Institute, n.d.); and Edison, inventor of the light bulb, phonograph, and motion pictures, built a chemical lab in his basement at age 10 (Tinker Lab, n.d.).

Aboriginal communities of North America were makers before the term was invented. They used available resources to harvest food, invent tools, and create games. To name a few inventions, we owe corn, wild rice, maple syrup, fish hooks, decoys, lacrosse, hockey and volleyball, sunscreen, surgical blades, diapers, asphalt and megaphones to the first nations' ingenuity (Landon & Macdonald, 2014). Black scientists and inventors (George Washington Carver, developer of hundreds of uses for the peanut, Elijah McCoy, inventor of the railroad self-lubricator that inspired the term "the real McCoy," and Lonnie G. Johnson (n.d.), inventor of the super-soaker water gun) show that discrimination could not stand in the way of their childhood curiosity and ability to *make* as adults.

Studies of other scientists and inventors strongly suggest that their childhood experiences of tinkering and play, involving construction and experimentation, developed their interest in science. The following three examples come from the lives of Nobel Prize winners: Albert Einstein's childhood play with a magnetic compass, puzzles, inventions, and model building, sparked his adult curiosity with phenomena and ideas (Frank, 1947; White & Gribbin, 1994). Einstein is credited as having said that imagination is more important than knowledge in an interview with the Saturday Evening Post (1929), indicating the value he placed on playing with ideas. Robert Burns Woodward, organic chemist, set up a basement chemistry lab as a child, According to his daughter, his lifetime work was playful, carrying "into mature forms of search and research" (Woodward, 1989, p. 248). Nobel

Prize winning physicist Richard Feynman recalled the importance of play in his autobiography (Feynman, 1985), describing the gadget making and general "piddling around" he did in his childhood home laboratory. As an adult, he reflected that he used to "enjoy doing physics" because he "used to play with it" (p. 157).

Ganschow and Ganschow (1998), reflecting on Watson and Crick's discovery of the structure of the DNA molecule as well as their own professional experiences, speculate that playfulness with science involves the satisfaction of curiosity. Arnold Beckman, inventor of the pH meter and the DU spectrophotometer, the first successful instrument for measuring absorption of ultraviolet light, began his career inventing toys as a child and developed his own chemistry lab at home after finding an old chemistry textbook at age 9 (Thackray & Myers, 2000). Neurologist Oliver Sachs (2002), best known for his book, *The Man Who Mistook His Wife for a Hat*, spent his childhood doing chemistry in his own lab and collected samples of the chemical elements as an adult. Charles Babbage, inventor of the first programmable computer, became fascinated with automata (moving toys) he was shown at a museum at age 8 (Johnson, 2016). According to Kean (1998), chemists often play with chemistry throughout their careers. These examples have been of famous scientists, but many successful tinkerers/inventors were, and still are, amateurs rather than professionals (Hitt, 2012).

What role has early childhood and elementary education played in developing interest in science? The scientists mentioned so far discussed parental influences and mentors, but most did not have good experiences in elementary school. Of 27 famous scientists who wrote about their childhood experiences, only three mentioned anything about elementary school (Brockman, 2004). Of the three, one mentioned a neutral experience in passing, a second mentioned teachers giving him especially interesting readings, and a third discussed being expelled from nursery school for not following orders. Clearly, their early childhood interests in science and technology were developed at home rather than at school.

In my research with scientists (Jarrett & Burnley, 2007), undergraduate science majors (Jarrett & Burnley, 2010), and preservice teachers (Bulunuz & Jarrett, 2010; Jarrett, 1999) on the influence of early experiences on interest in science, I have found links between play and experimentation as children and interest in science as adults. Seventy-three percent of the undergraduate science majors mentioned play with LEGOs as being their most important childhood influence. Studies of preservice teachers (Bulunuz & Jarrett, 2010; Jarrett, 1999) found that having memorable science experiences in elementary school was the best predictor of interest in science as an adult. Unfortunately, only one-third of the respondents could remember *anything* about science in elementary school. The second-best predictor was informal science experiences such as tinkering at home, play with science toys such as microscopes, chemistry sets, and LEGOs, and attending museum programs. Those preservice teachers with neither memorable science experience in elementary school nor strong informal experiences tended to be uninterested in science.

Current Tinkering Opportunities for Young Children

How do today's children develop interest in science? Not every family has a woodworking shop in the basement and freedom to tinker. Access to chemicals is more limited than it used to be as some of the more interesting chemicals in children's chemistry sets have been deemed too dangerous. Homeless children and children living in poverty may be especially disadvantaged in tinkering opportunities.

What about tinkering and making in schools? Once upon a time, schools routinely offered lessons in art, music, woodworking, cooking, and sewing where a degree of improvisation surely occurs. I envied my brother's ability to make a shelf in woodworking class. I really didn't mind taking cooking and sewing classes, but I also wanted to take woodworking, a class not allowed for girls. Our middle son had the opportunity to take cooking, but 13 years later, our youngest son had no shop or home economics classes. About 30 years ago, I knew a teacher of 4-year-olds who had a workshop center in her classroom where children used real tools to hammer nails in wood and saw pieces of styrofoam. A Google search shows that such centers still exist in Montessori and other private programs. Do public programs afford such building opportunities?

When personal computers were invented, many students learned to design their own programs. Papert (1993) introduced children to a *turtle* to program (code) using LOGO, a program he developed. Unfortunately, the decades-long focus on high stakes testing in urban high-poverty schools, exacerbated by No Child Left Behind and Race to the Top, has been accompanied by a decrease in playful classroom activities typically associated with social collaboration, creativity, and innovative thinking. By 2008, the school districts surveyed by the Center on Education Policy (McMurrer, 2008) had cut time for social studies, science, art, music, physical education, recess, and/or lunch to allow more time for math and literacy, the two subjects tested. Fifty-three percent of the districts cut at least 75 minutes from science per week. In recent years, computers have become used for test-taking with a possible decrease in creative uses. An entire generation of students, especially students in poverty, has had little opportunity at school for "playing around" with construction, art, and science materials. In other words, *tinkering*.

"Creativity is intelligence having fun," ascribed to Einstein (and others as well) illustrates a creditable relationship between playfulness, enjoyment, discovery, and invention. The relationships between play and learning and play, creativity, and innovation have been discussed in several recent books (Bateson & Martin, 2013; Gray, 2013; Honey & Kanter, 2013; Singer, Golinkoff, & Hirsh-Pasek, 2006).

The National Science Teachers Association (NSTA) Position Statement on learning science in informal environments (NSTA, 2012) mentions the value of science experiences in informal settings and cites research that provides "clear evidence that these experiences can promote science learning and strengthen and enrich school science" (p. 1). However, children who are learning the least science in school are likely the same students whose families cannot afford home workshops, microscopes, LEGO robotics, and museum visits or afford to provide the same enrichment activities during the summer holidays that give an academic boost to middle class children (Berliner, 2013). Through a focus on test-taking and isolated skills, many students have not acquired the cognitive, interpersonal, and intra-personal skills and motivations considered 21st century skills (National Research Council & Koenig, 2011). Unfortunately, some teachers have little interest or expertise in science, perhaps because of the lack of hands-on science and inventive projects in their own elementary school experiences (Bulunuz & Jarrett, 2010; Jarrett, 1999). An encouraging development is a new kind of summer school that focuses on fun rather than remediation (McCray, 2018). Noting that children in higher income families increase their academic performance during the summer while children from lower income families tend to decrease in academic performance, the new programs, which are free for students, include inventing and work on computers. One child was quoted as saying, "It's like learning, but they're making it fun" (p. A1). The success of the tinkering program that Aliya Jafri describes later in this chapter suggests that a focus on fun would be beneficial all year.

Gender Issues in Tinkering/Making and STEM

In the 21st century, more women are entering STEM professions. However, the science and engineering pipeline is still leaky for women, who continue to be under-represented in STEM (Blickenstaff, 2005). In 1999–2000, 80% of engineering and 50% of physical science Bachelor's degrees in the US were awarded to men as were 64% of engineering and 75% of the physical science Ph.Ds. In a small study of same-gender first and fifth grade dyads engaged in various hands-on science activities, with or without enough tools for each, girls tended to be more collaborative but boys were more inventive and exploratory (Jones et al., 2000). "Boys tended to use the materials outside of the guidelines for the science activity, while girls used materials within the boundaries of the teacher's directions" (p. 770). Although the girls were easier to control during tinkering activities, the boys did more actual tinkering.

As highlighted earlier, my tinkering experiences were very different from those of my brother, husband, and sons. While they took things apart, played with electronics, and built things, I made doll furniture, puppets, and sachets. Though my father was a mechanical engineer and my brother was studying metallurgical engineering, when I started off to the university in 1958, I did not even consider engineering. Women simply did not do that.

The list of famous scientists at the beginning of this chapter contained no women. No famous female American tinkerer was discussed in the history book on American tinkerers, *The Tinkerers: The Amateurs, DIYers, and Inventors Who*

Make America Great (Foege, 2013). The only woman tinkerer mentioned in the book was Blythe Masters, a British economist whose tinkering with credit derivatives was a possible cause of the 2008 recession! However, Swaby (2016) describes women scientists who have made a difference in technology, invention, astronomy and space exploration, health, medicine, and biology. Most of the women described in Swaby's (2016) book were strongly influenced by their fathers. Additionally, they showed amazing determination to overcome biases against them as women. Swaby (2016) did not mention women's school experiences or tinkering as children. However, one should not assume that the kinds of playful tinkering done by boys would not also influence girls.

Some years ago, I taught all the science for my son's third grade class, focusing on hands-on activities done in small groups. One week, we did some experiments illustrating the Bernoulli principle and then made paper airplanes. I suggested having a paper airplane design competition, judging the planes on distance, direction, loops, and so on. One of the girls said she did not want to participate, prompting me to give a mini-lecture to the class on the importance of tinkering. I noted that scientists and engineers tended to tinker as children and that girls who did not tinker might be shutting themselves out of possible science and engineering fields. The girl agreed to participate and was the winner for the plane that flew the furthest.

During the next few weeks, our class planned a series of science activities to share with students from other classes. A group of boys decided to set up a table where they taught our guests how to make airplanes. Half-way through the morning, several upset-looking boys sought me out. They told me that the girls from the other classes were not coming to their table, and they were afraid these girls would not have the option to become scientists and engineers! Having made such a point of this issue, I figured I needed to take them seriously. We decided that the guest classes would need to try all the activities, though they could spend additional time at the activities they liked the most.

Tinkering and Making: Current Influences

The Maker Movement

In 2005, Dale Dougherty launched a new magazine, MAKE, designed to give people ideas and to inspire them to invent and play with technology. The following year, he organized the first Maker Faire, a hands-on celebration of making. Perhaps as a reaction to stultifying trends in education and declines in manufacturing, MAKING has captured the imaginations of community makers creating makerspaces as well as home schoolers, school groups, and after-school tinkerers who participate in Maker Faires. In 2012, Dougherty established the Maker Educator Initiative in response to President Obama's Educate to Innovate initiative in which Maker Corps members work with young people (ages 12–18) at a series of informal education sites (Garcia-Lopez, 2013). However, since fourth grade is a time when many students, especially African American boys, begin to lose interest in school (Noguera, 2003), and fifth grade is the time when the achievement gap in mathematics is shown to have widened (Balfanz & Byrnes, 2006), it is important to introduce tinkering earlier, during the early childhood years.

Tinkering/making seems to have come into its own. A number of recently published books on the topic (Bateson & Martin, 2013; Gabrielson, 2015; Gray, 2013; Hargittai, 2011; Honey & Kanter, 2013; Martinez & Stager, 2013; Robinson with Aronica, 2013; Wagner, 2012) have focused on the connections between playfulness, creativity, and innovation. Research on informal science settings (Fenichel & Schweingruber, 2010) suggests that such activities as building one's own toolkits, designing T-shirts, building robots, and writing a book of their projects are highly motivating for students of all ages.

The Exploratorium Tinkering Studio

The other most important influence on tinkering is the Tinkering Studio, located within the Exploratorium, the Museum of Science, Art and Human Perception, in San Francisco. This special room opened on April 30, 2013, after three years of planning (Exploratorium, 2013). I had the opportunity to visit it shortly thereafter. The Tinkering Studio (n.d.) is open to children and adults for tinkering with a variety of materials. The materials vary day by day and include cardboard automata, cams, levers, and linkages; chain reactions; circuit boards with lights, switches, battery packs, motors, potentiometers, buzzers, and hand generators; squishy circuits made with Play-Doh, batteries, and LEDs; scribbling machines with off-center motors; marble machines with tracks; and animated stuffed toys that can be taken apart and reconfigured. The Exploratorium Tinkering Studio has taught online courses in tinkering through Coursera. I have taken two Coursera courses, 1) *Tinkering Fundamentals: A Constructionist Approach to STEM Learning* and 2) *Tinkering Fundamentals: Motion and Mechanisms*. Two of the course instructors, Mick Petrich and Karen Wilkinson, have written numerous book chapters, articles, and books on tinkering (Bevan, Gutwill, Petrich, & Wilkinson, 2015; Bevan, Petrich, & Wilkinson, 2014/2015; Petrich, Wilkinson, & Bevan, 2013; Wilkinson & Petrich, 2014), and also teach tinkering classes for teachers at the Exploratorium. The Exploratorium partners with the LEGO Foundation, the Lifelong Kindergarten group at MIT, Science Sandbox, Reggio Children, and the Lighthouse Community Charter School where they develop programs. They engage in research on methods of effective facilitation of tinkering and provide video clips of their findings (instructions available on the Tinkering Studio website—see Teacher Resources).

Tinkering in the Classroom

Guidelines for Tinkering in Early Childhood Education

According to V. S. Ramachandran, director of the Center for Brain and Cognition at the University of California, San Diego, "the best formula for success is to be around people who are passionate and enthusiastic about what they do, for there is nothing more contagious than enthusiasm" (Brockman, 2004, p. 211). Test preparation sessions do not tend to promote enthusiasm. Neither do "arts and crafts" projects where each child makes a similar object, whether a face on a paper plate to hang on the bulletin board or a pot holder from a pattern. I have observed that tinkering with stuff generates enthusiasm, whether by taking apart appliances that do not work, playing with circuit boards, marbles and tracks, or adding LEDs to fabrics. When tinkering, children are *doing their own thing*, but they are also able to observe others and get ideas from them.

Tinkering encourages the teacher to draw on funds of knowledge of the parents and the community (Gonzalez, Moll, & Amanti, 2005). Though children of scientists and engineers may have advantages at home, high-poverty neighborhoods also have expertise and materials to offer. A survey of parents, family members, and guardians could determine interest, expertise, and available materials, such as small appliances that no longer work (with the cords cut off to avoid shock). Visiting thrift shops for cheap materials that can be used for tinkering in the classroom is an inexpensive way to add resources.

What does tinkering look like? Much tinkering can be included in grade level content standards. However, since tinkering involves play with materials and student choice of projects, content covered will, to some extent, vary with the interests of the children; and it is likely that additional standards will be addressed. Trying to figure things out for themselves will help children behave like scientists and develop character traits such as self-control, social intelligence, curiosity, optimism, enthusiasm, creativity, and *grit*. What kinds of activities lend themselves to tinkering? Examples of possible projects to design, make, or use with connections to STEM include circuit boards, spinners, toys using magnets, musical instruments from household objects, kaleidoscopes, robots, generators or motors, puzzles, art with light and sound, and adding LEDs to paper or cloth. These projects can help teach content such as simple machines, forces and motion, electricity and magnetism, light, and sound.

Another way for teachers to encourage tinkering is to examine the STEM objectives and suggested ideas for projects. Assembling the materials and then letting children tinker with them, *messing around* to see what they can do with them, works well. Play will allow them to think creatively and be better prepared for whatever STEM challenge is suggested by the school curriculum. The play involved in tinkering allows for learning through exploration rather than the pressure or the need to get the right answer. By being able to make choices, children build confidence in their ability to DO. Tinkering allows children to experience, through exploration and play, the crosscutting concepts of the Next Generation Science Standards (NGSS) (Bybee, 2013): patterns; cause and effect; scale, proportion, and quantity; systems and system models; energy and matter (flows, cycles, and conservation); structure and function; and stability and change. Children should be allowed to tinker before being given formal assignments in STEM. For example, before children are challenged to build the tallest tower possible from drinking straws and chenille sticks (formerly known as pipe cleaners), they need to be able to "mess around" with the materials, connecting the straws and sticks to see which shapes are most stable. Before creating certain kinds of circuits, they should be allowed to tinker with batteries, wires, and bulbs to see how to light a bulb. Tinkerers may even be motivated to learn about patents and how they protect the rights of inventors. A free book on inventing is available from the U.S. Patent and Trademark Office (see Teacher Resources).

Next, I share the experiences of Aliya Jafri, a fourth-grade teacher. She and I both took an online tinkering class from the Exploratorium, and I have visited her class several times. Here is Aliya's story:

TINKERING IN THE CLASSROOM

By Aliya Jafri

I teach at a public charter school in a county in Georgia, USA. It has traditionally been one of the fastest growing refugee and non-English speaking communities in the state of Georgia. My fourth-grade classroom mirrors that description with 13 different languages and nationalities represented by my 24 students. To provide a hands-on experience to my students on simple machines, I requested Dr. Olga Jarrett offer a workshop. She offered an hour-long tinkering workshop. I was intrigued to see how some students who performed significantly below grade level in math and reading were particularly deft at taking things apart and tinkering. This workshop took place right after our school had taken our Winter Measures of Academic Progress (MAP) test, and our grade level team expressed frustration at how our Science MAP data were not representative of our students' understanding of fourth-grade science standards. Most school districts had switched to the NGSS at the beginning of the 2017–2018 academic year, but our school district chose not to. MAP was based on NGSS, and we were required to teach GSE (Georgia Standard of Excellence).

A few weeks later, Dr. Jarrett suggested we take an online tinkering course. The five-week course, offered by the Exploratorium in San Francisco, required a significant amount of reading and a new making challenge every week. I decided to create a makerspace in my classroom and opened it with the challenge to make a scribble machine using markers, a paper cup, length of tape, rubber bands, a motor, batteries, and wires. The students started out with a gusto; they figured out how to make a circuit and how to make the motor go; but every time they attached the motor to the cup, the motor weighed down on the paper cup and stopped working. The enthusiasm started to wane. It took the first group three sessions to accomplish their task. By this time some groups had given up and were frustrated, saying it was an impossible task. Some started playing with Play-Doh, some started to build using copious amounts of tape and craft sticks. However, as soon as the first group made their scribble machine, others gathered around to observe what they did to be successful and tried it out in their groups-some with more success than others. Later a student expressed that it was very hard to make the scribble machine because they couldn't make the motor run. Once another student showed them how to do that, they could put the machine together in no time.

In a nutshell, in the initial weeks of opening the classroom makerspace, I faced two problems: 1) my students were not used to having easy access to materials like pipe cleaners, tape, craft sticks, batteries, wires, and so on. The materials I had collected for the makerspace began to disappear. 2) Every time I offered a new challenge, most students got extremely frustrated, saying it was impossible. I noted that boys in my classroom gave up quicker than the girls. Instead of creating a fun learning environment, the projects made students feel angry and discouraged. I was not sure how to address both the issues right away, but knew that I had to continue offering making opportunities to my students and set some ground rules.

The first challenge of the Exploratorium tinkering course was to make a marble maze out of a pegboard. I decided to offer all the challenges from the course to my students as well. After Dr. Jarrett and I did a trial run ourselves using recycled materials like paper towel tubes, tape, and trifold boards at home, we opened the challenge to the class.

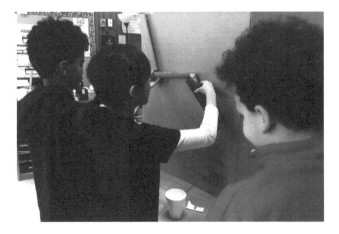

FIGURE 7.1 Marble Maze

They had to create a marble maze with the objective of catching the marble at the end of the maze. It was very exciting to see children work on their mazes. Some students found it hard to listen to others' ideas; some were creative thinkers, but not good communicators and were not able to explain their thinking to their team members, resulting in haws and hems from them. The overall experiment was successful: student teams were able to make multiple tracks, change angles, and soften the marble landing by cushioning the cup. One group used the egg crate and saw the marble bounce into one–three different egg cups. One child attached flashlights on either side to "light up" his maze. The second challenge was to make an automata requiring two or more cams to interact with each other to make the artwork on top of the cardboard box to move. That was a very frustrating process for me. I had to move away from it several times. What I considered the "end product" didn't match my aspirations. Surprisingly, were the automatas less challenging for the students, or were they building resilience?

FIGURE 7.2 Flying Crane Automata

The next challenge came from students themselves. They decided to make a game arcade to entertain K-5 students and raise funds. I had to get used to my classroom looking like a messy recycling center during the three weeks my students took to design their games. The games they were developing required time and often they had to leave things midway because the bell would ring for lunch, recess, or specials. The arcade was a huge success and everyone in the school was amazed at the students' agency.

FIGURE 7.3 Students Selling Arcade Entry and Lottery Tickets

They repurposed recycled materials into creative games, advertised for their event, made and sold tickets, and on the day set up and ran the arcade. They used the $150 raised at the arcade to paint the bathrooms.

After the arcade, the students chose their own projects, ranging from birdhouses, solar powered cars and iPad chargers, battery-powered boats, sensory bottles, rockets, necklaces, and airplane pillows. It was during the building of the arcade that I started to see a change: the students started to realize that random use of materials meant they may not have tape when they need it. When one student succeeded in making something, others gathered around to learn. It was heartwarming to see over time that the same students who shut down because they "failed," started to come back to their work and redesign with renewed energy.

The biggest gains were made by the students lowest in reading and writing. At the end of the school year, the students took the Spring MAP test. I am fully aware of the dangers of drawing conclusions by looking at data in isolation, so all I would say is that after obtaining virtually the same low scores in science as the other two fourth-grade classes in January, my students significantly outperformed the other two fourth-grade classrooms in May.

Based on observations in my classroom, I can safely conclude that tinkering helps develop grit and perseverance in and out of school. Adults and children have become used to instant results with smart technology at their fingertips. They are losing patience for longer, more drawn out inquiries. Tinkering is an opportunity to bring low and slow tech into the classroom. It is important to appreciate that many students may not have had those experiences, so it is going to be a slow process. Having a classroom makerspace, albeit a sparse one, has provided my students the opportunity to internalize design thinking. Students draw their design, label and describe what they are trying to accomplish, what is working, what is problematic and what would they change to improve upon their design. One of my quiet students said that having a classroom makerspace helped him not give up, but face the difficult tasks in makerspace and at school. Finding a medium other than English to express themselves, my English language learners (ELLs) are among the most successful makers.

Conclusion

In this chapter, I discussed the enthusiasm involved in tinkering with materials without the need to "get it right" and the importance of using one's hands. Most scientists and engineers tinkered as children and continued tinkering as adults as part of their work and hobbies. I recommend that young children have lots of time to engage in very open-ended tinkering in the classroom. Providing a tinker space with bins of materials that children can use in many ways each day can make a difference. Children need the self-motivation to play around with ideas and materials before being given a science or engineering lab assignment. Many young people whose families enabled their tinkering became interested in science and engineering in spite of their dreary experiences in school. Children whose parents cannot provide those experiences *need* tinkering experiences at school.

Not all children will, or should, become scientists and engineers. A thought-provoking article critiques the focus on STEM fields as a neo-liberal Trojan Horse (Beneze, Reiss, Sharma, & Weinstein, 2018). Pointing out that STEM leaves out inclusion of the liberal arts, including sociology, economics, anthropology, and philosophy, the article asserts that STEM fields do not sufficiently consider the human aspects and sometimes create problems (e.g., the petroleum industry aggravating global warming). I agree that American society has benefited tremendously from science and technology, but it also needs to discuss critically technologies that have damaged the environment and side effects of robots that replace workers. Creativity and curiosity should be encouraged in all children, and the tinkering mindset is valuable in many fields. Society also needs committed and curious teachers, social workers, bankers, artists, performers, business people, policymakers, and others. Those people need STEM literacy in their work and as informed citizens. And scientists also need the humanities, arts, and design to make them better scientists (Root-Bernstein, 2018). As suggested by Liritzis (2018), this new discipline might be called STEMAC (science, technology, engineering, and mathematics for arts and culture) to include cultural heritage (Liritzis, 2018).

Included next is a list of children's books, as well as tinkering books and downloadable resources for teachers. They are full of ideas teachers, after-school program staff, camp counselors, and parents can introduce and which children can adapt.

Making space for tinkering in the classroom can encourage curiosity, collaboration, innovation, confidence, and creativity. All children need these qualities to succeed in school and life. They also need to have freedom of choice to do things they enjoy doing. These opportunities promote ENTHUSIASM for being in school and for learning more.

Children's Literature About Inventors

Barton, C. (2016). *Whoosh!: Lonnie Johnson's super-soaking stream of inventions*. Watertown, MA: Charlesbridge. [Appealing and informative picture book of Lonnie Johnson's invention of the super-soaker.]

Beaty, A. (2013). *Rosie Revere, engineer*. New York, NY: Harry N. Abrams. [Fanciful story of a girl who invents an airplane. See also other books by this author.]

Hagar, E. (2016). *The inventors of LEGO toys*. New York, NY: Duo Press. [True history of the family invention of LEGOs. Interesting and informative.]

Jones, C. F. (1994). *Mistakes that worked: 40 familiar inventions & how they came to be*. New York, NY: Delacorte Books for Young Readers. [Informative and interesting stories of mistakes that became inventions. A good lesson for those afraid to make mistakes.]

Kamkwamba, W., & Mealer, B. (2010). *The boy who harnessed the wind: Creating currents of electricity and hope (P.S.)*. New York. NY: William Morrow. [Biography of the African boy who harnessed the wind to create electricity. Good background reading for the teacher.]

Kamkwamba, W., & Mealer, B. (2012). *The boy who harnessed the wind: Picture Book Edition*. New York, NY: Dial Books for Young Readers. [Inspirational picture book of an African boy who created a windmill generator from junk.]

Kamkwamba, W., & Mealer, B. (2016). *The boy who harnessed the wind: Young Reader's Edition*. London, England: Puffin Books. [Book for young readers about an African boy who created a windmill generator from junk.]

Sullivan, O. R. (2011). *African American inventors*. Hoboken, NJ: Wiley. [Biographies of 25 important African American inventors. Older elementary school readers.]

Tucker, T. (1998). *Brainstorm!: The stories of twenty American kid inventors*. New York, NY: Square Fish. [Inspiring to elementary school children to read about kid inventors.]

Wulffson, D. (2014). *Toys! Amazing stories behind some great inventions*. New York, NY: Square Fish. [Informative short stories on inventions of toys. Good background reading for teachers and upper elementary students.]

Teacher Resources

Baggett, S. (2016). *The invent to learn guide to Making in the K-3 classroom: Why, how, and wow!* Torrance, CA: Constructing Modern Knowledge Press.

Boston Children's Museum. *Tinker kit: Educators' guide*. Retrieved from http://www.bostonchildrensmuseum.org/sites/default/files/pdfs/Tinker_Kit_Educators_Guide_singles_web.pdf

Burker, J. (2015). *The invent to learn guide to fun*. Torrance, CA: Constructing Modern Knowledge Press.

Burker, J. (2018). *The invent to learn guide to more fun.* Torrance, CA: Constructing Modern Knowledge Press.

Ceceri, K. (2016). *Make: Edible inventions: Cooking hacks and yummy recipes you can build, mix, bake, and grow.* San Francisco, CA: Maker Media.

Clapp, E. P., Ross, J., Ryan, J. O., & Tishman, S. (2017). *Maker-centered learning: Empowering young people to shape their worlds.* San Francisco, CA: Josey-Bass.

DeVries, R., & Sales, C. (2011). *Ramps & pathways: A constructivist approach to physics with young children.* Washington, DC: National Association for the Education of Young Children.

Doorley, R. (2014). *Tinkerlab: A hands-on guide for little inventors.* Boston, MA: Roost Books.

Englehart, D., Mitchell, D., Albers-Biddle, J., Jennings-Towle, K., & Forestieri, M. (2016). *STEM play: Integrating inquiry into learning centers.* Lewisville, NC: Gryphon House.

Franklin Institute (n.d.). *Benjamin Franklin's inventions.* Retrieved from https://www.fi.edu/benjamin-franklin/inventions

Gabrielson, C. (2015) *Make: Tinkering, kids learn by making stuff* (2nd ed.). San Francisco, CA: Maker Media.

Gurstelle, W. (2016a). *ReMaking history: Early makers, Volume 1.* San Francisco, CA: MakerMedia.

Gurstelle, W. (2016b). *ReMaking history: Industrial revolutionaries, Volume 2.* San Francisco, CA: Maker Media.

Gurstelle, W. (2017) *ReMaking history: Makers of the modern world, Volume 3.* San Francisco, CA: Maker Media.

Heroman, C. (2017). *Making & tinkering with STEM: Solving design challenges with young children.* Washington, DC: National Association for the Education of Young Children.

Klepeis, A. (2017). *Explore Makerspace! With 25 great projects.* White River Junction, VT: Nomad Press.

Lonnie G. Johnson (n.d.) *Biography.* Retrieved from https://www.biography.com/people/lonnie-g-johnson-17112946.

Maker Ed Staff. (2017). *Setting up and facilitating tinkering workshops with educators.* Lexington, KY: Maker Education Initiative.

Moomaw, S. (2013). *Teaching STEM in the early years: Activities for integrating science, technology, engineering, and mathematics.* St. Paul, MN: Redleaf Press.

Smithsonian Institution. (2016). *Maker LAB: 28 super cool projects.* New York: DK Publishing.

Thomas, A. M. (2014). *Make: Making makers: Kids, tools, and the future of innovation.* Sebastopol, CA: Maker Media.

The Tinkering Studio. (n.d.) Retrieved from https://tinkering.exploratorium.edu/

The Tinkering Studio. *Tinkering our work: Learning and facilitation Framework.* Retrieved from http://tinkering.exploratorium.edu/learning-and-facilitation-framework.

U.S. Patent and Trademark Office. (2004). *The inventive thinking curriculum project: An outreach program of the United States Patent and Trademark Office.* Retrieved from https://intella-ip.com/free-patent-trademark-inventive-thinking-information/inventive-thinking/

References

About William (n.d.). Retrieved from http://www.williamkamkwamba.com/about.html

Balfanz, R., & Byrnes, V. (2006). Closing the mathematics achievement gap in high-poverty middle schools: Enablers and constraints. *Journal of Education for Students Placed at Risk, 11*(2), 143–159. doi:10.1207/s15327671espr1102_2

Bateson, P., & Martin, P. (2013). *Play, playfulness, creativity and innovation.* New York, NY: Cambridge University Press.

Bencze, L., Reiss, M., Sharma, A., & Weinstein, M. (2018). STEM education as "Trojan Horse": Deconstructed and reinvented for all. *Journal of Research in Science Teaching, 56*(6), 763–789.

Berliner, D. C. (2013). Effects of inequality and poverty vs. teachers and schooling on America's Youth. *Teachers College Record, 115*(12), 1–26.

Bevan, B., Petrich, M., & Wilkinson, K. (December2014/January2015). Tinkering is serious play. *Educational Leadership, 72*(4), 28–33.

Bevan, B., Gutwill, J. P., Petrich, M., & Wilkinson, K. (2015). Learning through STEM-rich tinkering: Findings from a jointly negotiated research project taken up in practice. *Science Education, 99*(1), 98–120. doi:10.1002/sce.21151

Blickenstaff, J. C. (2005). Women and science careers: Leaky pipeline or gender filter? *Gender and Education, 17*(4), 369–386. doi:10.1080/09540250500145072

Brockman, J. (Ed.). (2004). *Curious minds: How a child becomes a scientist.* New York, NY: Pantheon Books.

Bulunuz, M., & Jarrett, O. S. (2010). Developing an interest in science: Background experiences of preservice elementary teachers. *International Journal of Environmental and Science Education, 5*(1), 65–84.

Bybee, R. W. (2013). *Translating the NGSS for classroom instruction.* Thousand Oaks, CA: Corwin.

Exploratorium (2013). *Sketchpad: Opening day in the tinkering studio.* Retrieved from https://www.exploratorium.edu/tinkering/blog/2013/04/30/opening-day-in-the-tinkering-studio

Fenichel, M., & Schweingruber, H. A. (2010). *Surrounded by science: Learning science in informal environments.* Washington, DC: The National Academies Press.

Feynman, R. P. (1985). *"Surely you're joking, Mr. Feynman!" Adventures of a curious character.* New York, NY: Bantam Books.

Frank, P. (1947). *Einstein: His life and times.* New York, NY: Alfred A. Knopf.

Foege, A. (2013). *The tinkerers: The amateurs, DIYers, and inventors who make America great.* New York, NY: Basic Books.

Ganschow, R., & Ganschow, L. (1998). Playfulness in biological science. In D. P. Fromberg & D. Bergen (Eds.), *Play from birth to twelve and beyond: Context, perspectives, and meanings* (pp. 455–460). New York, NY: Garland Publishing.

Gauntlett, D., & Thomsen, B. S. (2013). Cultures of creativity: Nurturing creative mindsets across cultures. *Lego Foundation.* Retrieved from https://westminsterresearch.westminster.ac.uk/download/38225964b63ebf0282986e599e638bf8a5d12729f4062ccb69613b10483a2d77/3199158/Gauntlett_2013.pdf

Garcia-Lopez, P. (2013). *Maker education initiative: Every child a maker: Program Report 2012–2013.* Retrieved from: http://makered.org/wp-content/uploads/2014/12/Maker-Ed-2013-Program-Report-150dpi.pdf

Goertzel, V., & Goertzel, M. G. (1962). *Cradles of eminence.* Boston, MA: Little, Brown and Company.

Gonzalez, N., Moll, L. C., & Amanti, C. (2005). *Funds of knowledge: Theorizing practices in households, communities, and classrooms.* New York, NY: Routledge.

Gray, P. (2013). *Free to learn: Why unleashing the instinct to play will make our children happier, more self-reliant, and better students for life.* New York, NY: Basic Books.

Gurstelle, W. (2016a). *ReMaking history: Early makers, Volume 1.* San Francisco, CA: Maker Media.

Hargittai, I. (2011). *Drive and curiosity: What fuels the passion for science.* Amherst, NY: Prometheus Books.

Hitt, J. (2012). *Bunch of amateurs: Inside America's hidden world of inventors, tinkerers, and job creators.* New York, NY: Broadway Paperbacks.

Honey, M., & Kanter, D. E. (2013). *Design, make, play: Growing the next generation of STEM innovators.* New York, NY: Routledge.

Jarrett, O. S. (1999). Science interest and confidence among pre-service elementary teachers. *Journal of Elementary Science Education, 11*(1), 49–59.

Jarrett, O. S., & Burnley, P. (2007). The role of fun, playfulness, and creativity in science: Lessons from geoscientists. In D. Sluss and O. Jarrett (Eds.). *Investigating play in the 21st century: Play and culture studies, Vol. 7* (pp. 188–202). Lanham, MD: University Press.

Jarrett, O. S., & Burnley, P. (2010, March). Lessons on the role of fun/playfulness from a geology undergraduate summer research program. *Journal of Geoscience Education, 58*(2), 110–120. doi:10.5408/1.3534844

Johnson, S. (2016). *Wonderland: How play made the modern world.* New York, NY: Riverhead Books.

Jones, M. G., Brader-Araje, L., Carboni, L. W., Carter, G., Rua, M. J., Banilower, E., & Hatch, H. (2000). Tool time: Gender and students' use of tools, control, and authority. *Journal of Research in Science Teaching, 37*(8). 760–783. https://doi.org/10.1002/1098-2736(200010)37:8<760::AID-TEA2>3.0.CO;2-V

Kamkwamba, W., & Mealer, B. (2010). *The boy who harnessed the wind: Creating currents of electricity and hope.* New York, NY: Harper Collins.

Kean, E. (1998). Chemist and play. In D. P. Fromberg & D. Bergen (Eds.), *Play from birth to twelve and beyond: Context, perspectives, and meanings* (pp. 468–472). New York, NY: Garland Publishing.

Landon, R., & Macdonald, D. (2014). *A Native American thought of it: Amazing inventions and innovations.* Brantford, Ontario: W. Ross MacDonald School Resource Services Library.

Liritzis (2018). STEMAC (science, technology, engineering, mathematics for arts & culture): The emergence of a new pedagogical discipline. *Scientific Culture, 4*(2), 73–76. doi:10.5281/zenodo.1214567

Lundborg, G. (2014). *The hand and the brain: From Lucy's thumb to the thought-controlled robotic hand.* New York, NY: Springer.

Martinez, S. L., & Stager, G. (2013). *Invent to learn: Making, tinkering, and engineering in the classroom.* Torrance, CA: Constructing Modern Knowledge Press.

McMurrer, J. (2008). *Instructional time in elementary schools: A closer look at changes for specific subjects.* Washington, DC: Center on Education Policy. https://www.cep-dc.org/displayDocument.cfm?DocumentID=309

McCray, V. (2018, June 11), Making Summer School Cool. *Atlanta Journal Constitution,* A1, A9. Retrieved from https://www.ajc.com/news/local-education/narrow-academic-gaps-aps-tries-make-summer-school-cool/MXAtP4p3fsjVxXJR6UrLMM/

Morelle, R. (2015). Oldest stone tools pre-date earliest humans. *BBC News.* Retrieved from http://www.bbc.com/news/science-environment-32804177

National Research Council & Koenig, J. A. (2011). *Assessing 21st century skills: Summary of a workshop.* Washington, DC: The National Academy Press.

National Science Teachers Association (NTSA) (2012). *Position statement: Learning science in informal environments.* Arlington, VA: NSTA Press. Retrieved from http://www.nsta.org/about/positions/informal.aspx

Noguera, P. A. (2003). The trouble with black boys: The role and influence of environmental and cultural factors on the academic performance of African American males. *Urban Education, 38*(4), 431–459. Retrieved from https://doi.org/10.1177%2F0042085903038004005

Papert, S. (1993). *Mindstorms, children, computers, and powerful ideas.* (2nd Ed.). New York, NY: Basic Books of Perseus Publishing.

Petrich, M., Wilkinson, K., & Beven, B. (2013). It looks like fun, but are they learning? In M. Honey & D. E. Kanter (Eds.) *Design, make, play: Growing the next generation of STEM innovators* (pp. 50–70). New York, NY: Routledge.

Piaget, J. (1976). *To understand is to invent: The future of education.* Kingsport, TN: Penguin Books.

Piaget, J. (1970). Piaget's theory. In P. H. Mussen (Ed.), *Carmichael's manual of child psychology, Volume 1* (pp. 703–732). New York, NY: John Wiley & Sons.

Resnick, M. (2017). *Lifelong kindergarten: Cultivating creativity through projects, passion, peers, and play.* Cambridge, MA: The MIT Press.

Robinson, K. with Aronica, L. (2013). *Finding your element: How to discover your talents and passions and transform your life.* New York, NY: Viking.

Root-Bernstein, R. (2018). STEM education should get "HACD:" Incorporating humanities, arts, crafts, and design into curricula makes better scientists. *Science, 361*(6397), 22–23. doi:10.1126/science.aat8566

Sachs, O. (2002). *Uncle Tungsten: Memories of a chemical boyhood.* New York, NY: Vintage.

Saturday Evening Post, (1929, October 26). Retrieved from https://quoteinvestigator.com/2013/01/01/einstein-imagination

Singer, D. G., Golinkoff, R. M., & Hirsh-Pasek, K. (Eds.). (2006). *Play = Learning: How play motivates and enhances children's cognitive and social-emotional growth.* New York, NY: Oxford University Press.

Swaby, R. (2016). *Trailblazers: 33 women in science who changed the world.* New York, NY: Delacorte Press.

Thackray, A., & Myers, M.Jr. (2000). *Arnold O. Beckman: One hundred years of excellence.* Philadelphia, PA: Chemical Heritage Foundation.

Tinker Lab (n.d.). *Why is tinkering important?* Retrieved from https://tinkerlab.com/why-is-tinkering-important/

Vygotsky, L. S. (1980) *Mind in Society: The development of higher psychological processes.* Cambridge, MA: Harvard University Press.

Wagner, T. (2012). *Great innovators: The making of young people who will change the world.* New York, NY: Scribner.

Wilkinson, K., & Petrich, M. (2014). *The art of tinkering: Meet 150+ makers working at the intersection of art, science, and technology.* San Francisco, CA: Weldon Owen. Exploratorium Book.

Wilson, F. R. (1998). *The hand.* New York, NY: Vintage Books.

Woodward, C. E. (1989). Art and elegance in the synthesis of organic compounds: Robert Burns Woodward. In D. B. Wallace & H. E. Gruber (Eds.), *Creative people at work: Twelve cognitive case studies* (pp. 227–253). New York, NY: Oxford University Press.

White, M., & Gribbin, J. (1994). *Einstein: A life in science.* New York, NY: Dutton.

PART III

STEM Beyond the Classroom

8

EARLY STEM EXPERIENCES IN MUSEUMS

Gina Navoa Svarovsky

Early STEM Experiences in Museums

While conversations about STEM education in the United States can often to be focused heavily on school-based environments, it has been estimated that average Americans spend roughly only 5% of their lives within classroom settings, and that the public actually develops much of its understanding of science outside of school (Falk & Dierking, 2010). From well-established organizations like 4-H and Girl Scouts, to afterschool robotics clubs and youth programming at community centers, to institutions like libraries and museums, to everyday contexts like the home and grocery store, opportunities for STEM learning abound in settings beyond the classroom. Broadly defined as environments where learning takes place outside of the formal schooling structure, *informal learning contexts* can often be the places where unexpected interests are initially sparked and then ultimately nurtured into lifelong passions over time (National Research Council, 2009). Consider, for example, the paleontologist who experienced the awe and wonder of finding a first trilobite fossil on a "Dino Dig" led by a park ranger on a Saturday morning. Or perhaps the first-generation engineer who spent much of her childhood designing, measuring, building, and optimizing carpentry projects around the house with her immigrant father. Certainly, these first encounters with the STEM disciplines can be transformative for young people and lead to sustained engagement, both within the professional and personal arenas (Maltese & Tai, 2010).

As designed spaces, museums can play an essential role in the informal learning landscape for STEM education. With an estimated 70 million annual visits to nearly 400 science centers and museums across the United States (Association of Science and Technology Centers, 2017), these institutions have the opportunity to introduce the public to the STEM disciplines and engage visitors in meaningful and memorable experiences that leave lasting impressions. With an emphasis on highly interactive exhibits, a broad range of ongoing programming, and unique opportunities to interface with scientists, engineers, and other STEM professionals through events like *Family STEM Saturdays* and initiatives like Citizen Science projects, science museums are positioned at the intersection of society and the STEM disciplines. Museums are seeking to inspire and educate their visitors though activities focused on inquiry, exploration, and, increasingly, design (Bevan, 2016; Falk & Dierking, 2010; Honey & Kanter, 2013; National Research Council, 2009; Sheridan et al., 2014).

Traditionally, science museums have tended to focus on the design and development of exhibits and programs for families with school-aged children, with museum professionals colloquially using the phrase "8 to 80" way of describing the target age range for a given project. Children's museums, however, have always had an intentional focus on early learners from birth to approximately age 10. Dating back to the opening of the Boston Children's Museum in 1913, and the Children's Museum of Indianapolis in 1925, the first children's museums provided opportunities for young learners to study and observe collections and artifacts from around the world (Schofield-Bodt, 1987). During the 1960s, there became more of an emphasis on interaction with exhibits, artifacts, and objects in children's museums, thus forming the roots of the play-based, exploratory, and open-ended nature found in most children's museums today (Munley, 2012). There has been rapid growth in the number of children's museums around the world, with approximately 38 children's museums in the United States in 1975, to over 450 children's museums in 20 countries around the world combining for an estimated 31 million annual visitors a year (Association of Children's Museums, 2016).

Particularly over the last decade, science museums have devoted more time and resources to designing STEM-based experiences for early learners, while children's museums have built upon the inherent curiosity and tendencies for exploration of young children and their families to form connections to STEM content and practice within their exhibits and programs. Recognizing the need and opportunity in providing the youngest learners with productive and fun early STEM experiences, leading institutions from both sectors began to collaborate more intentionally and extensively to take on this challenge. Pioneering projects such as the National Informal STEM Education Network, along with professional organizations such as the Association for Science and Technology Centers and the Association of Children's Museums, began to provide ways for professionals from science museums and children's museums to enter into ongoing conversations. They discussed what engaging young children and their families in the STEM disciplines might look like and how to continue to work together to build a new frontier of informal STEM education.

This chapter will begin by providing an overview of experiences that early learners can encounter in both science and children's museums, which will be followed by a description of a common framework for informal learning and the constraints and affordances it presents when applied to young children and the ways they most commonly engage in museum settings. The chapter will then conclude with a brief discussion, highlighting implications for research and practice aimed at better understanding and implementing early childhood STEM in museum contexts.

Modes of Engagement Within Museums

Museums are intentional, multi-modal learning environments that invite visitors to engage in a wide range of activities. Unlike formal learning settings like classrooms, museums are contexts where visitors can choose to engage—or not—with the broad spectrum of experiences set before them. Decisions in *free-choice* learning environments (Dierking & Falk, 2003; Falk, Storksdieck, & Dierking, 2007) tend to be socially negotiated across the visitor group (e.g., a family or a group of friends) and can be motivated by a range of agendas, including different interests, educational goals, or practical and logistical needs. For example, a group's decision to engage with or avoid a particular experience could be motivated by the relevance of an exhibit topic to daily life, a desire to introduce someone in the visiting group to a new phenomenon or concept, or the need to make it on time to the IMAX film. Museum professionals design experiences and activities with these conditions in mind, seeking to appeal to different motivations, provide multiple entry points into an experience and supports and prompts to deepen engagement should visitors wish to do so (Bevan, Gutwill, Petrich, & Wilkinson, 2015; Gutwill & Allen, 2010; Humphrey & Gutwill, 2016; Pattison & Dierking, 2013).

Within museums, the two most common activity structures are *exhibits* and *programs*. Museum exhibits are generally defined as permanent or semi-permanent fixtures on the museum floor, such as a climbing structure within a children's museum or the water wave tank at the science museum. Temporary or traveling exhibits, when rented or borrowed by a museum, are often installed for a given time period ranging from a few months to a few years. These exhibits can be extremely large, such as the 14,000 square foot *Bodyworlds* exhibits, or quite small, such as the 400 square foot *Nano* exhibition (Svarovsky et al., 2013). Exhibits can be facilitated by museum staff or volunteers, such as in the *Cell Lab* at the Science Museum of Minnesota, where visitors engage with a trained facilitator who guides them through how to take a cheek swab, extract DNA, and view it under a microscope (Randi Korn and Associates, 2003). However, in most cases, visitors interact directly with the exhibit components on their own.

Museum programs, on the other hand, almost always involve some type of facilitation by museum staff or volunteers. Programs vary greatly in duration and delivery format. They might include: (a) activities such as traditional demonstrations of phenomena, (b) "cart" based demonstrations or activities where facilitators move around an area to engage visitors, (c) theater programs that involve actors performing a STEM-themed play or extended demonstration, (d) longer presentations on STEM topics, (e) drop-in programs for teens and families, (f) science café events that might happen off-site within the local community and (g) weekend workshops and summer camps (Bequette, Svarovsky, & Ellenbogen, 2011). Storytime sessions are also extremely common programming within children's museums.

Finally, it should be noted that a third type of museum activity structure, known as *dedicated makerspaces*, has been rapidly gaining in popularity over the past decade. Coinciding with the rise of the Maker Movement (Halverson & Sheridan, 2014; Honey & Kanter, 2013), makerspaces are areas on the museum floor that allow visitors to engage in using real tools and real materials to create. The types of tools and materials within makerspaces vary greatly, as do the types of activities that are emphasized. For example, some makerspaces emphasize using everyday, often recycled, materials while others focus more on electronic, digital, and computational components. Dedicated makerspaces, such as the *Tinkering Studio* at the Exploratorium in San Francisco or the *Creativity Jam and Studio* at the Minnesota Children's Museum, typically house several plain worktables, benches, and a multitude of materials and kits at the ready to support making activities, ranging from superhero masks to giant cardboard structures to wearable electronics. These spaces are most commonly facilitated by museum staff or volunteers, and visitors frequently spend extended amounts of time exploring and creating within these environments (Bevan, 2016; Honey & Kanter, 2013; National Research Council, 2009; Sheridan et al., 2014).

Currently within both science museums and children's museums, a wide array of opportunities exist for young children and their families engage in and with STEM across these three activity structures. In the following section, descriptions of such learning experiences will be provided for each of the STEM disciplines.

STEM-Focused Museum Experiences for Early Learners

Before providing examples of the ways in which young children and their families can experience science, technology, engineering, and mathematics in museums, it is useful to articulate a few caveats. First, throughout this chapter, the use of the term STEM refers to the collection of the four disciplines/areas, and not an integrated conception of STEM, which is an emerging construct in K-12 science and engineering education (see, for example, Moore & Smith, 2014; Moore, Tank, Glancy, & Kersten, 2015). Second, for the sake of clarity, each of the disciplines will be presented below in order, with science first, and mathematics last. For a variety of reasons—such as the intersection of the science communication field with the informal learning field, synergistic projects across these two intellectual communities, and the federal funding landscape for both formal and informal science education—informal science learning has a much longer and deeper history within museums than any of the other STEM disciplines. Finally, the examples highlighted below speak to the several common types of STEM experiences that can be found in museums for young learners, but certainly there are a growing number of these types of learning opportunities available to children and their families, and, therefore, the following is not meant to be an exhaustive list.

Science

Certainly, the alignment between exploration of natural phenomena as an essential science process and a natural tendency for young children has fostered the creation of some of the most common exhibits where early learners can engage in the science practices of observation, experimentation, and analysis. Science exhibits for early learners invite children and their families to interact with materials, objects, and phenomena while maintaining a significant focus on play. For example, one staple of museum-based science experiences for children is the water activity area, which of course resonates with the use of water tables for engaging young children in science within the early childhood classroom (Worth & Grollman, 2013; see Figure 8.1).

Ranging from a set of simple water tables with an assortment of cups, floating objects, and sources of flowing water to expansive, custom-built, room-size installations with complex jets, eddy currents, and topography, children are joyfully captivated by observing what happens when they interact with the exhibit in different ways. Similar types of exploration also can be fostered on wind-focused exhibits. For example, the simple wind tube (a horizontal fan placed closely underneath the bottom of a tall column where visitors can insert lightweight objects that are pushed up and over the column) or the more complex tornado tower, which allows visitors to control airflow conditions that can create a visible and active wind vortex as seen in Figure 8.2.

FIGURE 8.1 Water Activity Area at the Newly Renovated Children's Museum of Cleveland.

FIGURE 8.2 Tornado Vortex Simulation Station at (a) the Science Museum of Minnesota and (b) the Exploratorium

Of course, science and natural history museums commonly provide access to another early childhood favorite: dinosaurs and fossils. Young children can be experts in naming and classifying dinosaurs (Chi & Koeske, 1983), and the conversations that parents and children can have within the shadow of a T-Rex exhibit can lead to family conversations about evidence, theories, and the nature of science (Palmquist & Crowley, 2007; Svarovsky & Ellenbogen, 2011).

While these institutions will always maintain their dinosaur collections, new experiences for young learners and their families have been recently developed through the collaborative efforts of projects like the National Informal STEM Education (NISE) Network (nisenet.org). Currently, the NISE Network has over 600 member institutions, with a core development team that spans across several museum sectors, including science museums, natural history museums, and children's museums. In 2008, the NISE Network team developed its first set of activities for *NanoDays*, a national week-long festival dedicated to introducing the public to concepts and technologies related to nanoscale science, commonly defined as the science of extremely small things. Nanoscale science, technology, and engineering are quite ubiquitous in the current consumer marketplace; common examples include nanoparticles that reflect UV light in sunscreen, silver nanoparticles in fabrics that make clothing bacteria and odor resistant, and silica nanoparticles that are used to strengthen golf clubs and fishing rods without adding additional weight. For several of the NISE Network's children's museum partners, NanoDays was the first attempt at moving beyond purely exploratory experiences such as the water activity area to including current science and present-day discoveries into their museum repertoire.

During the early years of NanoDays, activities for young learners were mostly in the "cart demonstration" category, where facilitators would engage families in an interactive demonstration typically drawing on different senses to make observations about phenomena (Bequette et al., 2011). As the programming and collaboration within the Network evolved between core institutions (i.e., the Museum of Science, the Science Museum of Minnesota, the Oregon Museum of Science and Industry, Sciencenter in Ithaca, New York, the Children's Museum of Houston) and several others, additional formats were included in the NanoDays activities. Including formats for young learners such as creating storybooks like Alice in NanoLand, a giant floor puzzle and memory game about nano, and cart demonstrations tailored for younger audiences that invited young children to ask questions and explore concepts related to nanoscience. Lastly, as mentioned briefly above, the NISE Network embarked on an ambitious exhibit development project, *Nano*, as seen in Figure 8.3. *Nano* involved creating and testing a small-footprint, modular exhibit about nanoscale science and technology and then replicating it 50 times for distribution to Network partners (Svarovsky et al., 2013).

Nano was intentionally designed for intergenerational learning and use, and included a "living room" area with a couch, a "Build a Carbon Nanotube" large-size building activity, and nano-themed storybooks for early learning audiences. The exhibit was so successful in both science museums and children's

FIGURE 8.3 Nano exhibition at The National Museum of Nuclear Science and History in Albuquerque, New Mexico

museums that the Network ultimately created over 90 copies, the majority of which are still currently on display.

Technology

While science and exploration experiences for young learners and their families have become quite common, technology-focused opportunities continue to be somewhat sparse. It is also important to note that much like the formal education context, the field of informal learning continues to grapple with the many definitions of technology, as well as what it means to engage in and with it. Unlike science, engineering, and mathematics, technology in and of itself is not a defined discipline, but rather, a broader category that simultaneously attempts to encompass both the products of disciplines (e.g., technologies that are produced by engineering) as well as elements of specific disciplines themselves (e.g., coding and computer science). This ambiguity around the accepted and operational definitions of technology can translate into unclear goals and planning around learning experiences, particularly in informal education settings.

Despite this challenge, there are a growing number of museum experiences being created where young children and their families can engage in activities focused on specific aspects of technology. Two examples include the *Science of Pixar*, which was a large traveling exhibit originally developed by the Museum of Science in Boston, and the parent and child ScratchJr classes at the Boston Children's Museum. In the *Science of Pixar*, exhibit developers sought to introduce visitors to the science, math, and computer science practices involved in creating the blockbuster animated movies within the Pixar portfolio (Cahill, Mesiti, Paneto, Pfeifle, & Todd, 2018). Within the exhibit, there were both screen-based and physical material-based interactives, large immersive set pieces from different

Pixar films, a wide variety of videos, and opportunities for facilitated activities with museum staff or volunteers. While the target audience for this exhibit was 8 years and older, many families with young children frequently engage with the exhibit, with families reporting high levels of interest and enjoyment after the experience (Cahill et al., 2018).

At the Einstein's Workshop within the Boston Children's Museum, families can sign up for parent-child classes and work together to explore the ScratchJr interface (Flannery et al., 2013; Portelance, Strawhacker, & Bers, 2016; Strawhacker, Lee, Caine, & Bers, 2015) and experiment with the basics of block-based coding and computation. Other children's museums, such as the Children's Creativity Museum in San Francisco, California, and the Seattle Children's Museum in Seattle, Washington, offer coding-focused camps for children. Finally, the Children's Museum of Houston has recently opened a new exhibit, *Coding Hangout*, where young children and their families can interact with exhibits that engage visitors in core facets of computational thinking, including algorithmic thinking and decomposition. Clearly, these examples of technology experiences for young learners in museums suggest that this is an area that will continue to evolve quickly, which will also catalyze further discussion about more refined and clear definitions around technology for the field.

Engineering

Engaging young children in design-based engineering activities within museums has been a topic of increasing study since the late 2000s, with the first curriculum for preschool engineering—Wee Engineer, developed by the Engineering is Elementary team housed at the Museum of Science in Boston— just launched in 2018 (Major, 2018). In museums, engineering for early learners is becoming more common as makerspaces are incorporated into floor plans and visitors are invited to design and create with the wide range of tools and materials on hand. Within these experiences, museum professionals place an emphasis on the engineering practices of iterative design process, brainstorming and creativity, developing tool fluency, and taking exploratory design risks (Honey & Kanter, 2013; Wardrip & Brahms, 2015). Two of the first makerspaces that engaged young learners are the MAKESHOP in the Children's Museum of Pittsburgh in Pittsburgh, Pennsylvania, and the Design Lab and Makerspace in the New York Hall of Science in Queens, New York.

The MAKESHOP's targeted audience was built for early learners and their families. Visitors are encouraged to enter the space, take up an activity, and stay as long or as little as they like. Young children can build with a specialized construction kit, including boards, nuts, bolts, and hinges that can be easily placed and moved to create large structures. There are also other stations suited for early learners where they can engage in material exploration, including a magnetic marble run, an area with plexi-glass pegs that reflect and refract light, and different gear-related activities as seen in Figure 8.4. In addition, there are several stations that invite visitor groups with slightly older children to engage in creative activities like woodworking, circuitry, fiber arts such as sewing and weaving, and stop motion animation (Sheridan et al., 2014).

The expansive Design Lab in the New York Hall of Science (NYSCI) has five distinct areas that focus on different types of making and problem solving. Although designed for ages 8 and up, younger children can also engage in many of the creative activities, including building objects to cast interesting shadows, building with long connectors and dowels, and exploring circuits with specific circuit blocks and wires with alligator clips on either end. In addition, NYSCI has a Makerspace program which features workshops and events for younger learners and their families that take place in the Design Lab (Honey & Kanter, 2013).

Certainly, having a large, dedicated space on the museum floor for a drop-in Makerspace requires a high level of investment from a given institution. For many museums, such a space is simply not possible or practical to achieve; as such, museums have also begun to develop maker-style programming that can be cart-based or station-based and deployed flexibly, much like the NanoDays model described above. Examples of this type of programming are the *Play, Tinker, Make, Engineer* (PTME) events at the Science Museum of Minnesota (Causey & Braflaadt, 2016).

Every Saturday, PTME facilitators (consisting of museum staff and a specifically trained volunteer corps) set up 8–12 stations across the three floors of the museum, including activities tailored for young learners such as building large structures with plastic baskets, designing and playing a giant pinball game, and creating custom cookie cutters with metal and tools, as seen in Figure 8.5. Young children and their families spend extended periods of time at these stations engaging in a range of design practices and iteratively refining and optimizing their work (Svarovsky, 2014).

FIGURE 8.4 Gear Table at the MAKESHOP

FIGURE 8.5 Play, Tinker, Make, Engineer Station for Do It Yourself Cookie Cutters at the Science Museum of Minnesota

Mathematics

As perhaps the most abstract of the STEM disciplines, mathematics activities in museums can sometimes require more extensive design, development, and prototyping than other museum experiences before being launched (Dancu, Gutwill, & Hido, 2011; Dancu, Gutwill, & Sindorf, 2009; Selinda Research Associates, 2012). Museum professionals who design mathematics-focused activities are not only attending to the constraints and affordances of free-choice learning environments, but also common public perceptions and attitudes towards mathematics that tend to influence engagement—particularly for the parents within family groups, who have already formed their math identities and dispositions.

Much like science-focused experiences, exhibits and programs for young learners that focus on mathematics once again seek to encourage exploration and imagination, while simultaneously introducing early math concepts like numbers and operations, geometries and shapes, and patterns. Within children's museums, it is common to see light tables with Magnatiles—flat, plastic shapes with magnetic edges that attach to each other to form 3-D structures—for children and families to experiment with geometry and shapes. Another frequently seen activity is a shadow table, where a light is placed horizontally to project onto a screen, and items that can be moved closer or further from the light source to cast shadows of different sizes. Experimenting with these shadows can lead both to storytelling as well as interesting discussions about ratios, measurement, and lengths (Selinda Research Associates, 2016).

Two examples of exhibits focused on mathematics include the *Secrets of Circles* at the Children's Discovery Museum of San Jose, and *Geometry Playground*, a traveling exhibit developed by the Exploratorium. The Secrets of Circles exhibit was designed for children ages 3–10 and their families. The primary goals of the exhibit were to provide an engaging experience for visitors, introduce visitors to mathematical concepts about circles through interactive exhibits, and help visitors make connections between circles, science, and the world around them (Allen, 2007). The exhibit was also designed to be inviting particularly to families of Mexican and Vietnamese descent, two traditionally underrepresented populations in the local area that the museum was aspiring to engage. Children identified the Gears exhibit, the Build an Arch exhibit, and the Inventing the Wheel exhibit as their favorites, and demonstrated increases in confidence and fluency when describing geometric properties of circles and where circles could be found in everyday life (Allen, 2007).

Geometry Playground is an innovative exhibit built primarily for science museums that leverages multiple features commonly found in children's museums, including climbing structures, large puzzles, and building activities. The goals of the exhibit, designed for children ages 5–12 and their families, were to engage visitors and their families in full-body exploration of geometry and volume.

Summative evaluation findings indicate that visitors were able to increase the sophistication of their engagement and understanding about spatial reasoning, aesthetic aspects of geometry, and connections between geometry and daily life (Selinda Research Associates, 2012).

Characterizing Learning in Museums

The examples provide one snapshot of the constellation of STEM activities and experiences for early learners and their families in museums. Without doubt, these opportunities for learning are engaging for young children, as indicated by visitor observations, evaluation studies, and analysis of repeat visitation by museum professionals. However, the informal STEM learning field is in the nascent stages of developing research studies, measures, and theories exploring how engaging in these exhibits, programs, and makerspaces can help young children learn and develop.

Fortunately, there does exist a large body of literature focused on investigating science learning in museums, based on nearly three decades of research. In 2009, the National Research Council conducted an extensive review of the extant research on informal science learning available at the time, which resulted in a framework of six strands of informal science learning (National Research Council, 2009):

- *Strand 1: Developing interest in science.* A powerful construct in informal learning contexts, museums have been shown to support the development of excitement, awe, wonder, and interest in science.
- *Strand 2: Understanding science knowledge.* Museums have demonstrated the ability to engage visitors in learning science content, particularly high level content knowledge about specific topics.

- *Strand 3: Engaging in scientific reasoning.* Studies of visitors interacting with exhibits have shown that some museum experiences can prompt visitors to engage in deep questioning, explaining, and making sense of the world around them.
- *Strand 4: Reflecting on science.* While meaningful reflection by visitors interacting with stand-alone exhibit experiences is less common, there is ample evidence that briefly facilitated experiences can be successful in engaging visitors in thinking and reflecting on the activities encountered on the museum floor.
- *Strand 5: Engaging in scientific practice.* Museum-based experiences have demonstrated the ability to engage visitors in a range of scientific practices, particularly around the social practices of working together to explore and explain phenomena.
- *Strand 6: Identifying with the scientific enterprise.* Visitors often demonstrate different ways of finding relevance in science topics they encounter at museums, and engaging in authentic science practices can help visitors better understand and connect to the identity of someone who does science.

While these six strands have provided a useful framework for multiple large-scale studies of informal science learning (e.g., Svarovsky et al., 2013; Svarovsky, Tranby, Cardiel, Auster, & Bequette, 2014), there are at least three significant challenges to applying these six strands to examining STEM learning for young children in museums. First, the *singular disciplinary focus* on science can limit the applicability of the framework to experiences that focus on technology, engineering, and mathematics, not to mention integrated STEM experiences that combine the disciplines. Second, the description of these strands tends to reflect the traditional view that informal science learning is intended for members of the public who are approximately 8 years and older. Certainly, questions abound about how these strands would be adapted to be more *developmentally appropriate* for early learners, particularly given the extensive literature on early math and school readiness for young children, and the emerging research on early computational thinking (Flannery et al., 2013; Portelance et al., 2016; Strawhacker et al., 2015) and early engineering (Bagiati & Evangelou, 2016; Bairaktarova, Evangelou, Bagiati, & Brophy, 2011; Dorie, Cardella, & Svarovsky, 2014, 2015; Svarovsky & Cardella, 2013).

Finally, these six strands tend to *focus on the individual* as the unit of analysis: an individual can develop interest; an individual can develop fluency and familiarity with science content and practices; an individual can develop science identity. However, for young children in particular, attending to the engagement and learning of the entire family system—and measuring development for children, adults, and the family overall, with the family as the unit of analysis—can both provide better information about the learning and development that is happening through the types of activities and experiences described above. Indeed, while the

NRC framework has been fundamental to advancing the field of informal science learning overall, extending and expanding the six strands in order to address these limitations would make it more applicable and useful for examining early childhood learning around STEM in museums.

Few studies to date have measured STEM interest and learning outcomes for informal learning experiences at the family level of analysis, it should be noted that there has been a steady focus on family learning in science museums and how it influences an *individual* child's levels of interest and engagement, particularly through studies of parent-child interactions at exhibits, programs, and makerspaces (Crowley & Jacobs, 2002; Luce, Martin, & Callanan, 2015; Povis & Crowley, 2015; Rigney & Callanan, 2011; Tenenbaum, Prior, Dowling, & Frost, 2010). However, once again, the vast majority of these studies takes place within science-based informal learning activities, such as marine exhibits (Zimmerman, Reeve, & Bell, 2010) and dinosaur exhibits (Palmquist & Crowley, 2007). Only a small number of these studies are conducted in design-based informal learning settings, where elements of engineering design are incorporated (Wardrip & Brahms, 2015). Considering the documented role that parents play in occupational choice for underrepresented groups in engineering (Mannon & Schreuders, 2007; Matusovich, Streveler, & Miller, 2010), a better understanding of how parents can support children engaging in informal early engineering learning—as well as how parents' own engineering self-efficacy and identities can impact those interactions—is needed. In the following section, two studies, each focused on this intersection of parents, children, informal learning, and engineering, are described.

Families with Young Children Engaging in Engineering Learning

Study 1

The goal of the Gender Research on Adult-child Discussions within Informal ENgineering environmenTs (GRADIENT) project is to explore the development of early engineering interest and understanding for girls by closely examining parent-child conversations within museum-based informal engineering learning settings. One portion of the Institutional Review Board-approved study focuses on a museum-based drop-in program at a large Midwestern science center, where parents and young girls between the ages of 3–5 play with engineering-focused toys and engage in different aspects of the engineering design process (Dorie et al., 2014, 2015; Svarovsky & Cardella, 2013; Svarovsky, Cardella, Dorie, & King, 2017). The study investigates how the structure of the activities and the conversations between parents and children during these experiences can support or inhibit the participation of young girls in elements of the engineering design process.

Video observations of family groups were recorded at two different engineering challenges: (a) one that asked families to design a tower out of large foam blocks that was as tall as a large plant in the room, and (b) the other asked families to design a tower as tall as they could make it using Dado Squares. Dado Squares are firm plastic squares with notches on each edge for connecting to each other. Families were invited to engage with each challenge as long or as little as they liked. The two challenges were selected to capture variation in activity based on familiarity with the building materials; the children are typically familiar with the foam blocks, but not familiar with the Dado Squares.

In one portion of the analysis conducted on these videos (n=34), researchers examined the number and length of design iterations that family groups engaged in during both activities (Cardella, Svarovsky, Dorie, Tranby, & Van Cleave, 2013). An iteration was defined as beginning when either the child starts collaborating with the adult (series of joint activities/conversation happening close together in time), and purposefully places one block on the ground or puts two blocks together. An iteration ends under three different conditions: 1) when the children say they are finished, 2) when they leave the activity space, or 3) when 50% or more of the structure is removed. Children do not need to be touching blocks actively to be "building." Two researchers independently timed the versions and then compared their results until they reached a consensus.

This analysis focused on the practice of iteration due to its essential role in the engineering design process. Gaining an initial understanding of how much and how long families engaged in multiple iterations—within a free-choice learning environment like an activity station at a museum, which is very different than formal engineering learning environments where iteration is commonly more of a mandated endeavor—can inform museum professionals who are designing informal engineering experiences in the future.

Findings from the analysis suggest that even in a free-choice environment, family groups frequently engaged in multiple iterations of these activities. A total of 112 big foam block tower iterations (34 first iterations and 76 total subsequent iterations) was observed, with an average time of 2:15 for the first iteration, and 1:34 for the subsequent iteration(s). On average, a family group undertook three separate iterations, with a maximum of seven. For the Dado Squares activity, there were a total of 79 iterations (33 first iterations, as one group did not finish both tasks, and 44 total subsequent iterations) with an average time of 2:36 for the first iteration and 2:31 for subsequent iterations. The number of iterations per family group ranged from 1 to 14 with an average of 2 iterations.

These data indicate that once families get past an initial iteration, subsequent iterations tend to be shorter. This may suggest that families spend less time thinking through design decisions after the first iteration, which may function as a more exploratory iteration. In addition, adults tended to initiate iterations more frequently than children during the foam blocks activity, while initiating equally during Dado Squares activity, suggesting that perhaps the activity structure or materials may play a specific role during family learning about engineering.

Study 2: Head Start on Engineering

Head Start on Engineering (HSE) is a collaborative, National Science Foundation-funded research and practice project designed to develop and refine a theoretical model of early childhood, engineering-related interest development (Pattison et al., 2016; Pattison et al., 2018; Svarovsky, Pattison, Verbeke, Benne, & Corrie, 2017). The project focuses on Head Start families with 4-year-old children from low-income communities and is being carried out collaboratively by researchers, science center educators, and a regional Head Start program. The ultimate goal of the HSE initiative is to advance the understanding of and capacity to support early engineering interest development for young learners, especially for children from low-income families and traditionally underserved communities. Building on prior work that examined the conversations of parents and young children engaged in engineering design (Dorie, Carella, & Svarovsky, 2014; 2015), the beginning stages of HSE explore the perceptions, interactions, and interest development of young children and their parents while engaged in activities that incorporate elements of the engineering design process.

For the first two years of the project, the HSE team worked with teachers at one Head Start location to plan, gather input from families, and test new programs and activities. This early work was part of an IRB-approved front-end evaluation study (Svarovsky et al., 2017), which will be further described below. Approximately four months after the launch of the project, the HSE team offered two full-day professional development workshops for staff, during which teachers learned about engineering, explored examples of engineering and design in their own lives, tested new activities for families and young children, and provided input on future programs. Two months later, a group of Head Start families was recruited to participate in five months of program and research activities, including parent nights, home visits, take-home activity kits, and a field trip to the local science center.

For the portion front-end evaluation study described here, the primary data collection method was paper surveys administered to 79 Head Start parents. The surveys were developed in both Spanish and English in collaboration with Head Start staff members. The final parent survey included both closed- and open-ended questions and asked respondents to share information about their interests and their children's interests related to engineering, their associations with the words "engineer" and "engineering," their perceived importance of young children learning about engineering, and other questions related to the logistics of participating in the program. Analysis of responses included descriptive summaries of the close-ended questions and content analysis of open-ended responses to identify the most common response categories. Initial findings were shared with the project team and Head Start staff members from the primary implementation site so that the group could discuss and interpret the results collaboratively.

Findings from the front-end evaluation survey analysis suggest that interest and value for engineering were high for parents. When asked to rate how important they felt it was for their children to learn about engineering, 50% of the Head Start parents responded that it was "very important," 42% marked "important," and 8% marked "in the middle." Similarly, when asked how interested they would be in participating in the program, 60% indicated "very interested," and 30% responded "interested." Surprisingly, parents indicated a reasonable level of comfort talking about engineering with their children or doing engineering activities as a family. A total of 41% of adults said they were "very comfortable," and 43% responded that they were "comfortable."

Despite their excitement and interest, parents who responded to the survey indicated a somewhat narrow perception of engineering. Table 8.1 highlights the most common coded response categories for the frequency of responses within each category; responses could also be coded for multiple categories. Building and structures were by far the most common type of responses for parents (83%), followed by careers (46%), and planning and problem solving (34%).

These data were helpful to the HSE team as they developed the other activities and experiences that are part of the project, including the field trip to the local science center which had multiple engineering-themed exhibits, but targeted older children. By understanding parent levels of interest and parent perceptions of engineering, the project team decided to emphasize the ways in which engineering thinking could be embedded in everyday experiences, such as designing a custom shelving solution for a tight closet or creating a complex process for getting everyone out the door and to school and work every morning. This led to parents feeling much more comfortable and empowered around engineering as a topic, which could lead to deeper conversations and interactions with their young learners during engineering activities, both at home and at the museum.

TABLE 8.1 Frequency of Most Common Associations With the Terms "Engineer" and "Engineering"

Categories	Parents (n=79)	Example
Building, structures	83%	Construction sites, buildings
Planning, problem solving	34%	People who solve a problem with the help of technical knowledge
Careers	46%	Good Career, good money
Math	7%	Math and spatial awareness
Engineering-related values	0%	I think that more women are going into the field and I'm really glad about that

Adapted from Svarovsky et al. (2017)

Note. Responses could be coded within multiple categories.

Discussion and Implications

Museums offer a wide range of STEM experiences for early learners and their families. While open-ended and visitor agenda driven nature of free-choice learning environments can pose an array of challenges for museum professionals designing exhibits, programs, and makerspaces, these experiences can leave a lasting and lifelong impact on young children and their families. The experiences at times can catalyze the development of deep interest and commitment to a particular topic that can influence future schooling and career choices. Museums and other informal learning contexts can be a valuable and a non-trivial part of a family's learning ecosystem (Barron, 2006; Bevan, 2016), and, as such, can play an important role within the early STEM education landscape.

In terms of implications for practice, it seems that the early childhood education community, the child development and family studies communities, and the informal STEM education community would benefit greatly from increased conversation and collaboration. Of particular value would be research to practice partnerships (Bevan et al., 2015), which allow both scholars and practitioners to immerse themselves deeply in the application and generation of theory and effective informal learning education practices. It is also imperative to note that while the museum experiences described in this chapter are squarely positioned at the intersection of these fields, several other genres of informal learning also span these boundaries. Examples include: *The Brains On!*, a science podcast for kids and Citizen Science projects that engage families in authentic scientific data collection. There are apps such as *PBS Kids-ScratchJr* and *Early Math with Gracie and Friends* (Vahey, Reider, Orr, Presser, & Dominguez, 2018), as well as television shows such as *Peg+Cat* (McCarthy, Li, Tiu, Atienza, & Sexton, 2015) and *Splash and Bubbles*. Noteworthy, are the growing number of makerspaces and maker programming in public libraries (Halverson & Sheridan, 2014; Sheridan et al., 2014).

As interest in early STEM experiences continues to rise, museums and informal educators will look to develop robust ways to understand the family learning system as it relates to the STEM disciplines and young children. As such, it is essential for policymakers and educators to recognize and support not only early STEM initiatives in different educational sectors, but also meaningful research studies that look closely at the nature of the learning and interest development that takes place across these environments. Without doubt, there are powerful connections between the classroom, the home, the museum, and other informal learning experiences, which hold nearly limitless potential for meaningful STEM learning across and within these contexts. A potential that can quickly and effectively be realized with increased coordination and collaboration.

Acknowledgments

The author would like to express sincere thanks to Monica Cardella, Brianna Dorie, Zdanna King, Marjorie Bequette, Kirsten Ellenbogen, and the Science Museum of Minnesota Department of Evaluation and Research in Learning for their support and collaboration on the GRADIENT study; Scott Pattison, Marcie Benne, Pam Greenough Corrie, Veronika Nuñez, Cynthia Smith, and the OMSI and Mt. Hood Community College Head Start team for their support and collaboration on Head Start on Engineering; Christine Cunningham at Engineering is Elementary; and Elizabeth Kunz Kollmann at the Museum of Science and the entire NISE Network Evaluation and Research team. The author also wishes to thank the editors of this volume for their helpful suggestions and feedback. This material is based on work supported by the National Science Foundation under grant numbers 0532536, 0940143, 1136253, and 1515628. Any opinions, findings, and conclusions or recommendations expressed in this material are those of the author and do not necessarily reflect the views of the National Science Foundation.

References

Allen, S. (2007). *Secrets of Circles summative evaluation report*. San Jose, CA: Children's Discovery Museum.

Association of Children's Museums. (2016). *Association of Children's Museums Annual Report*. Retrieved from https://www.childrensmuseums.org/images/2016-ACM-Annual-Report.pdf

Association of Science and Technology Centers. (2017). *ASTC Science Center Statistics*. Retrieved from http://www.astc.org/wp-content/uploads/2017/09/ASTC_SCStats-2016.pdf

Bagiati, A., & Evangelou, D. (2016). Practicing engineering while building with blocks: Identifying engineering thinking. *European Early Childhood Education Research Journal*, *24*(1), 67–85. doi:10.1080/1350293X.2015.1120521

Bairaktarova, D., Evangelou, D., Bagiati, A., & Brophy, S. (2011). Early engineering in young children's exploratory play with tangible materials. *Children Youth and Environments*, *21*(2), 212–235.

Barron, B. (2006). Interest and self-sustained learning as catalysts of development: A Learning ecology perspective. *Human Development*, *49*(4), 193–224.

Bequette, M., Svarovsky, G., & Ellenbogen, K. (2011). *Year 5 Summative Evaluation of Exhibits and Programs*. St. Paul, MN: Science Museum of MN. Retrieved from http://www.nisenet.org/catalog/evaluation/year5exhibitsandprograms

Bevan, B. (2016, February 29). STEM learning ecologies. Relevant, responsive, and connected to practice. *Connected Science Learning*, 1. Arlington, VA: National Science Teachers Association. Retrieved from http://csl.nsta.org/2016/03/stem-learning-ecologies/

Bevan, B., Gutwill, J. P., Petrich, M., & Wilkinson, K. (2015). Learning through STEM-rich tinkering: Findings from a jointly negotiated research project taken up in practice. *Science Education*, *99*(1), 98–120. https://doi.org/10.1002/sce.21151

Cahill, C., Mesiti, L. A., Paneto, S. C., Pfeifle, S., & Todd, K. (2018). *The science behind Pixar: Summative evaluation report.* Boston, MA: Museum of Science.

Cardella, M. E., Svarovsky, G. N., Dorie, B. L., Tranby, Z., & Van Cleave, S. (2013). Gender research on adult-child discussions within informal engineering environments (GRADIENT): Early findings. In *Proceedings from the 120th American Society for Engineering Education Annual Conference & Exposition.*

Causey, L., & Braflaadt, K. (2016). *Play tinker make: An exploration of communities and making.* St. Paul, MN: Science Museum of Minnesota. Retrieved from https://padlet.com/keithbraafladt/makingconnections

Chi, M. T., & Koeske, R. D. (1983). Network representation of a child's dinosaur knowledge. *Developmental Psychology, 19*(1), 29–39.

Crowley, K., & Jacobs, M. (2002). Building islands of expertise in everyday family activity. In G. Leinhardt & K. Crowley (Eds.), *Learning conversations in museums.* Mahwah, NJ: Lawrence Erlbaum Associates.

Dancu, T., Gutwill, J. P., & Hido, N. (2011). Using iterative design and evaluation to develop playful learning experiences. *Children Youth and Environments, 21*(2), 338–359.

Dancu, T., Gutwill, J. P., & Sindorf, L. (2009). *Geometry Playground Pathways Study. The Executive Summary.* San Francisco, CA: Exploratorium.

Dierking, L. D., & Falk, J. H. (2003). Optimizing out-of-school time: The role of free-choice learning. *New Directions for Youth Development, 97*, 75–88. https://dx.doi.org/10.1002/yd.36

Dorie, B., Cardella, M. E., & Svarovsky, G. N. (2014). *Capturing the design behaviors of a young children working with a parent.* Paper presented at the 121st American Society of Engineering Education Annual Conference & Exposition, Indianapolis, IN.

Dorie, B., Cardella, M. E., & Svarovsky, G. N. (2015). *Engineering together: Context in dyadic talk during an engineering task.* Paper presented at the 122nd ASEE Annual Conference and Exposition, Seattle, WA. Retrieved from https://www.asee.org/public/conferences/56/papers/12602/view

Falk, J. H., & Dierking, L. D. (2010). The 95 percent solution. *American Scientist, 98*(6), 486–493.

Falk, J. H., Storksdieck, M., & Dierking, L. D. (2007). Investigating public science interest and understanding: Evidence for the importance of free-choice learning. *Public Understanding of Science, 16*(4), 455–469.

Flannery, L. P., Silverman, B., Kazakoff, E. R., Bers, M. U., Bontá, P., & Resnick, M. (2013). Designing ScratchJr: Support for early childhood learning through computer programming. In *Proceedings of the 12th International Conference on Interaction Design and Children* (pp. 1–10). New York, NY. https://doi.org/10.1145/2485760.2485785

Gutwill, J. P., & Allen, S. (2010). Facilitating family group inquiry at science museum exhibits. *Science Education, 94*(4), 710–742.

Halverson, E. R., & Sheridan, K. (2014). The maker movement in education. *Harvard Educational Review, 84*(4), 495–504. https://doi.org/10.17763/haer.84.4.34j1g68140382063

Honey, M., & Kanter, D. E. (2013). *Design, make, play: Growing the next generation of STEM innovators.* New York, NY: Routledge.

Humphrey, T., & Gutwill, J. P. (2016). *Fostering active prolonged engagement: The art of creating APE exhibits.* New York, NY: Routledge.

Luce, M., Martin, J., & Callanan, M. (2015). Two decades of families learning in a children's museum: A partnership of research and exhibit development. In D. M.

Sobel & J. L. Jipson (Eds.), *Cognitive Development in Museum Settings* (pp. 27–47). New York, NY: Routledge.

Major, A. (2018, August 3). *What Does Engineering Look Like in Early Childhood?* Retrieved September 10, 2018 from http://blog.eie.org/what-does-engineering-look-like-in-early-childhood

Maltese, A. V., & Tai, R. H. (2010). Eyeballs in the fridge: Sources of early interest in science. *International Journal of Science Education, 32*(5), 669–685. https://doi-org.proxy.library.nd.edu/10.1080/09500690902792385

Mannon, S. E., & Schreuders, P. D. (2007). All in the (engineering) family?—The family occupational background of men and women engineering students. *Journal of Women and Minorities in Science and Engineering, 13*(4). doi:10.1615/JWomenMinorScienEng.v13.i4.20

Matusovich, H. M., Streveler, R. A., & Miller, R. L. (2010). Why do students choose engineering? A qualitative, longitudinal investigation of students' motivational values. *Journal of Engineering Education, 99*(4), 289–303. http://dx.doi.org/ 10.1002/j.2168–9830.2010.tb01064.x

McCarthy, B., Li, L., Tiu, M., Atienza, S., & Sexton, U. (2015). *Learning with PBS Kids: A study of family engagement and early mathematics achievement.* San Francisco, CA: WestEd. Retrieved from http://www-tc.pbskids.org/lab/media/pdfs/research/Y4-WestEd-Learning_with_PBS_KIDS_FullReport_20151104C.pdf

Moore, T. J., & Smith, K. A. (2014). Advancing the state of the art of STEM integration. *Journal of STEM Education: Innovations and Research, 15*(1), 5–10.

Moore, T. J., Tank, K. M., Glancy, A. W., & Kersten, J. A. (2015). NGSS and the landscape of engineering in K-12 state science standards. *Journal of Research in Science Teaching, 52*(3), 296–318. https://doi.org/10.1002/tea.21199

Munley, M. E. (2012). *Early learning in museums: A review of literature.* Washington, DC: Smithsonian Early Enrichment Center.

National Research Council. (2009). *Learning science in informal environments: People, places, and pursuits.* Washington, DC: National Academies Press.

Palmquist, S., & Crowley, K. (2007). From teachers to testers: How parents talk to novice and expert children in a natural history museum. *Science Education, 91*(5), 783–804.

Pattison, S. A., & Dierking, L. D. (2013). Staff-Mediated learning in museums: A Social interaction perspective. *Visitor Studies, 16*(2), 117–143. https://doi.org/10.1080/10645578.2013.767731

Pattison, S. A., Svarovsky, G. N., Corrie, P., Benne, M., Nuñez, V., Dierking, L. D., & Verbeke, M. (2016). *Conceptualizing early childhood STEM interest development as a distributed system: A preliminary framework.* Paper presented at the National Association for Research in Science Teaching Annual Conference, Baltimore, MD. Retrieved from http://www.informalscience.org/conceptualizing-early-childhood-stem-interestdevelopment-distributed-system-preliminary-framework

Pattison, S., Weiss, S., Ramos-Montañez, S., Gontan, I., Svarovsky, G., Corrie, P. G., … Smith, C. (2018). *Engineering in early childhood: Describing family-level interest systems.* Paper presented at the National Association for Research in Science Teaching Annual Conference, Atlanta, GA.

Portelance, D. J., Strawhacker, A. L., & Bers, M. U. (2016). Constructing the ScratchJr programming language in the early childhood classroom. *International Journal of Technology and Design Education, 26*(4), 489–504. doi:10.1007/s10798–10015–9325–0

Povis, K. T., & Crowley, K. (2015). Family learning in object-based museums: The role of joint attention. *Visitor Studies*, *18*(2), 168–182. https://dx.doi.org/10.1080/10645578. 2015.1079095

Randi Korn and Associates. (2003). *Cell lab summative evaluation.* St. Paul, MN: Science Museum of Minnesota.

Rigney, J. C., & Callanan, M. A. (2011). Patterns in parent–child conversations about animals at a marine science center. *Cognitive Development*, *26*(2), 155–171. https://doi. org/10.1016/j.cogdev.2010.12.002

Schofield-Bodt, C. (1987). A history of children's museums in the United States. *Children's Environments Quarterly*, *4*(1), 4–6.

Selinda Research Associates. (2012). *Summative evaluation of Geometry Playground.* San Francisco, CA: Exploratorium.

Selinda Research Associates. (2016). *A longitudnal summative evaluation of visitor experiences in four Math Moves! exhibitions.* St. Paul, MN: Science Museum of Minnesota.

Sheridan, K., Halverson, E. R., Litts, B., Brahms, L., Jacobs-Priebe, L., & Owens, T. (2014). Learning in the making: A comparative case study of three makerspaces. *Harvard Educational Review*, *84*(4), 505–531.

Strawhacker, A., Lee, M., Caine, C., & Bers, M. (2015). ScratchJr Demo: A coding language for kindergarten. In *Proceedings of the 14th International Conference on Interaction Design and Children* (pp. 414–417). New York, NY: ACM.

Svarovsky, G. N. (2014). Engineering learning in museums: Current trends and future directions. In S. Purzer, J. Strobel, & M. E. Cardella (Eds.). *Engineering in pre-college settings: Synthesizing research, policy, and practices* (pp. 363–382). West Lafayette, IN: Purdue University Press.

Svarovsky, G. N., & Cardella, M. E. (2013). *Gender research on adult-child discussions within informal engineering environments (GRADIENT): Early findings from preschool playdates.* Presented at the Annual meeting of the American Educational Research Association, San Francisco, CA.

Svarovsky, G. N., Cardella, M. E., Dorie, B., & King, Z. (2017). *Productive forms of facilitation for young girls during engineering activities within informal learning settings.* Paper presented at the Annual Meeting of the American Educational Research Association, San Antonio, TX.

Svarovsky, G. N., & Ellenbogen, K. (2011). *Family conversations and the nature of science: Project summary.* St. Paul, MN: Science Museum of Minnesota.

Svarovsky, G., Goss, J., Ostgaard, G., Reyes, N., Cahill, C., Auster, R., & Bequette, M. (2013). *Summative study of the Nano mini-exhibition.* St. Paul, MN: Science Museum of Minnesota.

Svarovsky, G. N., Pattison, S. A., Verbeke, M., Benne, M., & Corrie, P. G. (2017). *Head Start on Engineering: Early Findings (Work in Progress).* Presented at the ASEE Annual Conference & Exposition, Columbus, OH.

Svarovsky, G., Tranby, Z., Cardiel, C., Auster, R., & Bequette, M. (2014). *Summative study of the NanoDays 2014 events.* St. Paul, MN: Science Museum of Minnesota.

Tenenbaum, H. R., Prior, J., Dowling, C. L., & Frost, R. E. (2010). Supporting parent-child conversations in a history museum. *British Journal of Educational Psychology*, *80*(2), 241–254.

Vahey, P. J., Reider, D., Orr, J., Presser, A. L., & Dominguez, X. (2018). The evidence based curriculum design framework: Leveraging diverse perspectives in the design process. *International Journal of Designs for Learning*, *9*(1), 135–148. https://doi.org/10.14434/ijdl.v9i1.23080

Wardrip, P. S., & Brahms, L. (2015). *Learning practices of making: Developing a framework for design*. In *Proceedings of the 14th international conference on interaction design and children* (pp. 375–378). New York, NY: ACM.

Worth, K., & Grollman, S. (2013). Science in the early childhood classroom. In S.W. Gilford (Ed.), *Learning from Head Start: A teacher's guide to school readiness* (p. 117–130). Lanham, MD: Rowman & Littlefield Education.

Zimmerman, H. T., Reeve, S., & Bell, P. (2010). Family sense-making practices in science center conversations. *Science Education*, 94(3), 478–505.

9

BLOCKSPOT®

A Supportive STEM Learning Community

Janet Emmons and Lynn E. Cohen

Is there a way for STEM to be integrated outside of the classroom in the community in a comprehensive FUN learning experience that works holistically? Absolutely! While there are increasing amounts of STEM programs for children, this chapter examines one particular program that is the first of its kind to combine a block play-based STEM educational concept into a retail space. Blockspot® is a 2,500 square foot state of the art block play-space in Southampton, New York. Over 10,000 wooden all natural unit blocks are organized and available to use (See Figure 9.1). Blockspot® offers after-school builders club, drop/in play, themed building nights, birthday parties, camp and school field trips. Summer months, Blockspot® has a

FIGURE 9.1 Blockspot®—A State of the Art Block Play-Space

partnership with a community summer camp. All children attending camp are given time to create and build with unit blocks.

Blockspot® was founded in 2013 based on the principles that older students had much to offer by way of inquiry, critical thinking, design, engineering and complexity of ideas. Additionally, the premise behind Blockspot® was the holistic social emotional disposition of the entire child would become enhanced by the experience. Play is the way in which children learn best and most naturally (Elkind, 2008; Hirsch-Pasek, Golinkoff, Berk, & Singer, 2009). Children learn to replicate their understanding of the way the world works and what they know through role-playing and imitation (Nielsen, 2012; Piaget, 1962). Unfortunately, children over age 5 have little time dedicated to true play (Miller & Almon, 2009). School curriculum, sports and specifically focused after-school activities have all but eliminated play from the elementary school-aged child's repertoire (Friedman, 2013; Gray, 2013, 2018). Recognizing that the days when children could come home and play outside in the neighborhood as not likely, Blockspot® was born with the idea of replicating what works best into a safe environment where PLAY is the center of it all.

Blocks and block play have been part of the early childhood curriculum from the nineteenth century. Blockspot® uses the wooden unit block as the tool to facilitate its entire curriculum and develop STEM concepts out of the classroom. This chapter examines a short historical overview of block play followed by how play at Blockspot® differs from the formal learning context of the classroom. A description of classes at Blockspot® for children ages 2-to-12-years in an out-of-school STEM learning environment are illustrated. Next, Blockspot®'s contribution to children's STEM learning with vignettes of children building complex block structures. The chapter concludes with the importance of Blockspot® as an out-of-school program to develop STEM experiences.

History of Unit Block Play

Frederich Froebel (1782–1852) developed a curriculum and educational methodology and opened a kindergarten in Germany. The founder of kindergarten and author of *The Education of Man* (1825/2005), he began a movement toward the use of blocks in classrooms. Froebel believed it was important to provide experiences in the early years in which children could be creative and make discoveries. He favored symbolic learning through the handling of materials in play (Cohen, 2006) and self-activity for young children. Froebel's contribution was the development of a series of 20 educational toys and materials called 'gifts' and 'occupations' (Provenzo & Brett, 1983). 'Gifts' are a series of geometric forms intended to provide children with pleasure and responsibility and 'occupations' were activities using craft materials such as sewing, origami, and modeling clay. Froebel believed the geometric forms of the 'gifts' were the building blocks of nature. In 'gift' play, the child first handles, observes, and compares the parts of the 'gift'. In Froebel's kindergarten curriculum, children would observe and describe properties of the objects (number, size, form, material) or compare objects to similar objects or contrast them with different objects (Cohen, 2006). The next process in working with the 'gifts' is to symbolically represent them to the larger world through forms. "Froebel named these Forms of Life, Knowledge, and Beauty to correspond with nature (the physical world), abstract knowledge (math/science) and art (design/pattern)" (Bultman, 2000, p. 6). In Forms of Life, the cube could represent a house or a table. The sphere placed on top of the cylinder could be a person. Friedrich Froebel began a revolution that emphasized the importance of wooden blocks for young children.

Following Froebel, in 1905, Patti Smith Hill, a faculty member of Teachers College, Columbia University, recognized children's need to play, and developed a set of floor blocks consisting of large blocks, pillars, wheels, and rods to give children the means to symbolically represent their environment and build houses, stores, and boats (Provenzo & Brett, 1983).

Inspired by Patty Smith Hill (her teacher), Caroline Pratt began her training in 1892 at Teacher's College, Columbia University, in Kindergarten Education where she observed children playing with the blocks (Winsor, 1996). During her training, she recognized the importance of blocks as a material to appropriate meaning for children. A simple geometric shape could become any number of things to a child; a barn, skyscraper, or entire community.

The most widely known blocks used in early childhood programs and Blockspot® are unit blocks that were developed by Caroline Pratt (Winsor, 1996). Unit blocks are the sole learning tool at Caroline Pratt's City and Country School in New York City (City and Country, 2018). The blocks are based on proportions of 1:2:4 (half as high as they are wide; twice as long as they are wide). Common block shapes include squares, triangles, rectangles, cylinders, curves, and arches. The cylinders conform in height to the unit. The curves are of similar width and thickness (Johnson, 1996).

In the 1900s researchers (Bailey, 1933; Guanella, 1934; Johnson, 1996) began to document the uses of blocks by children. These play scholars focused on the importance of block play for children's development, as well as symbolic functioning. At Blockspot® unit blocks serve as powerful objects to externalize, advance, and document children's STEM learning.

Blockspot® Programs

With blocks being the focus in a retail setting, rather than a prescribed classroom what makes STEM and more happen? Blockspot® offers typical classes throughout the week which provide opportunity for drop-in play and STEM learning. Here are a few samples of typical offerings.

Multi-Age Studio Saturday Classes—Ages 2–12

Saturday sessions are for multi-age children to explore architecture, engineering, balance, measurement, symmetry and geometry. Children of all ages spend time for an hour or more creating with blocks. Age-graded instruction is typical of most formal classroom settings. Peter Gray's (2011) research on mixed-age groupings found benefits to age-mixed play. "Older children enabled younger children to play games that they were not able to play with just age mates. Likewise, older children developed capacities to nurture and be compassionate" (p. 508). The Saturday multi-age studio at Blockspot® offers children the benefits of planning, building and sharing block-building experiences in a school setting that promotes mixed aged groupings rather than the age segregated, typical school classrooms.

After School Builders Club—Ages 5–12

The after-school program gives children freedom to learn and work on weekly activities planned on rotating topics created with blocks. Children learn about physics with ramps and roads, study architecture found in structures around the world, learn how blocks solve math questions, read and build story elements from their independent reading and replicate and design their own art in architecture. Children can try out their ideas by hypothesizing and observing while being encouraged to wonder and ask questions. The collaborative nature of the club helps to foster real-time life teaching and learning lessons among the children.

Nursery Nation—Ages 3–5

A session designed just for active learners. Blockspot®'s preschool program is a playtime building experience that provides guided play with a parent or teacher. Guided play is a blend of adult-scaffolding learning objectives but is child-directed. In guided play, adults initiate the learning process, constrain the learning goals and maintain focus on these goals as the child guides his or her discovery (Weisberg, Hirsh-Pasek & Golinkoff, 2013). Blockspot®'s Nursery Nation provides opportunities for parents and teachers to embed instruction in a number of domains (e.g., math, science, spatial relations, social interactions, pretend play, motor skills problem solving). Adults scaffolding for children can increase complexity of their block play and can be beneficial for developing and learning STEM concepts. Wolfgang, Stannard, and Jones (2001) found that block play complexity in preschool was related to math achievement in high school.

Field Trips for Public and Private Schools

Field trips are a type of experiential learning in which students are provided a new mode of learning out of the traditional classroom setting. The Association for Experiential Learning defined experiential learning as a methodology in which educators direct students to a specific experience, and then guide the students through reflection to "increase knowledge, develop skills, clarify values, and develop people's capacity to contribute to their communities" (Association for Experiential Education, 2017, para. 1, www.aee.org/what-is-ee). Learning on and from a field trip is a valuable supplement and addition to classroom learning (Nadelson & Jordan, 2012; Scribner-Maclean & Kennedy, 2007) and often meets Common Core standards (Cohen & Emmons, 2016; Kenna & Russell, 2015).

Blockspot®'s building block warehouse can accommodate up to 25 students building solo or in partner groups. It is designed to partner with educators as a curriculum resource for inquiry, practice, STEM exploration, and social development. Field trips bring the approaches based on Froebel, Piaget, Vygotsky, Caroline Pratt's theories and the ways children learn best to teachers and students out of the traditional classroom setting. Blockspot® teacher leaders help classroom teachers plan the perfect field trip. Classroom units of study are transformed into block-building experiences for preschool and elementary students.

Play-Based Learning at Blockspot®

When children are building structures at Blockspot®, one child may be in a corner building a tower alone. A friend comes over with another idea and the tower becomes an airport with an air traffic control tower. The play continues until an elaborate structure is designed using a variety of block shapes. The play and engineering of the structure involved time, problem solving, communication, and cooperation. This is an important consideration. Especially in light of the segmented way children are educated in schools today with an emphasis on English language arts and math. Typically, an elementary child's day is broken in time-periods of 30–40 minutes divided by subject. Elementary science is down to half an hour a week and little time for social studies instruction. The narrow curriculum is a national problem and equity issue as elementary teachers spend more time on English language arts and math (Saunders, 2015). Christie and Wardle (1992) examined the importance of time for play for preschool and kindergarten children. They found that constructive play with blocks requires a lengthy play period to reach its full potential. According to Christie and Wardle (1992) short play periods stifle the benefits of extended constructive play and "children resort to building very simple structures" (p. 29).

Why does this matter? Because, learning and life does not happen in isolation and because true focus and attention begin to peak 30 minutes into an activity. So just when concentration is flowing, children are asked to put the materials away and move on to something else. Blockspot® sessions allow for longer uninterrupted building time to capitalize on children's attention and for full realization of ideas. If the activity were shorter, one would never see the results as the children intended them. Most importantly, the children would be frustrated that their ideas never had the chance to come to fruition—because as mentioned before—this is their work. It is meaningful, planned, and purposeful and, most importantly, represents their creativity and thinking.

The lessons at Blockspot® are known to the children as *builders' challenges*. Each week children receive a simple set of intentions to guide their building. Some examples of these include (a) scavenger hunts, (b) coding, (c) measurements/area, (d) shape isolations, (d) ball challenges, and (e) loose parts. Through these "builders' challenges" the goal is to see children demonstrate, apply and practice the skills of analysis, definition of ideas and concepts, creating and evaluating. Evidence of these learning outcomes happen as the children work. Play-based learning is a process-oriented experience. Meaning that the best and highest form of learning happens through the experience of building and conversation of it. The result of the structure at Blockspot® often belies the brilliance behind the product. It is impossible to know everything by observation, so how are children's brilliant thoughts and ideas assessed when building? At the end of a building session, children share and describe their block-building structure with skillful adults listening carefully for evidence of the thought processes employed by the builders. Children need experiences with communication so they can learn how to make their own understandings explicit and sometimes to challenge and extend initial understandings, an important skill in all fields, including STEM. Children at Blockspot® may say, *"Well I was going to make it really tall, but this block kept slipping, so I needed to change to a different block." "I had to make many trips to the triangle shelf. I almost used all the triangles!" "I couldn't figure out how to get the ball to shoot out over here, so I asked Emma and we figured it out." "We didn't have a block that looked like the shape I needed, so I put these together instead."* Children at Blockspot® communicate their thinking and generalize meaning, contributing to their language and literacy development in meaningful and powerful ways.

Blockspot® and STEM

STEM disciplines is sometimes easiest to describe one topic at a time, but research is showing the importance of interdisciplinary connections for STEM learning. McClure et al. (2017) state,

> the stem acronym is more than an easy-to-remember word; it also makes explicit that the subjects under the STEM moniker – science, technology, engineering, and math are deeply interconnected and can be taught effectively in concert, with science and mathematics as anchors. (p. 17)

At Blockspot® STEM is emphasized and integrated, not isolated. It is impossible to isolate a subject when building with blocks. Math, science, technology, and engineering concepts are taught and learned as children build and design block structures.

Blocks are really the very foundation for STEM. They provide a natural inquiry based experience that leads to further exploration. If children are to be interested in a variety of pursuits throughout their lives, they need their freedom: freedom of exploration and play to discover what they are naturally attracted to by way of interest and talent. The past few years, research (Cohen & Emmons, 2016, 2017, 2018) has been conducted using video and audio observations at Blockspot® to identify ways features of block play is associated with STEM concepts and play. Data were collected through a series of naturalistic field observations during Blockspot® programs. The unit of analysis was based on Cook-Gumperz and Corsaro's (1977) interactive episode:

> Interactive episodes are those sequences of behavior which begin with the *acknowledged presence* of two or more interactants in an ecological area and the *overt attempt(s)* to arrive at a shared meaning of ongoing or emerging activity. Episodes end with physical movement of interactants from the area which results in the *termination* of the *originally initiated activity*. (pp. 416–417)

At the end of After School Builders and public and private field trip sessions children shared their block-building designs. These interviews of share sessions were additional data sources to understand the essence of block play and STEM-related behaviors.

Below are examples of verbal transcriptions taken from programs offered at Blockspot®. Pseudonyms are used in the following examples for the children's protection.

Example 1. A Vignette from a Nursery Nation Session

Charles, a preschool child, is building with his nanny. They are both sitting on the floor with blocks and a level. Nanny shows Charles the level and explains how the liquid in the middle needs to be even in order for the block structure to be level. Charles begins to build a house. Nanny asks, "What else do you have to do?" Charles looks over the blocks. Nanny points to other blocks. Charles picks up two more blocks the same size and slides them down until they fall into place. He reaches for the measuring tape. Nanny asks, "How long is it" Charles measures the block. Nanny asks, "How long to you want it to be, Charles?" Charles takes one more block to even out the building. He reaches for the tape measure again and hands it to Nanny's outstretched hand. She measured the structure and said it was 19 inches. He picks up one more block and adds it to the end of the structure. Nanny picks up a triangular block and asks, "What can you do with this block?" He places it halfway underneath the existing structure. Nanny has a triangular block and square blocks and asks him, "Are these blocks the same size as the one you just worked with?" Charles says, "Let me check." He goes over to the structure and measures it. He says, "No it's not." He measures the next one.

"Same!" Nanny asks, "How many do you need?" Charles responded, "A whole bunch across!" Nanny brings Charles some more blocks. Charles leaves the structure. Nanny asks, "Where are you going?" Charles replies, "I'm looking for cars to go down." He points to the triangular blocks slanted downwards then goes over to the shelf and gets the measuring tape out again. He gets two large cars and places them on the blocks slanted down. Nanny explains to him that in order to build a ramp they need to fix the structure so the cars can go up and down. Charles takes away the triangle blocks and builds a ramp.

This example illustrates the importance of adult scaffolding and encouraging inquiry to guide preschoolers with block-building activities. Inquiry is a concept that is central to science and is part of all science education. Nanny helped Charles experience and use the process of inquiry that resulted in building a ramp. Charles learned by trial and error to use materials and designs that lead to a stable structure. The use of spatial words (e.g. same, long, up, down) were used which are important for vocabulary and oral language development. Charles used the measuring tape to count the length of his structure, an important math concept. Charles was placing blocks to build an idea, which are design and engineering skills. In addition to the important STEM skills, Charles and Nanny were engaged in conversation and social interactions in an out-of-school learning experience.

Example 2. A Vignette from the After School Builders Club

The after-school builders club were given a challenge to build a roadway, bridge, tunnel or ramp. An 8-year-old girl, Anna, and 10-year-old girl, Xandra, took on the challenge to build a bridge. Xandra is holding up two large curved blocks and they are attempting to balance them atop the bridge. Anna holds a string as she is trying to figure out how to tie the curved blocks to hold them in place. Xandra suggests, "Maybe we can make a structure of like the twin bridges." Anna replies, "No, no I want to put this thing here... . I need another block," as she goes to the block shelf to get more blocks. Xandra and Anna continue to try to tie the two curved blocks together with string. Xandra is holding the blocks together, while Anna takes a longer string to tie around the blocks. Anna tells Xandra, "Maybe we should do it not on the blocks." She picks up the two curved blocks and puts them on the floor. "Here, just hold it like this." Anna shows Xandra how she wants them placed. Xandra holds them in place as Anna gets the string and wraps it around the blocks. Xandra exclaims, "Don't tie my hands!" Xandra holds it in place while Anna works to wrap the string around the blocks. Xandra says, "Hey, I have an idea! Maybe that could be like a tunnel and be like a decoration all on the top and the blocks could be like this (holds her hands parallel) so cars could go like under and stuff." Anna responds, "I really want the string to work." The teacher suggests Anna and Xandra use some different shapes to build their bridge. Xandra says, "Yeah, all those blocks could make a great tunnel." Xandra takes the curved blocks and places them on top as opposed to back-to-back in a curved X shape as Anna was attempting to do.

Xandra suggests, "This way cars could like enter here." Anna looks at it and considers it for a moment with a spool of string in her hand. Anna places another block between the two arches. Xandra says, "Put a block on top of here." Xandra claps her hands and gives a thumbs up to Anna. "Ok, cool!" she exclaims. Xandra brings over a matching large triangle block to place between the arches. Anna places a rectangular block across the top to balance on top. "Oooooh!" exclaims Xandra, as she examines their tower." Maybe we should do another one on this side." "Yes," replies Anna, "we should make it taller." "And then we go smaller and smaller," continues Xandra. Anna takes two smaller rectangular blocks and tries to balance them atop the structure. Xandra sounds worried, "Don't make it fall, don't make it fall! Maybe we should just keep it." Anna says, "No we're going to build it up until we need to share… . No we're going to build it up." Anna and Xandra continue to build up until they have a tall decorative bridge.

Blocks offered Anna and Xandra a unique opportunity to explore and investigate ideas related to equivalence. Both played around with spatial transformation and changed positions of the unit blocks repeatedly until satisfied with their tower. Anna was searching for a spatial design that was visually harmonious by attempting to tie curved blocks together with string. Yet, scientific exploration and engineering of block play are often driven by continuous visual feedback. Sometimes experimentation does not work. When it does not work, there is often no attempt to find out why, but instead something else is tried. Anna listened to Xandra and tried a new approach to her idea. Stringing two curved blocks one on top of another with a string, so mathematical concepts of line, part-whole relationships, aspects of number, area, patterning, and volume are evident as they completed their bridge. The structure was engineered and designed as an aesthetically, symmetrical tower (see Figure 9.2).

FIGURE 9.2 Two 8-Year-Old Children Build a Tower

Example 3. A Vignette from the After School Builders Club

The after-school builders in this vignette engaged in science and engineering practices when they designed and built their own technology to move small rubber balls. The vignette below demonstrates how three boys developed practical understanding of Newton's laws of force and motion in relation to inclines (Counsell, Uhlenberg, & Zan, 2013). Two 8-year-old boys, Greg and Clyde, one 9-year-old, Brad, and one 6-year-old, Sean were given the challenge to use five different types of blocks and connect to another team of block builders. The dyads, Greg and Brad, are one team, and Sean and Clyde, another team, as they build separate structures.

Greg has started building a structure with several unit and double unit blocks. He goes to the shelf for ramps and places one ramp at the end of his structure, hanging off the edge. He goes back to the shelf and gets three more unit blocks. He places them under the ramp for support. He straightens up his ramp. Clyde brings Greg more unit blocks. Greg tells Clyde, "We're gonna send each other balls." Clyde says, "Yeah. Wait, can you, can we send each other balls? Cause this is gonna, like, cause this is like an outpost ship." Clyde replies, "This is kind of like an outpost ship because it's on the water. It's an on the water outpost ship." Greg brings over two plastic PVC tubes and places it on the ramp. He takes the second tube and connects it to Clyde's structure. Greg kneels down and pushes a rubber ball through the tube. Greg shouts, "It works!" The rubber ball makes it through the tube and stops approximately one foot from the end. "Ugh!" says Greg. Sean runs over and kneels down next to the end of the tube. "Watch this!" "Watch this!" says Sean. Sean blows into the tube and the rubber ball comes out the other end. Greg walks to the other end to retrieve the rubber ball. He picks it up and turns around. Greg walks to the other end of the tube and places three balls inside of it. Sean exclaims, "I just blew!" Sean runs to the end of the tube. Greg blows into the tube and the three balls fall out the other end. Greg says, "A little wind!" Greg and Clyde pick up another ramp and make another connection. Greg walks to the other end, picks up some rubber balls and one by one pushes the rubber balls through the PVC tube (see Figure 9.3).

The four boys are now trying to connect their structures and complete the challenge. Clyde takes a unit block and places it under a section of his ramp to secure his structure. Sean continues to build his structure to connect to Greg and Brad's structure. Sean takes several double unit blocks and creates a row to connect to Greg's ramp. Clyde is building another ramp to connect to Greg's ramp. Clyde realizes his ramp needs more support, so he gets two unit blocks and places them under the end of the ramp. Sean says, "We work together!" Clyde continues to work on his ramp. Sean runs over placing another double unit block in a line to connect to Greg's ramp. It doesn't quite reach, so he goes to the block shelf and gets more blocks. He brings back a unit block. He tries to fill the space between his structure and Greg's structure to make the connection but the unit

FIGURE 9.3 Newton's Law of Force and Motion Using Blocks, Ramps, and Objects that Roll

block is too small. Sean goes back to the block shelf, picks up a double unit block and again attempts to make a connection. The double unit block is too big to fit the gap between his structure and Greg and Brad's structure. To solve the problem, Brad pushes the row of blocks back, and slides the double unit block in place to fit and make a connection between the two block structures. Brad helps Sean straighten his connection.

Clyde adds another section of ramp to his structure and connects to Greg and Brad's building.

This vignette is evidence that Blockspot® provides elementary children with many opportunities to plan, investigate, and analyze outcomes by the Next Generation Science Standards (NGSS) for science. Engineering practices are further aligned with the K-PS2 and 3-PS2 Motion and Stability: Forces and Interactions (K-PS2–1, 3-PS2–1 and KPS2–2 and 3PS2–2) when children use ramps to create new structures with an intended purpose or function (NGSS, 2013). The use of unit blocks with ramps, and objects that roll (e.g., marbles, ping pong balls, rubber balls, pom-poms, and balls with different surfaces) provide the boys the opportunity to make choices and decisions as well as explore and investigate according to their own interests and curiosities. This physical science experience allowed the children to make a ball roll down a PVC tube and were able to observe immediate results and change the variables (height and length of the ramps) as needed. They worked independently and in dyads to decide what they wanted the balls to do according to their own problem and questions. Good physical science activities using blocks, ramps, and objects that roll encourage and motivate children to figure out how to make something happen (DeVries & Sales, 2011).

A task was given and the boys worked cooperatively without any struggles or arguments. Sean reinforced this with his comment, "We work together!" The mixed ages of the group indicates that children of all ages exert their full attention and energy toward investigating and finding solutions to block-building problems to achieve goals. Through block building, children of all ages employ a basic engineering design process, as described by Cunningham (2018) in which children ask, imagine, plan, create, and improve their structures according to what they want happen.

Example 4. Second-Grade Field Trip to Blockspot®

Public- and private-school administrators arrange two or more field trips to Blockspot®. The first field trip visit serves as a pre-assessment and children are given a choice as to what they want to build. The second and subsequent field trip are post assessments of classroom curricula. Students work with the classroom teacher and develop a plan related to a curricular area. Blockspot® field trips allow students opportunities to ask and develop questions and use knowledge learned in the classroom and represent their ideas with blocks. The students are implementing science-integrated engineering design thinking as classroom knowledge is transformed into block structures.

A second-grade New York State social studies curriculum is *My Community and Other Communities*. Students described where stores were located and made connections between stores. Additionally, they described the goods and services their local community produces. This chapter includes photos (Figure 9.4 and 9.5) along with student interviews describing two community block structures engineered and designed during a field trip to Blockspot®.

STUDENT 1: "So we was planning to build a city, but instead of building a whole entire city we just build half of the city. So, so then we made like one Walmart, see, like you see that little… . 'scuse me, you see that little store, that kinda is CVS and these are… that's K-Mart. And you'll see some people driving out and going some places. That's our gas station right over there. You see over here, there's some like, workers and some people like driving home from and stuff. I split the part so we can have some like McDonald's and some Subway."

STUDENT 2: "And some like store here"

STUDENT 3: "And- and then we- we- we"

STUDENT 2: "Build Walmart"

STUDENT 1: "Build Walmart first, so you see a little."

STUDENT 3: "The like the- like, like there's like a lot of toys and food and everything inside. There's like a lot of people there."

STUDENT 1: "And then there's markers and here's our sculptures and there's our rooms right there. And…"

STUDENT 3: "And these are—and this are the toys… food… and…"

STUDENT 1: "And here's…we called this the bridge so they can come back and stuff just crashing in the building so…"

FIGURE 9.4 Second-Grade Social Studies Unit—Recreating Walmart, CVS Store, and Gas Station

TEACHER: "Can I make an observation? On all three of your buildings, there is an inside. So you boys spent some time on the details on the inside, and I'm noticing that some stores are very broken up into purposeful areas. And it looks like maybe this person works here, and I'm not sure if those people are shopping. And maybe this is merchandise, is that, is this the stuff you buy, you guys?"
STUDENT 2: "Yea"

The next community structure that children in the second grade built was a train station. Below is a an excerpt from a sharing session. The students built the train station by stacking quadruple blocks on top of elliptical curved blocks to represent the wheels of the train. This vignette demonstrates how children plan, design, and problem solve when ideas do not work. They worked through the problem of not having wheels and improvised by turning the elliptical cursed blocks upside down using double unit blocks for support.

STUDENT 1: "I made this whole thing. It's like where you could come into the train stations and get your tickets here and then you can sit on the bench to wait. And I have no idea how oh, how that got there…and then we all—we both made this train and Amelia made the train track and I helped her make the ceiling. And I also…" "Well we tried to finish it and put people and animals on the top."

STUDENT 2: "And we weren't supposed to put them on the top…"

STUDENT 1: "No, like here."

TEACHER: "The hardest—the hardest part of your train was what?"

STUDENT 1: "The wheels."

TEACHER: "The wheels"

STUDENT 2: "Because it was. we had to put like little stands."

STUDENT 1: "like these little stands."

STUDENT 2: " so that—so that they wouldn't roll when we put like this on top of it."

The Importance of Blockspot® as an Out-of-School Program

Learning block-building skills outside of school can directly affect STEM learning inside the classroom. Strategies that support STEM learning such as hands on learning, inquiry based pedagogy, connecting STEM to everyday life, and building strong communication skills are widely applied at Blockspot®. The structural features of Blockspot® (e.g., hands-on-activities, ungraded building activities, opportunities to communicate and share block-building structures, multi-age groupings, fluid uses of time) extend children's interest and developing understanding of STEM.

FIGURE 9.5 Second-Grade Social Studies Unit—Recreating a Local Train Station

There are implications that demonstrate Blockspot® contributes to children's understanding of and interest in STEM. First, Blockspot® is located in the local community and taught by adults who live in the community. Important role models and community connections are provided that encourage children's pursuit of STEM learning. Second, longitudinal studies of practicing scientists find that their experiences at home and in their community were important for developing a passion for the STEM disciplines and choosing a STEM career (Christensen, Knezek, & Tyler-Wood, 2015; Jones, Taylor, Forrester, 2011). Christensen et al. (2015) gathered data from 342 high school students participating in a STEM academy on a university campus. Data indicated students were interested in STEM careers due to self-motivation, high school course work and parental support. Jones et al. (2011) asked 37 scientists and engineers about their in- and out-of-school experiences and memories of significant people who influenced their careers. The scientists and engineers reported that teacher and family mentoring, tinkering and building models, and out-of-school experiences were the factors that were most influential.

The National Research Council (2015) offers three criteria for identifying and developing productive out-of-school STEM learning programs: 1) engage young people intellectually, socially, and emotionally, 2) respond to young people's interests, experiences, and cultural practices, and 3) connect STEM learning in out-of-school, school, home, and other settings. Does Blockspot® meet these three criteria for a productive out-of-school program? Yes!

First, Blockspot® provides children with first-hand cognitive and social experiences with unit blocks so they are able to engage in sustained STEM practices. The scientists and engineers in Jones et al.'s (2011) study reported that building models and out-of-school experiences influenced them to choose a career related to STEM. Blockspot® provides unit blocks and an open space to develop the questions that interest children as they collaborate and build structures in dyads and teams.

Second, Blockspot® teachers support and build upon children's STEM interests by providing building challenges. In example 2, the after-school builders club was given a challenge to build a roadway, bridge, tunnel or ramp. The challenge in example 3 was to use five different types of blocks and connect to another team of block builders. Blockspot® teachers are also responsive to children's prior interests and experiences. Children who take field trips to Blockspot® use their school experience and prior knowledge to build communities, including stories heard at home and in school, or games played during recess.

Last, Blockspot® makes connections in and across settings and programs to broker opportunities to engage in block building and STEM learning activities. Blockspot® has an ongoing partnership with a community camp to provide campers with block-building STEM learning experiences. Blockspot® offers Saturday programs for mixed-age children, parent-child programs for preschool children, field trips for public and private schools and its After School Builders Program.

Conclusion

When we think about children as adults in the job-place, we can see a connection between the children's experiences at Blockspot® and careers in math, science, technology, and engineering. Additionally, employers are seeking analytical, evaluative and creative skills. Why do we hear of executives harking the need for more STEM in our schools? Because jobs like Software Developer, Civil Engineer, Cost Estimator, IT Manager, Industrial Psychologist, and Architect require STEM. Add into the STEM mix and the workplace the interpersonal skills required for success, such as collaboration, risk taking, communication, resiliency, listening, and creativity and it is easy to see why blocks are the perfect tool for STEM learning.

References

Association for Experiential Education (AEE). (2017). What is experiential education? Retrieved July 6, 2018 from http://aee.org/what-is-ee

Bailey, M. (1933). A scale of block constructions for young children. *Child Development, 4,* 121–139.

Bultman, S. (2000). *The Froebel gifts. The building gifts 2–6.* Grand Rapids, MI: Froebel USA.

Christensen, R., Knezek, G., & Tyler-Wood, T. (2015). A retrospective analysis of STEM career interest among mathematics and science academy students. *Journal of Learning, Teaching and Educational Research, 10*(1), 45–58.

Christie, J. F., & Wardle, F. (1992). How much time is needed for play? *Young Children, 47*(3), 28–33.

City and Country School. (2018). Retrieved from http//www.cityandcountry.org

Cohen, L. E. (2006). *Young children's discourse strategies in pretend block play.* Dissertations Abstracts International, (67)02A (UMI No.3208578).

Cohen, L. E., & Emmons, J. (2016). Block play: Spatial language with preschool and school-aged children. *Early Child Development and Care, 187*(5–6), 967–977. doi:10.1080/03004430.2016.1223064.

Cohen, L. E., & Emmons, J. (2017). *Metacognition and talk in block play: In-school and out-of-school playful contexts.* Paper presentation of The Association for the Study of Play 43rd International Conference. Rochester, NY: The Strong Museum of Play.

Cohen, L. E., & Emmons, J. (2018). Block play: Spatial language with preschool and school-aged children. In D. Wisneski & J. Nicholson (Eds.), *Towards social justice and equity: Reconsidering the role of play in early childhood.* New York: Taylor & Francis.

Cook-Gumperz, J., & Corsaro, W. A. (1977). Social-ecological constraints on children's communicative strategies. *Sociology, 11*(3), 411–434.

Counsell, S. L., Uhlenberg, J., & Zan, B. (2013). Ramps and pathways early physical science program: Preparing educators as science mentors. In S. Koba & B. Wognowski (Eds.), *Exemplary science: Best practices in professional development* (pp. 143–156). Arlington, VA: National Science Teachers Association Press.

Cunningham, C. M. (2018). *Engineering in elementary STEM education. Curriculum design, Instruction, learning and assessment.* New York, NY: Teachers College Press.

DeVries, R., & Sales, C. (2011). *Ramps and pathways. A constructivist approach to physics with young children.* Washington, DC: National Association for the Education of Young Children.

Elkind, D. (2008). The power of play. *The American Journal of Play,* 1(1), 1–6.

Friedman, H. L. (2013). *Playing to win: Raising children in a competitive culture.* Berkeley, CA: University of California Press.

Froebel, F. (1826/2005). *The education of man.* (W.N. Hailmann, Trans.). New York and London: D. Appleton and Company.

Gray, P. (2011). The special value of children's age-mixed play. *American Journal of Play, 3*(4), 500–522.

Gray, P. (2013). *Free to learn. Why unleashing the instinct to play will make our children happier, more self-reliant, and better students for life.* New York: Basic Books.

Gray, P. (2018). *The Promise of Play.* Keynote address at The Association for the Study of Play, Melbourne, FL.

Guanella, F. M. (1934). Block building activities of young children. *Archives of Psychology, 174*, 5–91.

Hirsch-Pasek, K., Golinkoff, R. M., Berk, L. E., & Singer, D. (2009). *A mandate for playful learning in preschool: Applying the scientific evidence.* New York, NY: Oxford University Press.

Johnson, H. (1996) The art of block building. In E. S. Hirsch (Ed.) *The block book.* (pp. 9–25). Washington, DC: National Association for the Education of Young Children.

Jones, G., Taylor, A., & Forrester, J. H. (2011). A retrospective look. *International Journal of Science Education, 33*(12), 1653–1673. doi:10.1080/09500693.2010.523484

Kenna, J. L., & Russell, W. B. (2015). Tripping on the core: Utilizing field trips to enhance the Common Core. *Social Studies Research and Practice, 10*(2), 96–110.

McClure, E. R., Guernsey, L., Clements, D. H., Bales, S. N., Nichols, J., Kendall-Taylor, N. & Levine, M. H. (2017). *STEM starts early: Grounding science, technology, engineering, and math education in early childhood.* New York: The Joan Ganz Cooney Center at Sesame Workshop.

Miller, E., & Almon, J. (2009). *Crisis in kindergarten: Why children need to play in school.* College Park, MD: Alliance for Childhood.

Nadelson, L., & Jordan, J. (2012). Student attitudes toward and recall of outside day: An environmental science field trip. *Journal of Educational Research, 105*(3), 220–231. doi:10.1080/00220671.2011.576715

National Research Council. (2015). *Identifying and supporting productive STEM programs in out-of-school settings.* Committee on Successful Out-of-School STEM Learning Board on Science Education, Division of Behavioral and Social Sciences and Education. Washington, DC: The National Academies Press.

Next Generation Science Standards (NGSS). (2013). *Next generation science standards. For states, by states.* Retrieved from http://www.nextgenscience.org/sites/ngss/files/NGSS%20DCI%20Combined%2011.6.13.pdf

Nielsen, M. (2012). Imitation, pretend play and childhood: Essential elements in the evolution of human culture. *Journal of Comparative Psychology, 126*(2), 170–181. doi:10.1037/a0025168

Piaget, J. (1962). *Play, dreams, and imitation in childhood.* New York: W.W. Norton.

Provenzo, E., & Brett, A. (1983). *The complete block book.* Syracuse, NY: Syracuse University Press.

Saunders, S. (2015, February). *Emphasis on ELA and math is pushing aside science, social studies and other important subjects.* Retrieved from https://www.nysut.org/news/nysut-united/issues/2015/february-2015

Scribner-Maclean, M., & Kennedy, L. (2007). More than just a day away from school: Planning a great science field trip. *Science Scope, 30*(8), 57–60.

Weisberg, D., Hirsh-Pasek, K., & Golinkoff, R. (2013). Guided play: Where curricular goals meet a playful pedagogy, *Mind, Brain, and Education*, 7(2), 104–112.

Winsor, C. (1996). Blocks as a material for learning through play. In E. Hirsch (Ed). *The block book* (3rd ed). (pp. 2–7). Washington, DC: National Association for the Education of Young Children.

Wolfgang, C. H., Stannard, L. L., & Jones, I. (2001). Block play performance among preschoolers as a predictor of later school achievement in mathematics. *Journal of Research in Childhood Education, 15*, 173–180.

In the summer of 2019 Blockspot will be closing its Southampton location in pursuit of reaching a broader audience through a new location in the New York City Metro area and franchise opportunities. Any inquiries can be made by emailing info@blockspotlearning.com

10

STEM IN OUTDOOR LEARNING

Rooted in Nature

Monica Wiedel-Lubinski

STEM in Outdoor Learning: Rooted in Nature

Science, technology, engineering, and math have roots in the natural world. As children engage with nature, STEM knowledge blossoms. Experimentation, inquiry, observation, problem-solving, and comparison are just a few of the ways young children form knowledge through child-led outdoor learning (Kramer & Rabe-Kleberg, 2011, cited in Cremin, Glauert, Craft, Compton, & Stylianidou, 2015). Children ask and, in time, answer, basic questions about their surroundings and their place within it. Cycles of life and death, changing seasons, growth and decay, light and dark, weather and climate, time and space, the plant and animal kingdoms—all mysteries of earth, space, and sky—call to be examined (Tunnicliffe, 2017). To this end, nature provides endless, play-filled opportunities for STEM concepts to come alive (Cremin et al., 2015).

Before further discussion, it is helpful to note a few terms that give context to STEM-based outdoor learning. "Outdoor learning" refers to any learning that happens outside. All educators, no matter the curricular model, can open the door and take learning outside.

"Nature-based learning" refers to curriculum, activities, or experiences that use nature as a central organizing concept, which other learning builds upon. The natural world provides the underlying skeletal structure for all learning and skill development. While nature is at the heart of nature-based learning, developmentally appropriate practices and skill development flesh out a fully realized curriculum. Outdoor learning and exploration are paramount in nature-based early-learning programs. In fact, some nature-based early childhood programs occur solely outdoors in all weather, utilizing shelter in only the most extreme conditions. Yet, there are many nature-based early childhood programs that move between indoor and outdoor learning environments. Natural materials, plants, animals, and artifacts enrich nature-based classrooms.

These terms are highlighted because a program can engage in nature-based learning indoors or out. But outdoor learning is always outside, and it is not exclusive to any one curriculum or set of learning standards. Outdoor learning is available to all.

One additional term, "nature," is also important to note. "Nature" typically refers to wild places, like a forest, beach, or garden. This interpretation insinuates that nature only exists in specific locations, separating people from places where nature is found (Tunnicliffe, 2017). In the context of this chapter, however, nature applies to *all outdoor settings*. Nature is the ground beneath our feet, even if it is paved. It is the sky and the wind, the rocks and the rain. All the elements in the ecosystem, including people, are captured in this definition of nature. Nature is everywhere—in cities, suburbs, and rural areas alike. This is a significant distinction for teachers who want to harness nature for outdoor learning. Nature is not a destination; it is not somewhere far away. Nature is an integral part of every community and every aspect of our lives. It may require a shift in mindset to grasp fully this concept of nature, but it is essential for teachers to understand if they want to access nature in whatever form it exists at their schools.

With a basic understanding of these terms in place, we move on to consider how the natural resources available in various settings can support STEM-based outdoor learning.

Hands-On Nature

Curious Discoveries

Unlike typical classrooms, nature is full of surprises: a soft tuft of moss at the base of an old tree; the heavy scent of rain after summer storms; the tickle of a tiny ladybug; or the sight of the first golden leaves of autumn. There are new discoveries in every season. These discoveries engage emotions, senses, and a child's curiosity. Sometimes changes in nature happen on a grand scale, like a fresh blanket of snow or a dogwood in bloom. Other times change is slow and gradual, like a sprout that will grow into a vine, ripe with pumpkins. When children participate in frequent outdoor learning, discoveries like these help children hone observation skills and become keen observers of nature's phenomena (Esser, 2017). Inquiry and investigation naturally emerge.

Any educator or parent can speak to the wonder and inquisitive nature of young children. Questioning is an essential aspect of early learning. Children naturally wonder and ask questions to better understand themselves, their experiences, and their surroundings. When learning moves outdoors, curiosity drives a great deal of interest in STEM-based concepts. Seasonal elements in the schoolyard or neighboring park are far less predictable than the four walls of a familiar classroom. Curiosity is amplified because the environment is always in flux, which stimulates rich inquiry. Nature is always willing to reveal surprises for those who venture outside.

Learning Through Direct Experience

The Experiential Learning Theory (ELT) provides context for the role of direct experiences in STEM-based outdoor learning. ELT presents a holistic view of learning as a process. It values children's ideas and their abilities to test and refine ideas to construct new knowledge (Armstrong & Fukami, 2009). Constant adaptation occurs between the environment and children's reconciliation of thoughts and feelings as new ideas and learning emerges (Armstrong & Fukami, 2009). The ebb and flow are continuous between child, environment, experience, culture, physical sensation, emotion, inquiry, and reflection. Evolving ideas are constantly in motion as these factors collide to shape and re-shape learning.

Torquati, Cutler, Gilkerson, and Sarver's (2013) research explains, "direct experiences with nature provide opportunities to see firsthand the intricate interdependencies among living things and elements" (p. 726). These direct experiences outweigh simulated ones because children can fully engage with all their senses and interact with physical matter.

Tree Reality

Imagine participating in a lesson about trees as a young child. In this example, the teacher passes around a laminated picture of a maple tree. *If you were in a classroom holding this picture, what would your body be doing? What other objects and activities might surround you? What might the teacher and other children be doing as you hold the laminated picture? What truths could you come to know about trees?*

Now imagine the same lesson outside, beneath a maple tree on a windy day. *What would your body be doing? What other objects might surround you? What might the teacher and other children be doing under the tree? What else might you discover about the tree? What other inquiry could emerge?*

Considering these two approaches to a tree lesson, which best reveals the properties of a tree? Which provides deeper inquiry? Which experience is more engaging and memorable to a young child? Such a stark comparison demonstrates the power of experiential learning, even when it is held in one's imagination.

Local Knowledge

The tree example also brings up the significance of place-based education. Local habitats and communities are paramount to children's cultural and personal experiences, and therefore provide a meaningful context for learning. In other words, should one even teach about maple trees if there are not any in the area?

Or penguins, for that matter? Place-based education, "injects value and meaning into the school experience" because it is relevant to children in their immediate communities (Smith & Sobel, 2013, p. 42). It may not make sense to learn about trees, or specifically maple trees, in every environment. Learning about plants and animals should be relevant to the places that children call home. If the native landscape is made up of cacti or coniferous trees, learning about maple trees will not access children's lived experience, thereby making learning less meaningful. Place-based education hinges on connection with the immediate surroundings and explores the natural and cultural significance of place (Sobel, 1996, 2004). This approach is an important underpinning in education, and takes special precedence when teaching about habitats, wildlife, and seasonal topics related to STEM-based outdoor learning.

Water Play

Puddles are another place to find STEM learning, and they certainly are not found in a classroom! Indoor water bins and sensory tables foster fun water play and inquiry, for example, by measuring and pouring. But what if children learn about the properties of water outside? How is a puddle different from a water table, in terms of what children can observe or experience?

- Living things drink from and swim in outdoor puddles
- Animals make tracks and lay eggs in puddles
- Puddles often lead to creeks or gutters
- Puddles change in shape, size, and volume
- Things float and sink in puddles
- The earth changes beneath puddles
- Outside temperatures impact puddles
- Natural objects fall into puddles
- People can move and splash water in puddles, with hands or feet
- Plants can grow in puddles
- Large objects placed in puddles can change how the water flows or moves
- Natural surroundings are not damaged from messy exploration of puddles

This illustrates an array of STEM concepts available for children to explore in a puddle. While some of these experiences may be possible with an indoor water table, they could never replicate the same degree of richness or surprise.

Indirect vs Direct Learning

It is easy to see why the ELT is an effective approach to learning. Here we apply more examples. The following chart (Table 10.1) offers examples of content that many early childhood educators implement as part of a well-rounded science curriculum. On the far left are common seasonal topics and examples to describe

TABLE 10.1 Examples of Seasonal Comparison of Indirect and Direct Learning Experiences in a Science Curriculum

	Examples of indirect learning	Examples of direct learning outdoors
Trees	Teacher shares photos or books about trees Teacher provides a worksheet to teach about parts of a tree Teacher leads art project to make tree silhouettes with the children's handprints	Children feel the wind as it blows through grass and trees Children discover and smell fresh blooms on trees in spring Children taste ripe fruit from trees Children observe changes in the same tree over time, in each season Children investigate life on a rotten log or uprooted tree Children collect leaves and seeds for sorting, grouping, or counting Children observe and compare tree silhouettes with and without leaves for tree identification Children mimic how squirrels and birds use trees and tree parts to build nests
Frog life cycle	Teacher provides worksheet for children to cut, color, and sequence stages of frog metamorphosis Teacher shows a video with time lapse video of frog life cycle Teacher places plastic frog life cycle toys in water table	Children listen to frogs calling Children search for frog nurseries in stream, wetland, vernal pool, or pond Children catch slippery tadpoles and frogs Children observe frog eggs, how tadpoles swim, and how frogs hide, jump, or swim Children explore local habitats to discover what frogs need to survive
Bird migration	Teacher reads story about birds flying south in the winter Teacher shows map with migration routes Teacher plays matching game with laminated pictures of birds or other animals that migrate	Children listen to Canada geese honking overhead and observe flight pattern Children create sound maps indicate where birds are most active on school grounds Children use journals to record resident birds observed throughout the year, noting habits, patterns, and absence of various species Children feed birds and/or plant food sources for birds to help them prepare for migration Children observe birds to discriminate between species, male and female, juvenile and adult morphs, etc.
Hibernation	Teacher shows pictures or video of bears in hibernation Teacher shows casts of bear paws or tracks Teacher explains hibernation	Children go outside in winter and pretend to be bears searching for a warm, protected den Children gather leaves, sticks, pine needles or other natural materials to build a winter shelter Children search for bear clues like tracks in the mud and snow, clumps of fur, and scat Children forage for nuts and seeds and hide them as they pretend to prepare a cache of food like a chipmunk, mouse, or squirrel

	Examples of indirect learning	Examples of direct learning outdoors
Snow	Teacher shows pictures of snowflakes Teacher instructs children to fold and cut paper snowflakes Teacher invites children to look out the window at the snow	Children roll or sled down a snowy hillside Children construct igloo snow dens or forts with snow bricks Children measure, graph, and photograph snow drifts and note changes over time Children record temperatures of shady and sunny locations and make predictions about snow that falls at each site Children observe feeding habits of native animals after snow fall Children examine, measure, make predictions, and follow animal tracks in snow Children experiment with seeds by hiding them and trying to locate them in the snow; in spring they may discover sprouts from buried seeds

how some teachers might introduce them. Examples on the left are primarily teacher-directed activities that offer limited, indirect learning about the content. In contrast, the examples on the right describe direct learning approaches to engage with the content in more meaningful ways outdoors.

Most teachers offer some form of interactive, child-directed learning despite the selection of activities on the left. These examples are not meant to undercut the potential value of such activities, depending on their context. They do, however, make the point that hands-on outdoor learning is an obvious choice for teaching about seasonal content, and it is right outside the door.

Outdoor learning activates the senses, invites physical play, and promotes child-directed inquiry (North American Association for Environmental Education, 2019). It also offers amazing possibilities for hands-on, experiential learning that are simply not an option inside.

Nature for All

Fortunately, every teacher and child can access nature and outdoor learning. Sky, sun, wind, rain, soil, stones, plants, animals, clouds, moon, and stars—they can be found everywhere, in all settings. These "big nature" elements, as Dr. Mary Rivkin refers to them, surround us (Rivkin, 1995). As educators, it is our duty to help young children connect to the communities in which they live and to access nature in those settings. Even in the proverbial concrete jungle, bees visit dandelions peeking out of sidewalk cracks. Birds rest on wires. Squirrels build leafy drays atop trees. Rain puddles freeze. And the sun sets in the west. Too often teachers (and children) believe that nature is something they must visit by bus or field trip, when in fact, nature is everywhere. It is not reserved

FIGURE 10.1 Tessa Touches a Toad

FIGURE 10.2 Exploring Nooks in the Forest

for the wealthy or privileged few. It is ours to share but remains invisible if we remain inside.

Real and Perceived Barriers to Outdoor Learning

Some teachers may read the previous examples and immediately spout off reasons they cannot facilitate outdoor learning with their students. The following are some of the most common reasons teachers cite for staying indoors. Each is paired with solutions for teachers to help children access outdoor learning.

1. We Don't Have Nature Here

Look again. Even at urban school grounds paved with blacktop, the rain falls, sun shines, wind blows, plants and animals thrive. Nature manifests differently in cities than in wild habitats, but it is nature nonetheless. City parks and preserves are often within walking distance of urban schools, but teachers must take initiative to find them.

For teachers seeking more natural spaces, projects that help re-wild urban school grounds and play spaces are a great way to involve the learning community in STEM-based outdoor learning. Projects can be as straightforward as potting herbs in oversized pots or transforming upright pallets into unlikely planters (both too heavy to be picked up and carried away). The source of the complaint about "no nature" lies within the teachers' understanding of it, and their ability or willingness to harness the potential of the existing site (Torquati et al., 2013). This perpetuates the notion that nature is somewhere else, far away, and reinforces a disconnect with the natural world. It also underscores the need for on-site teacher training (Torquati et al., 2013).

2. It's Not Safe Outside

This is a valid concern. Children need to be physically and emotionally safe, first and foremost, before they can access the true benefits of outdoor learning. First, we should consider real versus perceived danger outside (Louv, 2008; Rivkin, 1998). In some instances, the influx of information from media and online platforms causes teachers, administrators, and parents to overreact and keep children inside (Louv, 2008). Busy roads, fear of crime, poor air quality, and other forms of pollution also contribute to the indoor learning trend (Louv, 2008; Rivkin, 1998). But other factors, like indoor air conditioning and daily use of electronics, are just as detrimental when it comes to outdoor learning, or lack thereof. They keep people in the climate-controlled confines of indoor spaces (Rivkin, 1998).

Second, we should consider what is meant by keeping children "safe." Educators should dig into school policies to understand the nuances of the word *safe* and what being *safe* means to school administration. For example, one school may encourage children to examine insects on the playground, while another may forbid it. One school may encourage children to collect seed pods, while another may be fearful of allergic reactions. It is important for teachers and administrators to have candid discussions about learning goals to ensure policies align with the school's vision and curriculum. A well-informed teacher can help point out incongruent or ineffective policies that hinder learning.

It is also useful to define "hazard" versus "risk" when we consider what is safe. In areas where teachers routinely come across weapons or drug paraphernalia on the playground, obviously there is real cause for concern. These are hazards that present immediate danger, and children are not responsible for assessing or removing such hazards on their own. Unlike beneficial risks, hazards are dangerous, and can cause serious injury, harm, or even death. Adults are responsible for identifying, removing, and/or avoiding hazards for young children. A site assessment is a useful tool for teachers as children move between outdoor spaces.

By contrast, risk implies choice on the part of the child. Risk-taking involves thoughtful consideration and a thought process by which a child decides how to proceed. Children can choose whether they want to take a risk. This is a liberating but scary prospect because risky play is thrilling and exciting, yet usually carries a degree of potential physical injury (Sandseter, 2009). For example, balancing on a log presents some degree of risk. A child may consider the following: The log could wobble or roll. The log could be slippery. It may be difficult to balance and walk from one side of the log to the other. An insect or animal could be under the log. Other children may compete to play on the log. This illustrates how physical, emotional, social, and cognitive forms of risk can overlap. It is up to the child to determine if the risk is worth the satisfaction or mastery it presents.

There are many benefits to risk-taking during outdoor learning and play, not least of which include determination, resilience, and self-confidence (Carter, 2014; McFarland & Laird, 2018). Risk, while it may result in minor inquiry, does not pose a danger to the child's health or well-being (Carter, 2014). Researchers assert that children are innately curious about the natural world and are more willing to take risks during outdoor play (Arreguín-Anderson, Alanis, & Gonzalez, 2016). Safety can be a relative term and out of an abundance of caution, well-meaning teachers can preclude the very skills they hope to develop in young children.

3 There Are Too Many Children

If class size is a concern, one can consider how to involve families and volunteers during outdoor learning. With ingenuity and outreach, large classes can be managed successfully. Smaller outdoor learning groups with parent or volunteer support may be one solution. Additional help from the community is another solution. The school Parent Teacher Association (PTA), nearby retirement community, church, or local university can all be sustainable sources for dedicated volunteers. Consider recommendations in the *Best Practices Guidelines in Nature-Based Education* to see what ratio is ideal for a specific outdoor setting (NAAEE, 2019).

4 The Children Don't Behave Appropriately Outside

This is difficult to accept, especially if the children have had few or no opportunities to establish routines and expectations for outdoor learning. Just as children adjust to new procedures and equipment in a gymnasium or library, they adjust to expectations during outdoor learning.

5 We Don't Have Enough Time

Thoughtful planning can also alleviate this concern. The adage is true: where there's a will, there's a way. One can collaborate with other teachers who want to facilitate more outdoor learning and see if there are ways to help one another. One popular solution is to begin or end the day outside. This alleviates all the lag time involved with kids putting on gear because they are already bundled up when they arrive or prepare to go home.

Note: Recess should not be replaced with outdoor learning. They are not the same. Recess is a sacred, unstructured, wholly child-directed time for children to break from teacher-directed goals and curriculum while socializing with peers. Recess is shrinking in many public-school districts, so we should all advocate for recess and never attempt to substitute it with any other forms of curriculum-driven learning.

6. We Don't Have Gear

There are several ways to remedy this, but they all require effort by teachers, administrators, and/or parents. At minimum, schools can offer a gear bank made up of donated gear from families and the surrounding community. This is a great way to spark buy-in with the school's PTA and recruit their support.

Small grants are often available to assist with outdoor education, including the purchase of supplies and gear. Local banks, power utilities, or watershed organizations may all be sources of grant funding.

ITEMS FOR THE GEAR BANK

Rain boots
Rain pants or rain suits
Hooded rain jackets
Fleece pullovers or mid-weight jackets
Heavy winter coats
Snow boots
Snow pants or snow suits
Hats
Neck warmers (not scarves)
Ear muffs
Waterproof mittens
Warm socks

---

7. Parents Don't Want Kids to Get Dirty

This is where parent education proves invaluable. There are cultural, socio-economic, and personal factors that impact parents' views about getting messy. Unless parents understand the significant benefits of outdoor learning, teachers may not have their support. Defining why outdoor learning can enhance academic achievement (among other things) and explaining safety measures can put parents' minds at ease. A letter home along with a gear list and option to use the gear bank is a terrific way to communicate outdoor learning expectations. Once parents realize how valuable these learning experiences are, and the level of the school's commitment to outdoor learning, parents will rally behind these efforts—or at least become more aware.

8. Administration Won't Let Us Go Outside

Not unlike parent concerns, administrators must understand the benefits of outdoor learning to support student and staff engagement. They must also balance the benefits of risk with the need to keep children safe (McFarland & Laird, 2018). Administrators who read current research and policy can develop a firm understanding of the positive outcomes correlated with academic achievement. Once informed, they can help teachers decide how best to implement STEM-based learning outside.

It takes time to change the mindset of a school, especially if it is steeped in teacher-directed [indoor] instruction. But if outdoor learning is to be a sustainable aspect of a school's learning model, it must come from a sincere, informed place within the school's walls.

Adults Who Shape STEM Outdoor Learning

Given the teaching methods required for effective outdoor learning, it is helpful to consider how teachers, administrators, and parents can provide strategies for success. Rachel Carson eloquently states, "if a child is to keep alive his inborn sense of wonder…he needs the companionship of a least one adult who can share it, rediscovering with him the joy, excitement and mystery of the world we live in" (Carson, 1956, p. 55). Each role below is a strand in the web that makes such magical outdoor learning possible.

Role of Teachers

Teachers face many expectations regarding STEM-based curriculum, sometimes dueling for attention. Research demonstrates the power of hands-on, sensory, child-directed learning (Cremin et al., 2015). Though, in many classrooms, students are spoon-fed exactly what questions to ask, when to ask them, and how to arrive at the [teacher's] desired outcomes. Teachers should examine their roles and teaching styles to gauge how much didactic teaching they are doing versus how much time is spent stimulating and facilitating learning experiences. The latter are far more effective in STEM-based approaches (NAAEE, 2019).

There is an important balance between emergent learning experiences, which are led by the children, and intentional teaching practices, which are almost exclusively teacher directed. To facilitate the most meaningful STEM-based learning, teachers should strive to facilitate learning rich in inquiry, experimentation, and trial-and-error, rather than "teach" content.

Note: Several training programs and courses exist to support early childhood educators who want to facilitate emergent curriculum in nature-based programs. Some include Eastern Region Association of Forest and Nature Schools (ERAFANS.org), the Vermont Wilderness School (vermontwildernessschool.org), and Cedarsong Nature School (cedarsongnatureschool.org).

Role of Administrators

As administrators develop a deeper understanding of the value of outdoor learning, they have a responsibility to children to make it happen. In some instances, a lead administrator fully embraces outdoor learning, but has the challenge of training reluctant staff who are perfectly comfortable with the status quo. Conversely, it can be difficult (but not impossible) to persuade an unwilling administrator to take learning outside. With either administrators or educators, the real and perceived barriers discussed previously are likely to be the culprits. Administrators should train and encourage staff regarding how to facilitate outdoor learning experiences. Administrators should also share policies about risk and safety, as well as how to align outdoor learning with curriculum goals. Finally, they should identify and share potential locations for outdoor learning, along with budget implications for materials and gear.

Role of Parents and Guardians

Family involvement is a powerful motivator for children's attitudes and behaviors regarding any form of learning. Taking advantage of back-to-school events or parent workshops to educate families about the benefits of outdoor learning can help. In addition to speakers or lecture-style events, planning outdoor workshops for families to connect outdoors is an effective strategy. Stargazing, campfire sing-alongs, or a picnic with hide-and-go seek are fun ways to activate a sense of community and belonging in nature. This support can carry over into STEM-based outdoor learning, at home and at school, and may help recruit volunteers.

Science, Technology, Engineering, and Math...Outside!

Children are enticed by natural objects, artifacts, plants, and animals that have hidden stories to tell. Next, we explore specific ways outdoor learning develops children's understanding of science, technology, engineering, and math.

Note: The following examples can crisscross disciplines and skill development, and they surface across multiple learning domains. Examples are not necessarily exclusive to any one STEM discipline, but they are organized by content area to relate to standards and curriculum frameworks.

Living Science

Scientific thinking is a natural part of child development. Children can observe, explore, and discover how the world works from a tender age, thus forming a basic understanding of science-relevant ideas (National Research Council, 2012).

The definition of science is broad but can be distilled to its essence for early childhood educators: science is the process and pursuit of obtaining new knowledge through active engagement, observation, experimentation, and exploratory play, combined with the subsequent questions and inquiry that often follows (NSTA, 2014). This definition captures not only the experience of "doing" science, but also the cyclical nature of how it is conducted (Ashbrook, 2014). Playful trial-and-error, prediction, collaboration, and reasoning are all skills afforded by science as children investigate the world around them (NRC, 2012; NSTA, 2014). Outdoor learning helps children fully unlock the potential for scientific thinking. To exemplify this point, Table 10.2 correlates with outdoor experiences with a sampling of the Next Generation Science Standards for Kindergarten through 2nd Grades (NGSS Lead States, 2013).

These examples highlight how seamlessly outdoor learning supports science standards and reveal a natural path to meaningful inquiry.

Through this lens, the scientific method is on display in miniature fashion as children engage in outdoor learning (see Figure 10.3). Unlike the formal stages of the scientific method, a modified version is presented here to demonstrate how unstructured outdoor learning promotes inquiry without teacher direction or predetermined outcomes.

The Modified Scientific Method for Outdoor Inquiry begins when children **observe and explore the outdoors**. Observation and exploration can be likened to the research stage in the traditional scientific method. Children do their own research to understand how nature works through child-directed, sensorial experiences (Torquati et al., 2013). Children try to reconcile their newly forming ideas with their innate curiosity (Cremin et al., 2015; Armstrong & Fukami, 2009).

This is the basis for further inquiry as children **wonder and ask questions**, born from outdoor observation and exploration. Questions bubble up as children take in their surroundings, observe changes, and want to know more. Curiosity is strong motivator for the purest forms of child-directed inquiry. Rachel Carson muses, "many children, perhaps because they themselves are small and closer to the ground than we, notice and delight in the small and inconspicuous" (Carson, 1956, p. 76). Wonder-filled questions, especially when a child focuses on one

TABLE 10.2 Outdoor Learning Helps Children Fully Unlock Potential for Scientific Thinking

Outdoor Experiences	Next Generation Science Standards, K-2
Children experiment with ice outdoors to see where ice and snow melts quickly or more slowly.	K-PS30–1 Weather and Climate Make observations to determine the effect of sunlight on Earth's surface.
Children observe sunlight filtering through autumn leaves; children experiment with leaves and flower petals to discover the transparency or opacity of natural materials.	1-PS4–3 Waves and Their Applications in Technologies for Information Transfer Plan and conduct investigations to determine the effect of placing objects made with different materials in the path of a beam of light.
Children observe and compare parent birds and hatchlings in nest boxes. Children observe dandelion seedlings and mature dandelions in bloom. Children gather acorns and investigate the full-grown oak trees they fell from.	1-LS3–1 Heredity: Inheritance and Variation of Traits Make observations to construct an evidence-based account that young plants and animals are like, but not exactly like, their parents.
Children make frequent visits to explore the same outdoor locations and observe where shadows fall at the same time of day.	1-ESS1–1 Earth's Place in the Universe Use observations of the sun, moon, and stars to describe patterns that can be predicted.
Children observe the change in light as clouds pass in front of the sun, the change in temperature in shady and sunny areas, the change in weather with a passing storm, the change in composition of a rotting log.	2-ESS1–1 Earth's Place in the Universe Use information from several sources to provide evidence that Earth events can occur quickly or slowly.
Children seek and discover dry high ground and low-lying ground where puddles, creeks, or intermittent pools form; children observe changes in puddles in winter and spring.	2-ESS2–3 Earth's Systems Obtain information to identify where water is found on Earth and that it can be solid or liquid.

Adapted from NGSS Lead States (2013)

specific question, is an alternative to the more formal statement of a problem or hypotheses stage of the scientific method (Gerde, Schachter, & Wasik, 2013). Questions emerge, and curiosity baits further inquiry.

Children **tinker, investigate, and experiment to answer questions** and test their informal hypotheses. The result is a glorious outpouring of experimentation with materials in the natural world. They may use plentiful natural objects or combine natural materials with tools and props provided by a teacher. Children may engage in experimentation in pursuit of one question for days, weeks, or even months at time through frequent outdoor learning opportunities. This is illustrated in the text box titled, *What is Emergent Curriculum?*

Some children may pursue a question on their own and answer it relatively quickly. For example, "What's inside this round green husk?" After some banging, smooshing, rolling, and pounding, they may come to learn that a nut lies inside.

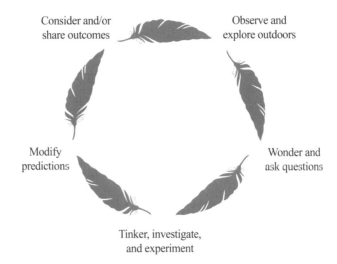

Consider and/or
share outcomes

Observe and
explore outdoors

Modify
predictions

Wonder and
ask questions

Tinker, investigate,
and experiment

FIGURE 10.3 Modified Scientific Method for Outdoor Inquiry

But other questions are not so easily answered. Children make and **modify predictions about questions** as result of experimentation. Outdoor inquiry often sparks collaboration among a community of learners as children seek input from each other. Sometimes experimentation is a silent, steadfast pursuit while at other times it is a joyful ruckus of failure and success. Both are forms of analyzing a hypothesis and adjusting as needed.

WHAT IS EMERGENT CURRICULUM?

Children can form their own questions and directions for learning without advanced teacher-directed goals or intentions. As children explore their surroundings and materials therein, learning emerges. Teachers who facilitate emergent curriculum utilize documentation during the learning process to reveal interests and skills that unfold. This "looking backwards" approach sheds predetermined teacher-directed and curricular goals. Instead, it stimulates child-directed development and interests. This is a highly individualized approach to natural learning processes and relies on teachers to be researchers and facilitators more so than traditional "teachers."(Edwards, Gandini, & Forman 2012)

The process comes full circle as **children consider and/or share outcomes of experimentation**. Sharing may take place with a teacher or peers, especially if the question is one that others acknowledged or made contributions to during investigations. But not necessarily. It is also intrinsically satisfying for a child to ask and answer a question without the need for validation from another person. As conclusions are reached, the cycle of observation, exploration, and further inquiry begin anew.

In addition to (or perhaps an extension of) inquiry, outdoor learning lends itself to identification of plants, animals, and other elements found in the natural world. First, it must be stated that it is not nearly as important to know the names of plants and animals as it is to connect with them on a deeper plane, the deeper knowing that occurs through frequent outdoor learning (Carson, 1956). In David Sobel's essay, *Beyond Ecophobia*, he explains the role of empathy in early childhood as the primary vehicle for young children to connect with nature and elaborates on the role of unstructured wild nature play (Sobel, 1996). Neither is usually factored into the overarching goals of science education, they should be.

When children have frequent encounters in nature during outdoor learning, one can expect an enthusiastic response to identification and classification of flora, fauna, and inanimate natural objects found there. Fortunately, there are many developmentally appropriate ways for young children to do so, especially where taxonomy is concerned. The following list offers ideas for identification and classification in the context of outdoor learning:

- Use sweep nets in grassy areas or edge habitats to gather, examine, and compare invertebrates
- Lift rocks, bricks, or logs to see what lives underneath to study and sort invertebrates
- Find 5–10 kinds of flowers and photograph them. Make a chart to show where each flower was found, what light and soil conditions were present (sun/shade, sandy/rocky/clay), and what other plants were observed nearby. Note observations of insects or other wildlife also near flowers
- Go birding to observe a range of bird species, where they fly, what they eat, where they roost, and other characteristics. Notice how they are adapted for the habitats where they dwell
- Search for clues left behind from invertebrates which may include cicada molts on tree bark, bess beetle shells, holes in trees or soil, nibbled leaves, and so on.

Note: Always gently place logs or stones back into position and return animals back to their habitats after exploration.

When children identify and classify wildlife through direct experience, they can readily observe physical and behavioral adaptations at the same time. This is an excellent way to develop appreciation for survival mechanisms, life cycles, and interdependence among natural communities of living things.

STORIES IN A NUTSHELL

As children triumph or fail with outdoor experiments, storytelling can help children justify their predictions and methods of experimentation. By encouraging daily storytelling, children can explain what took place sequentially, what was discovered, what they want to know more about, and how they might try again (Arreguín-Anderson et al., 2016). The act of speaking about experiments may spark new inquiry, and at the same time, it informs teachers about the children's interests and skill development.

Storytelling also enhances expressive and receptive language skills.

The Nature of Technology

When the topic of technology comes up, tablets, television, computers, e-books, or video games may spring to mind. Electronic, digital technology is ubiquitous in most home and work settings. It is increasingly found in restaurants, stores, libraries, childcare settings, and schools, making it difficult, if not impossible, to avoid. Not surprisingly, young children are inundated with digital technology.

Some research proposes benefits of high-tech media for specific purposes and in small doses (NAEYC & FRC, 2012). However, electronic technology simply cannot replace experiential outdoor learning. Nature provides the ultimate interactive, 3-D, sensory learning experience. Electronic technology is one means, but not a superior means, to enhance skill development when compared to the dynamic nature of outdoor learning (Mitra, 2013).

The joint position statement from the National Association for the Education of Young Children (NAEYC) and the Fred Rogers Center for Early Learning and Children's Media indicates the importance of setting clear limits on screen time and digital technology use (NAEYC & FRC, 2012). Among their recommendations they note that early childhood educators should "prohibit the passive use of television, videos, DVDs, and other non-interactive technologies and

FIGURE 10.4 Life on a Log

FIGURE 10.5 Adella Found a Snail

media in early childhood programs for children younger than 2, and discourage passive and non-interactive uses with children ages 2 through 5" (NAEYC, 2012, p. 11). They go on to define "interactive technology" as content designed to encourage active and creative use and social engagement with other children and adults (NAEYC, 2012). This definition is useful as it compares passive technology and media, but still leaves unanswered questions about its application. The term "active" is misleading if a child is sedentary playing an app or video game. The term "social engagement" is also ambiguous, especially if there is no dialogue, body language, physical presence, or relationship-building with caring people in children's lives, but is instead replaced with social engagement of strangers on an internet gaming platform. Electronic technology is often an easy go-to for teachers to access because they are indoors where plugs and screens are aplenty. Teachers may also be more comfortable – and certainly encouraged – to incorporate digital technology long before they ever consider the immense benefits and skill development waiting on the other side of the door. When learning moves outdoors, it is not reliant upon electronic technology, passive, interactive, or otherwise.

More broadly speaking, technology is the application of knowledge for practical purposes, and encompasses the tools and equipment developed to do so. Despite the word technology being used synonymously to mean "high-tech," technology is much more (NGSS Lead States, 2013).

Low-Tech Tools and Machines

If children are not plopped in front of screens, what other forms of technology are available, and how are they implemented in outdoor settings? Low tech tools and simple machines that magnify a pushing or pulling force can help children explore ideas in science, math, and engineering (Woodford, 2018). Table 10.3 provides examples.

Engineering Wonder

The Next Generation Science Standards include engineering, which applies scientific principles to practical solutions and design (NGSS Lead States, 2012). The low-tech tools previously described go hand-in-hand with engineering concepts.

Children spontaneously experiment with natural materials to invent solutions to problems during outdoor learning (Cremin et al., 2015). Engineering combines experimentation, resourcefulness and creative problem-solving with grit and determination. These are arguably the traits that have ensured human survival in every corner of the planet. Instinctively children create using natural materials

TABLE 10.3 Examples of Low-Tech Tools and Simple Machines

Tool or Simple Machine	Examples
Pulley	Pulley is made to transport items from one place to another with at least two wheels, rope, and pail
Levers	Shovel, mallet, tongs, scissors, knife, wrench, nutcracker, whisk, spatula, hand trowel, wheelbarrow, or tweezers
Inclined planes and wedges	Ramp is used to move or transport an item from one place to another; hammerstone and mallet can be used as wedge and lever to break or split wood
Wheel and axle	Heavy items like logs, stones, or water jugs can be moved great distances with use of wheels and axles
Screw	Hand drill with brace crank and bit demonstrates how screws pull wood out of logs when drilling into the wood
Mortar and pestle	Used since ancient times, a mortar and pestle can be used for finely grinding leaves, roots, nuts, and other seeds into fine paste or powder

Adapted from Woodford (2018)

that surround them, which is why outdoor learning is also ideal for nurturing engineering skills.

It is typical to see children create problems intentionally so that they can build or invent their own solutions. If one has ever heard the phrase "children's work is their play," this is what it means. Children find and create problems as part of their work during purposeful play. This playful engineering is rich in symbolic high-order play and creative problem-solving.

Natural Loose Parts

Nicholson's (1971) theory of loose parts articulates that plentiful materials in the environment can be freely manipulated and combined for building (Nicholson, 1971). Children can access a plethora of natural materials (loose parts) that are freely available for construction and engineering projects during outdoor learning. Consider how children might use these in their engineering endeavors:

- Twigs and small branches
- Large branches
- Felled logs or tree cross-sections (tree cookies)
- Pine cones or magnolia seed pods
- Pine needles
- Leaves
- Pebbles and stones
- Soil and clay
- Water (from puddle, creek, pond, or rain barrell)
- Acorns, hickory nuts, black walnuts
- Milkweed seeds and pods
- Flowers and flower petals
- Feathers
- Berries and fruits (edible or not)
- Grasses
- Corn cobs

Note: Adults always perform site assessments and monitor for potential hazards outdoors.

Engineering Takes Flight

As children develop an understanding of creatures in the local landscape, they can take a closer look to see which animals are engineers. Beaver, crayfish, chipmunks, birds, wasps, mice, squirrels, and a host of other animals all construct dwellings for shelter and to raise young. Animals' physical adaptations are marvelous such as gopher claws for digging, webbed duck feet for paddling, woodpecker beaks for drilling, fish fins for swimming, butterfly tongues for drinking, frog legs for jumping, and bat wings for flying.

The NGSS define crosscutting concepts that feature interdependence and influence of engineering, technology, and science on society and the natural world (NGSS Lead States, 2013). The standards and coordinating examples of outdoor experiences are given in Table 10.4

Math Unfurls

Many teachers shy away from teaching math due to their own negative experiences. But when mathematical concepts are considered outdoors, a new realm of

TABLE 10.4 Examples of Outdoor Experiences and Their Relationship to the Next Generation Science Standards for Kindergarten through Second Grade

Outdoor Experience	Next Generation Science Standards, K-2
Children observe cloud shapes and record daily weather, then invent a system to make weather predictions based on their knowledge about clouds and observations of the sky.	K-ESS3–2 Earth and Human Activity Ask questions to obtain information about the purpose of weather forecasting to prepare for, and respond to, severe weather.
Children experiment with call-and-response calls and songs to determine which animal call is most effective and what else may help amplify calls.	1-PS4–4 Waves and Their Applications in Technologies for Information Transfer Use tools and materials to design and build a device that uses light or sound to solve the problem of communicating over a distance.
Children design, construct, and mimic a fort to stay warm and dry in, based on observations of squirrel nests.	1-LS1–1 From Molecules to Organisms: Structures and Processes Use materials to design a solution to a human problem by mimicking how plants and/or animals use their external parts to help them survive, grow, and meet their needs.
Children gather and determine which branches make the best for bows, slingshots, or walking sticks.	2-PS1–2 Matter and Its Interactions Analyze data obtained from testing different materials to determine which materials have the properties that are best suited for an intended purpose.
Children compare eroded streambanks and healthy stream banks, then design a solution to restore the degraded streambank.	2-ESS2–1 Earth's Systems Compare multiple solutions designed to slow or prevent wind or water from changing the shape of the land.
Children observe maple seeds fall from trees, then trace or sketch maple seeds to understand how its design is ideal for flight and seed dispersal.	K-2-ETS1–2 Engineering Design Develop a simple sketch, drawing, or physical model to illustrate how the shape of an object helps it function as needed to solve a given problem.

Adapted from NGSS Lead States (2013)

possibilities unfurls. For example, children happily gather natural objects like seeds, insects, or leaves during outdoor exploration, which can then be used for counting, grouping, measuring, or ordering from largest to smallest. The math standard "recognize that numbers (or sets of objects) can be combined or separated to make another number" is a concept that plays out, organically, time and time again, during outdoor learning. There is no herculean effort involved in helping children count, combine, or count sets of objects—nor any need for a PowerPoint demonstration. Children count worms in a pail, flower petals, pine cones, twigs, or stones, and teachers do not have to tell them to do it! Teachers may provide additional support for intentional skill development, but nature already provides an organic way for children to learn math ideas.

Outdoor learning adds an experiential layer to math, complete with sunshine, fresh air and active play, thinking beyond little plastic rods and tiles! There are countless ways young children can develop an understanding of mathematical ideas through outdoor learning. Here are a few favorites:

- Measure diameter of trees, tree stumps and logs
- Gather seeds, then sort by size or shape
- Create a graph to demonstrate quantity of items you find outside (e.g., leaves, nests, or flowers)
- Organize natural objects from largest to smallest (e.g., rocks, feathers, or sticks)
- Measure and chart the length of shadows at different times of day
- Count and sort insects and other invertebrates—gently!
- Count the legs of various invertebrates found outside (e.g., worms, millipedes, slugs, grasshoppers, or ants)
- Count plentiful plants by tens, up to 100 (e.g., milkweed seeds, acorns, or clovers)
- Create symmetrical patterns inspired by moth or butterfly wings
- Arrange natural materials to create a mandala with radial symmetry
- Practice addition and subtraction using natural materials
- Observe and photograph the movement of a plant in 30- or 60-minute intervals
- Identify geometric shapes in nature
- Use storytelling to share a word problem, then challenge the children to act out a solution through nature play (e.g., addition or subtraction of bees pollinating flowers, seeds being eaten by a mouse, or frogs hopping away from a pond)
- Keep a class moon journal to develop an understanding of passing of time
- Search for spider webs and take photographs after gently misting them with water; see how many sizes, shapes, and patterns of webs can be found

Like all STEM concepts, math is easy to tap into outdoors once the idea of learning math shifts from worksheets and apps to bugs and acorn caps.

> ## DOCUMENTATION OF STEM-BASED OUTDOOR LEARNING
>
> Teachers can capture STEM-based concepts in bloom during outdoor learning with photo and video documentation. These formats clearly illustrate stages in the learning process, rather than a final product.
>
> Avoid obvious use of cameras or phones, as they can be intrusive and distract from the learning it aims to witness. But assuming one can be invisible with a camera, then learning can become visible to all.

Outward Bound

As children and teachers become comfortable with outdoor learning, they gain confidence in their abilities to master STEM content. Teachers quickly realize how motivating and exciting it is for children to learn outdoors, which makes teaching more enjoyable and effective. Children improve their skills and take risks in new ways with greater affordances that outdoor learning provides. No matter the school or learning environment, teachers can inspire deeper understanding and connection with content in science, technology, engineering, and math. Take the children—and the learning—outside!

References

Armstrong, S. J., & Fukami, C. V. (Eds.). (2009). *SAGE handbook of management learning, education and development.* Thousand Oaks, CA: Sage Publications.

Arreguín-Anderson, M. G., Alanís, I., & Gonzalez, I. S. (2016). Using acorns to generate an entire alphabet! *Science and Children, 53*(6), 76–81.

Ashbrook, P. (2014). The nature of science in early childhood. *Science and Children, 52*(1), 24–25.

Carson, R. (1956). *The sense of wonder.* New York, NY: Harper & Row.

Carter, M. (2014). Seeing risk as benefit. An interview with Laurie Cornelius. *Exchange, 36* (3), (No. 217), 27–31.

Cremin, T., Glauert, E., Craft, A., Compton, A., & Stylianidou, F. (2015). Creative little scientists: Exploring pedagogical synergies between inquiry-based and creative approaches in early years science. *Education 3–13, 43*(4), 404–419. doi:10.1080/03004279.2015.1020655

Edwards, C. P., Gandini, L., & Forman, G. E. (Eds.) (2012). *The hundred languages of children: The Reggio Emilia experience in transformation.* Santa Barbara, CA: Praeger.

Esser, J. (2017). Looking closely. *Exchange, 39*(1) (No.233), 89.

Gerde, H., Schachter, R., & Wasik, B. (2013). Using the scientific method to guide learning: An integrated approach to early childhood curriculum. *Early Childhood Education Journal, 41*(5), 315–323. doi:10.1007/s10643-013-0579-4

Louv, R. (2008). *Last child in the woods: Saving our children from nature-deficit disorder.* Chapel Hill, NC: Algonquin Books.

McFarland, L., & Laird, S. G. (2018). Parents' and early childhood educators' attitudes and practices in relation to children's outdoor risky play. *Early Childhood Education Journal, 46*(2), 159–168. doi:10.1007/s10643-017-0856-8

Mitra, M. (2013). Reflection: Nature connections in preschool. *Exchange Press, 35*(6) (No. 214), 96.

National Association for the Education of Young Children & Fred Rogers Center for Early Learning and Children's Media. (2012). *Position statement: Technology and interactive media as tools in early childhood programs serving children from birth through age 8.* Washington, DC: National Association for the Education of Young Children.

National Research Council (NRC). (2012). *A framework for K–12 science education: Practices, crosscutting concepts, and core ideas.* Washington, DC: National Academies Press. Retrieved from http://static.nsta.org/pdfs/PositionStatement_EarlyChildhood.pdf

National Science Teachers Association (NSTA). (2014). *NSTA position statement: Early childhood science education.* Retrieved from http://www.nsta.org/about/positions/early childhood.aspx

NGSS Lead States. (2013). *The Next Generation Science Standards: For states, by states.* Washington, DC: National Academies Press. doi:10.17226/18290

Nicholson, S. (1971). How not to cheat children: The theory of loose parts. *Landscape Architecture, 62*(1), 30–34.

North American Association for Environmental Education (NAAEE). (2019). *Early childhood environmental education programs: Guidelines for excellence.* Submitted for publication. Washington, DC: NAAEE Publications.

Rivkin, M. (1995). *The great outdoors: Restoring children's right to play outside.* Washington, DC: National Association for the Education of Young Children.

Rivkin, M. (1998). Happy play in grassy places: The importance of the outdoor environment in Dewey's educational ideal. *Early Childhood Education Journal, 25*(3), 199–202.

Sandseter, E. B. H. (2009). Characteristics of risky play. *Journal of Adventure Education & Outdoor Learning, 9*(1), 3–21. doi:10.1080/14729670802702762

Smith, G. & Sobel, D. (2013). Bring it on home. *Independent School, 72*(3), 94–102.

Sobel, D. (1996). *Beyond ecophobia: Reclaiming the heart in nature education (Nature Literacy Series, Volume 1).* Great Barrington, MA: The Orion Society.

Sobel, D. (2004). *Placed-based education: Connecting classrooms and communities.* Great Barrington, MS: Orion Society.

Torquati, J., Cutler, K., Gilkerson, D., & Sarver, S. (2013). Early childhood educators' perceptions of nature, science, and environmental education. *Early Education & Development, 24*(5), 721–743. doi:10.1080/10409289.2012.725383

Tunnicliffe, S. D. (2017). Emerging environmental science in early years education. *Environmental Education, 115*, 15–17.

Woodford, C. (2018, May 16). *Tools and simple machines.* Retrieved from https://www.explainthatstuff.com/toolsmachines.html

ABOUT THE EDITORS AND CONTRIBUTORS

About the Editors

Lynn E. Cohen is a professor in the department of teaching and learning at Long Island University/ Post. She holds a PhD from Fordham University. Prior to joining the faculty at LIU/Post, she worked for over 25 years as a preschool, kindergarten, and literacy teacher. She enjoys the mixing of teaching, mentoring students, providing service to local school districts, and producing scholarly research. Dr. Cohen was the recipient of the prestigious David Newton Award for Excellence in Teaching in 2017 at Long Island University. Dr. Cohen is a founding member of the Play, Policy Practice Interest Forum of National Association for the Education of Young Children (NAEYC), secretary for the Association for the Study of Play (TASP), and active member of the American Educational Research Association. Her research interests include young children's play, language development, emergent literacy, dual language learners, early childhood technology, school readiness, and contemporary literacies

She has co-edited four books with Sandra Waite-Stupiansky: *STEM in Early Childhood: How Science, Technology, Engineering and Mathematics Strengthen Learning* (Routledge, 2019), *Theories of Early Childhood: Developmental, Behaviorist, and Critical* (Routledge, 2017), *Learning across the Early Childhood Curriculum* (Emerald, 2013), *Play: A Polyphony of Research, Theories, Issues* (University Press of America, 2012). Dr. Cohen's work has appeared in numerous peer-reviewed journals including *Contemporary Issues in Early Childhood Education, Young Children, International Journal of Early Childhood, Early Childhood and Development and Care*, and *Journal of Research in Early Childhood*. (See https://www.researchgate.net/profile/Lynn_Cohen and www.lynnecohen.com.)

Sandra Waite-Stupiansky is Professor Emerita at Edinboro University, Pennsylvania, where she taught undergraduate and master's degree students for 23 years before retiring in 2015. As part of her responsibilities, Dr. Waite-Stupiansky also taught PreK through fourth grade at the Miller Laboratory School on the grounds of Edinboro University for ten years, where she also served as Principal. Her research interests include recess in elementary schools, children's moral development, children's play, and applications of Piagetian theories. Before joining the faculty at Edinboro, she taught in public and private schools in Ohio, Indiana, and California. Dr. Waite-Stupiansky holds a PhD from Indiana University, Bloomington, and is a founding member of the Play, Policy, and Practice Interest Forum of NAEYC, where she served as a co-facilitator and managing editor of *PPP Connections* for nearly 20 years. She has written multiple articles and books published by Scholastic and NAEYC. This is her fourth co-edited book with Lynn Cohen. After retirement, she become a certified Master Gardener through Cornell University Cooperative Extension, volunteering much of her time teaching children and adults the wonders of the natural world.

About the Contributors

Aikaterini (Katerina) Bagiati is currently a research scientist working at the MIT Office of Open Learning. After graduating with a Diploma in Electrical and Computer Engineering and a Master's degree in Advanced Digital Communication Systems from Aristotle University in Thessaloniki, Greece, Dr. Bagiati was one of the first graduate students to join the pioneer School of Engineering Education at Purdue University. In 2011, she acquired her Doctorate in Engineering Education, followed by a post-doctoral associate appointment within the MIT-SUTD Collaboration at the Massachusetts Institute of Technology (MIT). She is actively involved in development and assessment related to MIT's national and international educational projects. She conducts research at the PreK-12 and higher education levels. Dr. Bagiati's research interests are in the areas of early engineering, educational technologies, STEM curriculum development and teacher training, and Design Based Learning and has numerous publications related to early engineering.

Marina Umaschi Bers is a professor in the Eliot-Pearson Department of Child Study and Human Development and an adjunct professor in the Computer Science Department at Tufts University. She heads the interdisciplinary Developmental Technologies research group. Her research involves the design and study of innovative learning technologies to promote children's positive development. She serves as director of the graduate certificate program on Early Childhood Technology at Tufts University. Her research interests include designing, studying, and implementing programming languages and robotic systems for early childhood education and their associated curricular and teaching materials, assessment instruments and professional development strategies. She has authored numerous articles and the books *Coding as a Playground* (Routledge, 2018), *Designing Digital Experiences for Positive Youth Development: From Playpen to Playground* (Oxford University Press, 2012), and *Blocks to Robots* (Teachers College Press, 2008). Dr. Bers received prestigious awards such as the 2005 Presidential Early Career Award for Scientists and Engineers (PECASE), a National Science Foundation Young Investigator's Career Award for her work on virtual communities of learning and care, and the American Educational Research Association (AERA) Jan Hawkins Award for Early Career Contributions to Humanistic Research and Scholarship in Learning Technologies.

Douglas H. Clements is Distinguished University Professor and the Kennedy Endowed Chair in Early Childhood Learning at the University of Denver, Colorado. Doug has published over 146 refereed research studies, 26 books, 90 chapters, and 300 additional publications on the learning and teaching of early mathematics; computer applications; creating, using, and evaluating research-based curricula; and taking interventions to scale, mostly with colleague and wife, Julie Sarama. He served on the U.S. President's National Mathematics Advisory Panel, the *Common Core State Standards* committee, and the National Research Council's Committee on early mathematics, and is co-author each of their reports Additional information can be found at http://du.academia.edu/DouglasClements, and http://www.researchgate.net/profile/Douglas_Clements/.

Janet Emmons is founder of Blockspot®. She has over 20 years of experience in education, research, and business, which culminated in the creation of Blockspot®. Blockspot® is the first of its kind to marry education and block play within a retail concept. Ms. Emmons' understanding of how children think, play-based learning, and the direct link to emotional development are put into practice every day at Blockspot®. Blockspot® demonstrates the power of emotional and intellectual intelligence coming together in purposeful and holistic synergies. Her ability to focus solely on multi-age group, play-based learning and curriculum through blocks has led to some compelling discoveries. Currently, Blockspot® operates a 2,500 square foot state of the art facility in Southampton, NY. www.blockspotlearning.com

Demetra Evangelou has research and policy experience relevant to the advancements of technological and scientific literacy. She is credited with introducing the concept of *Developmental Engineering*, a new area of research and education that explores engineering and human development. In 2011, she was awarded by President Obama the Presidential Early Career Award for Scientists and Engineers (PECASE), which is the "the highest honor bestowed by the US Government on Science and Engineering professionals in the early stages of their independent research career." The award citation read "for outstanding research into how early experiences can lead children to pursue engineering later in life and for working with teachers from diverse schools to develop new teaching materials and methods that can help students become innovative and more technologically literate." Dr. Evangelou has served on the faculty of Purdue University, Aristotle University, and the University of Thessaly. She holds a PhD from the University of Illinois at Champaign-Urbana and is a member of several scientific and professional societies, including the Sigma Xi Science Honor Society. In 2009, she was awarded the prestigious National Science Foundation Career Award.

Lynn C. Hartle started her career as a Montessori directress in schools in Michigan and founded a children's house in Cookeville, Tennessee. Her passion for understanding and using deeper learning strategies led her to pursue her graduate preparation at Tennessee Technology University and The Pennsylvania State University in Curriculum and Instruction, Early Childhood Teacher Education Specialization. Her career included undergraduate and graduate teaching positions at East Stroudsburg University, the University of Florida, Florida Gulf Coast University (as a founding faculty member in 1996), and the University of Central Florida. Her current position brought her back to The Pennsylvania State University, Brandywine. Throughout the last 30 years in higher education, she has helped to shape and redesign teacher preparations programs. She has also led global learning trips with students to Greece and Cuba. Her research interests include teacher preparation, play, learning through the arts, and appropriate uses for digital media.

Dr. Hartle has presented at numerous national and regional conferences, most frequently at the National Association for the Education of Young Children (NAEYC) and American Education Research Association (AERA) conferences. She has authored or co-authored chapters in books and over 20 journal articles. As service to the research community, she is a frequent peer reviewer for the *Early Education and Development* and *Young Children* journals.

Dr. Hartle has held leadership positions with the National Association of Early Childhood Teacher Education and the NAEYC interest forums. She was awarded the *2008 Children's Champion Award* by the Central Florida Association for the Education of Young Children and the *2016 Edgar Klugman Award for Lifetime Contribution of Research and Leadership in the Field of Early Childhood and Play* by the Play, Policy, and Practice Interest Forum of the NAEYC.

Aliya Jafri is currently the academic coach and International Baccalaureate (IB) coordinator of the International Community School in Decatur, GA. In her teaching career of 17 years, she has taught in both public and private schools locally in the US and Egypt, Pakistan, India, and Switzerland. She went to Reggio Emilia, Italy, to participate in their International Study Group and observe the approach first hand. As a fourth grade teacher at the International Community School, a school that serves refugees and immigrants with local children, Ms. Jafri introduced a makerspace to her students. She realized that the refugee students, who were not on grade level for reading and math, excelled at tinkering and making.

Olga S. Jarrett is Professor Emerita of science education in the Department of Early Childhood and Elementary Education at Georgia State University. Her research interests include recess, service learning, play and social justice, and the role of playfulness in the development of interest in science. Dr. Jarrett is a past president of The Association for the Study of Play (TASP) and The American Association for the Child's Right to Play (IPA/USA).

Pamela S. Lottero-Perdue is a professor of Science and Engineering Education in the Department of Physics, Astronomy and Geosciences at Towson University, where she has integrated engineering into courses for PreK-8 teacher candidates and developed and directed a graduate STEM program for PreK-6 teachers. She has partnered with teachers to develop and implement high-quality PreK-8 engineering learning experiences. She has co-authored numerous engineering-focused articles for the teacher practitioner journal, *Science and Children*. She presents her research regularly through the American Society for Engineering Education Precollege Engineering Education Division, a division she has chaired. Her current research includes investigating how K-5 students plan, fail, and productively persist.

Gina Navoa Svarovsky is an Assistant Professor of Practice at the University of Notre Dame Center for STEM Education. For nearly two decades, she has been interested in how young people learn science and engineering in both formal and informal learning environments. Specifically, her research interests are focused on exploring how youth from traditionally underrepresented populations in engineering develop engineering skills, knowledge, and ways of thinking as a result of participating in a variety of learning experiences. Dr. Svarovsky holds a joint appointment in the College of Engineering at Notre Dame, where she has taught in the First Year Engineering program. She also directs the Evaluation and Research team within Notre Dame's Institute for Educational Initiatives. Prior to joining the faculty at the Center for STEM Education, Dr. Svarovsky worked as a Senior Evaluation and Research associate at the Science Museum of Minnesota. She earned a BS in Chemical Engineering from Notre Dame, and a PhD in Educational Psychology from the University of Wisconsin.

Emily Relkin is a PhD candidate in the Department of Child Study and Human Development at Tufts University. She is a research associate in the DevTech Research Group at Tufts where she takes part in the creation of new technologies designed to promote positive development in young children. Ms. Relkin's doctoral research focuses on new methods for assessing computational thinking abilities in children 4–7 years of age using a variety of coding platforms.

Julie Sarama is Distinguished University Professor and the Kennedy Endowed Chair in Innovative Learning Technologies at the University of Denver,

Colorado. She has taught high school mathematics and computer science, gifted, and early mathematics. She directs eight projects funded by the National Science Foundation, the Institute of Education Sciences, and others and has authored over 77 refereed articles, 6 books, 55 chapters, and over 80 additional publications, along with 50 computer programs, many with colleague and husband, Douglas H. Clements. Her research interests include children's development of mathematical concepts and competencies, implementation and scale-up of educational interventions, professional development models' influence on student learning, and implementation and effects of software environments. See https://www.researchgate.net/profile/Julie_Sarama and http://portfolio.du.edu/jsarama.

Monica Wiedel-Lubinski holds a BS and Master's Degrees from Towson University, Maryland.

She is a leader in the field of nature-based education and brings over two decades of leadership to local, regional, national, and international platforms to help others develop deeper connections with the natural world. Her career began at the Irvine Nature Center in 1997. Later, she founded and directed Irvine's nature preschool (2010), an internationally recognized model, then became the force behind Irvine's Forest Dreamers (2016), a 100% outdoor forest kindergarten. As Director of Early Childhood Education, she created programs including parent and child series, homeschool programs, professional development courses, summer camps, school field trips, nature birthday parties, and community events. She coordinated exhibit design for Irvine's indoor exhibit hall and was a key collaborator in the design of their celebrated Nature Explore Outdoor Classroom. She spear-headed the Nature Preschool Conference (2012), which earned a 2016 *Innovator of the Year Award* under her leadership. The Outdoor Classroom was named in her honor in 2016, and she was awarded the O'Neill Award to recognize outstanding achievements in nature-based early childhood education in 2017.

Ms. Wiedel-Lubinski is currently contracting with Baltimore City Recreation and Parks (BCRP) as the co-founder of Wild Haven Forest Preschool and Childcare, which aims to offer greater access and immersive outdoor learning for young children throughout the local park system.

She is a member of the Natural Start Alliance's Advisory Board of the North American Association for Environmental Education (NAAEE). She is the co-chair of the Council of Nature and Forest Preschools and one of ten authors selected to write the first national *Best Practices Guidelines in Nature-Based Early Childhood Education* (expected in 2019).

Karen Worth has been a faculty member at Wheelock College for over 40 years, where she teaches early childhood and elementary education with a focus on science education. She works closely with the Mathematics and Science Department to enhance the mathematics and science preparation of pre-service students at the college. She also coordinates the Integrated Elementary and Special Education program at the graduate level. Ms. Worth worked as a senior research scientist at Education Development Center, Inc, for more than 25 years, leading a range of programs focused on science curriculum development, professional development, and systemic reform. She has been a consultant and advisor to a number of museums including the Boston Children's Museum and the Chicago Children's Museum. She has advised public television stations including WGBH and PBH and community organizations across the US and internationally. She is a recipient of the Exploratorium's Outstanding Educator Award for her work in science education, the international purKwa prize for the scientific literacy of the children of the planet, and the NSTA Distinguished Service Award. She is the author of numerous articles and book chapters and was the principal investigator in the development of *The Young Scientist Series* (Redleaf), *Worms, Shadows and Whirlpools* (Heinemann), *Insights, An Elementary Hands-On Science Curriculum* (Kendall Hunt), *Science and Literacy: A Natural Fit*, and *The Essentials of Science Literacy* (Heinemann).

INDEX

Made in United States
Troutdale, OR
07/16/2023

11274947R00136